AT LAST! IT'S ___
TO LOVE ___ ___!

LOVING A YOUNGER MAN

Victoria Houston

POCKET BOOKS

New York   London   Toronto   Sydney   Tokyo   Singapore

Grateful acknowledgment is made for permission to reprint the excerpt on pages 168-171 from "The Cold Literal Moments" by Dorothy Pitkin, edited by R. C. Townsend. Reprinted from *The Massachusetts Review*, copyright 1974 The Massachusetts Review, Inc.

POCKET BOOKS, a division of Simon & Schuster Inc.
1230 Avenue of the Americas, New York, NY 10020

ISBN: 0-671-66882-X

First Pocket Books printing April 1989

10 9 8 7 6 5 4 3

For Brant

Contents

I felt that way. And I never expected to find myself
in book numbers—I was so sure I was alone.

Preface

"It's hard not to like somebody who loves you so much right from the start, is so thrilled that you're there, is just so enchanted by you. It makes you feel good! It's like Christmas. I've been having such a good time, it's hard to resist, but you have to think of other things. . . ."

 —Lynn, age 37,
  talking about dating a younger man

I want to tell you about a very silly woman. Me.

Eight years ago, I met and fell in love with the man of all my dreams—then I tried to turn around and walk away from him. I almost said no to the best thing that had ever happened to me.

Why? Because he was nine years younger than I am. I let that nine years get in the way of our lives. I let myself be intimidated by what I thought others might think of us. And I imagined all kinds of silly reasons that our relationship shouldn't work. I can say they are silly reasons today, but they were nightmares just a few short years ago.

Today I am married to that man. His name is Brant. I love him dearly, and I am so proud of us and our marriage that I often take a moment to stop whatever I'm doing and thank all the good spirits that made it possible. But even as I knock on wood and give credit elsewhere, I know in my heart that the good spirits are really our own courage and our own willingness to go ahead and do something that just didn't seem right at first.

In fact, our being together seemed so wrong that I was sure it would appall and anger all the people who mattered to us, like our families and our good friends. What shocks me today when I realize how happy we are is how close I came to letting it all go.

The truth is, we did not appall anyone. And, more important, I now know the luxury of having a husband who is also my very best friend, and I can't imagine ever doubting that our relationship could work. We laugh together at funny, little stuff like "Peewee's Playhouse." And when our Siamese cat, who truly ruled our household, curled up one night, proud and elegant as always, to die quietly in Brant's arms, we discovered that we can weep together, which is probably as important as laughing.

Everything isn't perfect, of course. We always breathe a sigh of relief when we make it through our taxes without a divorce. Sometimes our schedules are so frantic that we wonder if we'll ever have time together. But as much as our two-career household can be frustrating at times, it is exactly what makes our life together fascinating for us. And I believe that's one of the big reasons we do so well together: we both work.

We got to know each other because of our work, even though the kind of writing each of us does is very different. That means we not only understand the pressures each of us faces daily, but we also value what each of us accomplishes. We frequently use each other as sounding boards for new ideas or to seek advice when a writing or reporting project isn't working. *Respect* may not be a word we use a lot, but it sure is a word we would use to describe our feelings for one another.

Partners is another word I'd use to describe us. Brant and I are partners in this business of marriage. We may share good times, but we sure as hell share the bills for them as well. We hassle and we bargain, but we try to go 50-50 every step of the way so neither one of us feels overwhelmed or overburdened by carrying the whole load. And when the bills are paid, we divvy up the housework, decide whose turn it is to take an animal to the vet, and try to remember which one of us cooked the last Sunday breakfast. At all times, however, we stay tuned in to each other's work schedules so neither one of us gets too weighed down with both house and office responsibilities at once.

So why do I keep saying that I almost walked away from this man with whom I do all this good stuff? Because that nine-year age difference seemed so monumental to me at times that I was sure it could sabotage us. What would my kids say? Would he mind my wrinkles? Would he still love me in 10 years?

If this book does nothing else, it will explain just how and why I was wrong, wrong, wrong. I don't want anyone to waste five years as I did—not even one year, not even a second—thinking that it somehow isn't right for a woman to consider falling in love with a younger man or that it can't work out. *Loving a Younger Man* lets you in on what it took me five years to learn the hard way and what men who marry younger women have always known: love works no matter what ages we are!

On The Brink of Change

For me, it all started on a sunny April day as I boarded a plane in the midwestern town I called home. It was more than a simple departure. Not only was I making a brief trip back to the college I had attended, but I was also trying to leave my marriage of 16 years. I had just turned 35, and I knew my life was at a major turning point. In my bones, as I waited on the runway for that plane to take off, I sensed I might return a different person.

The man I was leaving was a good man, but we were leading distant, parallel lives under one roof, lives that might touch one another physically but seldom made any contact emotionally. Even though we shared three children, a house, and two cats, we never talked about the things that really mattered to us as individuals. After years of trying, including an intensive period of marriage counseling rigorously pursued by both of us, it still seemed that we just didn't know how to talk about important issues with each other.

The one thing we did share was a mutual frustration on one critical point: my work. I wanted to work. I felt that I *had* to work, although I couldn't say exactly why. Ever since our marriage, which took place the summer after he graduated from college and I finished my sophomore year, I had tried to finish school in order to start a career, but it was always an inconvenience to my husband. For him it meant late meals, his having to help with children, or my getting to bed late, which then ruined his sleep and affected him the next day. And, as he pointedly remarked, my plan to work after finishing school would actually cost us more money because it would put us into a higher tax bracket. Finally, he put his foot down—no full-time career for the woman in *his* household.

I gave in, feeling like some dried-up leaf blown aimlessly by a cold, harsh wind. Powerless. I didn't want the money; he made enough for all of us. I wanted me, a forgotten me. I wanted to be a whole human being. I knew I had skills, even if I lacked experience. And I wanted to know that I could survive if something ever happened to him or to us.

I gave in, but I didn't give up. I admitted to myself that it was my fault, that I hadn't told him before we married that I always envisioned myself as a wife, a mother, *and* a woman with a career. I also vowed I would never let this happen again. If I should ever remarry, my new husband would know how important my work is to me—*before* we made a long-term commitment.

And so, as my plane took off, I had already made the decision to seek a divorce. I just didn't know exactly what the first steps would be. I felt that I needed some direction, especially job-wise, before I consulted a lawyer. Nevertheless, I had reached a point where I looked at my marriage as one between two people pulled in different directions but yoked by a decision we had made when we were still kids.

I recognized I was responsible for some of the differences between us. After all, I had married a man who expected a traditional family life. As a young woman, a young wife, I had been afraid to do the unconventional and be more outspoken about my hopes for a career. My husband's first reaction to my attempts at starting a career may have been extremely negative, but it was not surprising. He said he felt family, friends, and business colleagues would think that he couldn't adequately provide for us. At that time, I listened to him and thought, Well, maybe what other people think *is* more important. He must be right.

What I did then, in my early twenties, was allow my husband to become the authority figure in my life, the man who would tell me what to do as my father had done before him. I did not yet have the confidence in myself to recognize that my needs might be different from his. In addition, I was confused by his lack of respect for me and my goals. I did not understand his attitude, but I saw it in the husbands of my friends, too. And so, confused and uncertain over which of us was right, I allowed him to make me feel bad about wanting to defy convention and return to school or go to work. I agreed to be the kind of wife he expected.

However, I was deeply unhappy. Our two older children had been born during the first two years of our marriage and just before we moved to a major city for my husband's first job after graduate school. Right after the move, I went through a severe depression. I had no friends and no sense of identity beyond folding diapers and cleaning house. Knowing that I had to do something because I felt close to committing suicide, I finally got myself a part-time clerical job on Saturdays and used my meager self-earned dollars to pay a sitter and take one course at a time at a local university. Seems like a small change, but it worked! With my self-esteem as a thinking person bolstered, I became a better mother and a happier person.

Then we moved again—this time to the midwestern town where my husband had grown up. Again, he made it very clear that he didn't want me to work. He felt that, as a senior executive in top management, he would be embarrassed if his friends and professional colleagues knew I worked as a receptionist or a clerk. But that left me with a classic Catch-22: we couldn't afford my education unless I had such a job. That meant I couldn't get the degree I needed to have in order to apply for the kind of position that would reflect well on my husband. And so we grew away from each other, my husband tightening the bonds of tradition just as I was trying to force them loose. Over the years, I began to realize that always being the subordinate partner in our marriage, sharing his dream for the future but never having a dream of my own, wouldn't work. I wanted our lives to change so I could be more of a person, and I had begun to recognize that maybe, just maybe, *I didn't care what people thought*.

A Long Trip Home

The plane took me to a tiny jewel of a campus in the Green Mountains of Vermont, a campus famed for its radical politics, liberal arts education, and a reputation (from the 1950s and early '60s) for encouraging "free love." I was returning to a school I had entered 18 years earlier as a young woman addicted to rebellion, Camus, and motorcycle boots. Enthralled with the revolutionary zeal of Simone de Beauvoir, I was convinced I, too, could be a woman who would change the world.

But that April day, I returned as a well-tailored, well-mannered member of the alumni council, an enthusiastic but hardly revolutionary crowd. In the years that had passed, I had done nothing to change the world. Instead, I had become the perfect corporate wife of a man who had attended all the right schools, where he had learned to make all the right decisions. I made *my* important decisions in silk blouses, playing tennis at country clubs, and making sure invitations were sent to all the right people.

The only real failure I could point to during those "country club'' years was a second depression, in my early thirties, that brought me to the brink of alcoholism and, once again, to the brink of suicide. What helped me stay alive was the same thing that was destroying my marriage—a step-by-painful-step return to the role of an independent woman. I now knew how much I needed to work, to produce. I recognized that I was a person who wanted urgently to reach beyond the perimeters of my comfortable home and family and that I was willing to give up comfort and security in order to do that.

As I stepped out of the cab onto the sunny green lawn of the college, I remembered with embarrassment that I was still two years short of a college degree, that I had excused myself from any involvement in the women's movement because I was busy having babies, that I had joined a consciousness-raising group five years after everyone else. I was, however, writing. After three years of hard work, and in spite of the friction it caused in our household, my art criticism was appearing in our local newspaper and in two national art magazines. I was receiving small commissions for my advertising copywriting. Maybe I wouldn't have to mention that my work was only ''part-time.'' Also, I had been invited to join the alumni council even though I was not a graduate because I had supported the college by making donations and interviewing prospective students from the Midwest.

For a moment, as I walked up the cement stairs past the familiar college post office on my way to the alumni meeting, I felt like that 18-year-old girl again. A bittersweet memory of excitement and fear swept over me. Once more, I felt excited by all the intelligence and aggressive thinking going on around me, fearful of how well I could do. Suddenly, I realized I had let that fear conquer me.

In that second, standing there on the post office steps, I understood for the first time that my marriage after my sophomore year had come more out of a need for security and the urge to do the right thing than out of love. I saw in a flash what I hadn't seen before: I had listened to the people around me who said that this was the right man for me—smart, on the way up, outgoing, financially stable.

And I had let the right man tell me that I had to marry him then or lose him. I didn't know then what I know now—that I should follow my own instincts instead of listening to others.

Eighteen years is a hell of a long trip home. But, standing on those steps, I was grateful for the insight that I knew would change my life for the better—and better late than never.

Within minutes, I was part of a crowd of women whose high energy level was infectious. As we waited for the meeting to begin, we shouted at each other, everyone talking at once. Dry wit and irreverent humor made us all sound more like school kids than grown-ups. Among the self-conscious and socially insulated types with whom I had just spent a decade of my life, I always felt like my remarks and my jokes were a little unseemly, a little too raunchy, not quite proper. I felt like my ideas pushed the boundaries of what was acceptable to consider, much less to do. But here I fit right in. I sat back and relaxed with a big smile on my face. I felt like a little kid at a party with all my favorite friends.

As we sat waiting for the meeting to start, several of us were anticipating our first glimpse of the kind of men who had been admitted to the college after it went coed in the '70s. We'd had our doubts about the wisdom of that decision. Now there were three men on the alumni council. How would they fit in?

I noticed the first two with mild curiosity. Then, just as the meeting started, a third rushed in. That one I noticed. I watched him walk to his seat. He was of medium height with red hair and a face . . . well, I thought to myself, if the college had admitted men who looked like that when I was there, my life might have been very different. Not bad. Not bad at all. He was introduced as Brant, graduate of the class of '76, nine years after mine.

Later, during the meeting, he challenged a point I had made to the group. Since I considered myself experienced in the type of volunteer activity under discussion, I disagreed with him. Patronizingly. After all, I had 10 years on the kid. What did he know about volunteer activities and how to run a bunch of women?

He didn't take the reprimand. He told me I was wrong. I resisted the impulse to tell him just to shut up. And I wondered who he was that he had that kind of confidence.

I made sure to sit next to him at dinner, just so I could look at him. He told me later that he had made sure to sit next to me, too. We discovered we were both writers. He was an investigative reporter, full-time of course. I found myself telling him about a political scam I'd uncovered during a recent feature story assignment.

Something clicked in that conversation. At some point, I stopped looking at him and started listening. We found out that we shared the same kind of ethics, that we were both easily outraged by people who take advantage of others' weaknesses. We went after things the same way. We got so carried away talking that we almost forgot to eat our dinner or to talk to anyone else at the table. I was so happy. After all these years, I'd found someone I could really talk to.

I discovered something else too: age has nothing to do with wisdom or having an intelligent point of view. Brant might have been nine years younger than I, but at dinner that night, discussing politics and corruption, literature and financial markets, I found him to be as bright, witty, and well informed as any of the older men from Harvard, Yale, and Stanford who had been my dinner partners during the previous decade. In fact, what I liked most was that, as smart and articulate as I found him to be, he seemed to think the same about me.

With no hesitation, I turned down an invitation to disappear into a bridge game with some women my age and older that night. Instead, I hung out at a local bar with Brant and the younger members of the council. We drank beer and listened to old rock and roll on the jukebox. Later, as the evening was winding up, I looked over the glass I had raised to my lips and studied Brant's face. He was so full of life. I thought he was wonderful. Too bad, I thought, that he's too young for me.

I had a hard time getting to sleep that night. Instead of

going to sleep, I sat up in the dark, a million thoughts racing through my mind. I thought first of myself, and so many women like me, locked into a marriage that was easier to submit to than to change. How it seemed safer to compromise than to alter the course of my life and head into uncertainty and the pain my changes would be sure to cause others.

I thought of my years of effort to be the best mom, the best cook, to do needlepoint, to socialize properly. While I loved motherhood, the rest of homemaking left me convinced that the praise heaped on women who excel at needlepoint and cookery is really a subversive male tactic designed to keep us occupied and out of the work force. I had just spent an evening with women who were married, had families, *and* worked. And they were the most interesting, delightful people I had met in ages.

And Brant. He was evidence that there are men who can be friends with a woman without flirtation and sexual innuendo. I had been observing men for a good 20 years, and finally I had found one who would like me as a thinking person, not just as an attractive female. That meant there had to be more men out there like him. It also made me hope that my relationship with such a man could be extended into a more intimate relationship. Can't the person you love be the person you most enjoy talking to and sharing your dreams with as well?

My last thought that night was to wonder if it was too late to find that 18-year-old again, with her enthusiasm for life and her willingness to charge ahead even if some days were frightening. Was I going to capitulate and turn into a mewling wreck of a woman, always cursing what might have been— or could I make a fierce break for a new life? It was a curious symmetry, I thought, that placed such a decision in my life right when I was back in the same place I'd been in when I decided to marry nearly 20 years earlier.

I boarded the plane home knowing I had found the momentum I needed to leave my marriage and to try to recapture a new life for myself. All the people I had just seen, especially Brant, had reinforced my own self-esteem and demonstrated that I could fit in somewhere. People connected with the college had already hinted at job offers if I were to move east. And Brant—well, I was sad to say good-bye to such a good new friend. In fact, I made a mental note to be sure to introduce him to one of my sisters who is just his age—I thought he would be the perfect man for her! I knew he could never be the right man for me—he was much too young.

The Impossible Dream?

I felt the same sadness, mixed with anticipation, when I learned two months later that I would see Brant again. He had to attend a national news conference in the city where I lived. I didn't tell him when he called that I had received a job offer from the East and that I would be divorced by fall. Nor did I tell him that my children had chosen to remain with their father rather than move with me, which worried me.

Since my two oldest children were in their early teens, our state's child custody laws allowed them to choose their custodial parent. We talked about this for hours—my three children (aged 6, 13, and 14), their father, and I. The kids wanted to remain close to school friends and other family members rather than move across the country to a new and unknown life. I decided not to challenge their decision. At the time, it was a relief because I wouldn't be changing their lives drastically. I knew I would miss them, but I thought I could stay in close touch.

But I told Brant none of this until after I saw him again. Instead, swallowing my fear of his reaction to seeing me in my usual circumstances, I said I would love to see him.

I was sure that, when he saw me in my suburban roles as wife, mother, and housekeeper, he would be disappointed. He might think that the woman who bloomed at the college alumni meeting did not really exist. I knew I wasn't sure that she did—yet. But I was so wrong!

He greeted the news of my job offer with encouragement. And it was clear from the minute I saw him again that our mutual interests and pleasure in talking together still existed. The more we talked, the more energy we seemed to generate.

Within an hour of greeting him, I was telling Brant all my worries about the future. He understood what I meant because he had experienced the same feelings when his own marriage ended. So we talked about the emotional pain, the guilt, and the grief that go into that awful rendering of lives that's called divorce.

Finally, I made a decision to do something I never had the courage to do before—I showed him a suspense novel I had been working on for three years. He was the first person I trusted with it, and I wondered if he would laugh. But he didn't. He said something wise and so encouraging that it was the one remark that would get me over the most difficult times of my life, which were soon to follow: "I admire the kind of work you've put in on this. Even if this book doesn't sell, it shows you have the drive and all the skills that are necessary. I don't know anyone who has been able to do this kind of thing. I'll bet you get somewhere with it."

Meanwhile, the fun of being with him again was having a devastating effect on me. I remember one episode very clearly. Invited to my home for dinner, he turned the radio dials until he found a Rolling Stones song. Guessing correctly that I'd never really listened to the Stones, he waited for a strategic Jagger scream, then twisted the dial up full blast. I jumped and turned and caught a look on his face of such mischief and pleasure that it gave him a totally charming, devilish appeal. And at that moment, I fell head over heels in love.

I also kept it to myself. I thought it was absurd that I felt this way. I reminded myself that I was nine years older than he, and if I told him how I felt, he would be shocked.

It was midnight of the day he returned home that I sat alone at my makeshift desk, my children asleep, and thought about him. I opened the journal I was keeping, and my hand trembled as I wrote—"Is this the kind of man you give up everything for? What am I doing? What is happening to me?"

I put the pen down and cried and cried. I felt as if I was going mad. I was leaving my marriage, leaving my children, and fantasizing about a man I could never be with. Not only was he married, but the nine-year age difference made my even thinking of him ridiculous. I figured I was more desperate than I had ever imagined.

But once I accepted that I was on the edge of insanity, I decided it was no great loss to go ahead and imagine the impossible. So, even as I admitted it would never work, I decided to keep tuned in to Brant's life. I might just take a chance. It was an absurd thought, but at that time I had nothing to lose.

I had no idea how he felt until another two months had passed. By that time, I had begun work in Boston, and Brant had moved there, too, taking a new job with a local news agency. It was a wonderful coincidence for me. At first, we met to work on plans for a newsletter for the alumni council. Afterward, we would have a drink together and share the common woes of people who are dealing with divorce. I let myself enjoy his company more and more, but I was always aware of our age difference. He told me later that he never thought about it. But I was so frightened.

One night, he took me to dinner and for a long walk afterward.

"What are you thinking?" he asked me.

I could have given lots of answers. I could have said, "This weather is too hot, and my crummy apartment is awful." I could have cried a little and said, "I don't know if I'm doing the right thing; I miss my kids so terribly."

But I didn't. Instead, I said, "I think I'm falling in love with you."

He stopped walking and reached out to touch the back of my neck. I started to cry. "It's dumb, I know, but I am. I also think that the most I would ever ask for is just one year with you." I couldn't believe the words coming out of my mouth.

I have never felt so naked. And all because I was too old to be saying this. Too old.

But he disagreed with me. Just as he had in that first meeting, he let me know my opinion wasn't necessarily correct.

So, less than six months after we met, we began to see each other as man and woman, not as younger man and older woman. It was a wonderful time of discovering another person and rediscovering myself. We never ran out of things to say to each other. More than anything, we reaffirmed, day by day, how much we *liked* each other.

I admired his work even more when I observed it firsthand. Meanwhile, my own self-esteem skyrocketed when I discovered that my meager journalistic experience was suddenly in demand because I had worked extensively with the commodity markets in my recent position as news editor for a wire service specializing in commodities, making me a valuable asset to the computer firms developing software for investors. Over the next 10 weeks, I received some dandy offers that made me feel like a million.

It was also wonderful getting to know Brant. My heart overflowed with happiness and energy. In 10 weeks, I came to a new understanding of what love could be between two people whose interests and passions and dreams meshed so well. It was difficult to believe, it was so perfect. The fact is, I didn't believe it at all.

I just knew it couldn't last. Already I missed my children too much. Until I'd tried to live so far away, I never quite knew how important mothering was to me—not what I did *for* my kids, but the emotional wealth that I drew *from* them. So even though I could now say that this was a man with whom I would love to have a future, my despair over my children got in the way. When I put my sons on a plane home after a brief visit and cried steadily for the next week, I knew I couldn't survive without them.

Just short of a nervous breakdown, I turned down a dream job that would have paid me over $50,000 a year, got into my car, and drove back to that midwestern city where my children lived. I had my last $250 in my pocket and everything I owned in the world packed into my Chevrolet. I had said good-bye to Brant, who had asked if he could visit sometime.

"No," I'd said. "It can never work between us."

Saying No for All the Wrong Reasons

On my return to the Midwest, my career took a big leap forward—I became executive director of a statewide political campaign—and, to my great surprise, things began to work out right away. I got joint custody of my kids, and I got back on track emotionally. I was able to rent a room from a good friend for a while, and soon I found a lovely little house to rent.

I didn't forget Brant. We talked every day by phone, but I discouraged his plans to visit. After all, I tried to tell him, I was back in real life now. And in real life, sensible women don't get involved with younger men, especially when they have children and family and lots of friends to think about.

Brant disagreed, of course, but I held fast. In my warped way, I looked at the depth of his feelings for me as evidence of immaturity, of a lack of understanding of how the world really works. I was sure time would prove me right.

I told him I had to date men my own age. So I did, and I was bored out of my mind. I would come back from a tedious date with a man with whom I had nothing in common and think of the long, wonderful talks I'd had with Brant while jogging on the esplanade along the Charles River. Or I'd recall the wintry Saturday afternoons when we would roam the streets of Cambridge and stop to splurge on huge sandwiches or meander through bookstores and record shops. I remembered how much fun it had been to go to rock concerts and listen to all the great music that I had tuned out for the last decade. It was so funny—at a couple of those concerts I saw men my age with younger women. They were having as good a time as I was, and I felt proud of myself for keeping up with the boys for a change. Still, even as I ached for the new and exciting part of me that I left in Boston, I couldn't think of Brant and me as a couple because I had returned to living by all the old rules.

But Brant was determined to see me again. One night he

called to say he had a ticket to arrive for my birthday in March.

I tried to sound happy on the phone, but I dreaded his coming. Two memories paralyzed me every time I tried to think of a future for us together. Both were of women I knew who had become involved with younger men.

The first was the wife of a prominent executive I knew. The executive was a beefy kind of guy who took pride in his romantic pursuit of the secretarial pool. He was renowned for his heavy drinking and for waking up Saturday mornings still downtown, quite naked, with at least one woman in his bed. I had met his wife at a party once and watched her closely. A very young wife myself, I looked for some sign of misbehavior on her part that would justify *his* behavior, but all I saw was a friendly, straightforward woman who took her husband home early that night because he was so drunk he could barely walk. Several months later, we heard that she had left him—for their 19-year-old gardener. She would have been in her mid-thirties at the time.

The men in our circle, including my husband, snickered. The women mumbled softly about what a sad case she was. Even the wives who had been her friends managed to disown her. Everyone saw her move as a desperate one, an incredibly stupid one. They pitied her husband. That was my first image of a woman with a younger man.

The second one was even scarier to me because it involved a woman who I thought was much more courageous than I could ever hope to be.

She was a woman I knew in college—we'll call her Erin— who was a year ahead of me and who everyone thought was stunning. Tall, with a lovely, expressive face and a ripe, full-breasted body, Erin carried herself with such assurance that people would stop in their tracks to watch her pass. A talented writer, she was also a gifted actress and singer. I didn't know a person, male or female, who wasn't immediately impressed upon seeing her. Erin had everything, including a flair for romantic rebellion. If any woman could flaunt convention with spirit and fire, it was Erin.

Ten years after I last saw her in college, I read in the newspaper that Erin would be coming to our city to perform a benefit concert. By this time, she had become famous, a confidante of people like Bob Dylan and other icons of our generation. What a beautiful, successful woman! I got in touch with her and arranged to have lunch. We caught up on news of mutual friends, and then she told me that she was soon to be married. She was thrilled. Just to make conversation, I asked her, "How old is he?"

Talk about a conversation stopper! Erin blanched. She dropped her head and looked away.

"Will you keep this confidential?" she asked me, all the happiness drained from her voice. "Please don't tell anyone . . . he's four years younger than I am."

"Oh . . . ," I said, understanding. "I promise," and I reached over to touch her arm, "I won't tell anyone."

And I never did—until now. Now something has changed. Erin's husband may have been four years younger, but his age has not made a difference; they have enjoyed a long and good marriage.

So Brant was on his way to visit me from Boston. It was hopeless. I was sure the visit would be a miserable time for us both. I just could not see a way to make a relationship between the two of us seem right, much less take off with the kind of love and mutual support that any couple needs in order to move ahead together.

I called him to say a final no to his visit, to any future between us. And he had an interesting response: he agreed.

"Okay," he said, "but I want you to know I've decided to start seeing other people. I have to get on with my life. I'm taking out a woman I used to know next week."

"Good," I said, and I hung up. I started to tremble. The trembling turned into shaking, and I leaned down to put my head between my knees. I felt faint. I felt nauseated. I tried to calm myself and think hard about what I was doing.

Here I was trying to tell myself that I could change my life for the better, yet I was turning away the most loving, honest man I had ever met, one of the kindest, brightest human beings I had ever known. Why? Because I was intimidated by the fact that I was older than he was.

I took a good hard look at myself. Was I really worried about what people would think of me with Brant? Didn't I realize they already thought I was a fool to have walked out on my marriage? To have left my children? To have put myself in a position where I had to earn my own living, a pretty puny living, at the age of 35? I had nothing to lose on that front.

What is wrong with you? I asked myself. You've just spent months talking about how you don't care about what these people do or think—so why are you doing this? What the hell does it matter what anyone else thinks? It's your goddamn life! You are still buying into the same dumb program that almost destroyed you.

Dozens of thoughts raced through my mind as I held my arms tightly and the tears streamed down my face.

What do I think people will say? That I'm desperate? That I have a gigolo? That I am weak and silly? So what? I know that's not true. What matters isn't what others think of me but how I will react to that. Don't I have the strength to believe in myself, in Brant, and in the full worth of our lives as they might be together?

Be smart for once, I told myself. This is a good man who thinks he loves you. Think about what that means to you. Take care of yourself. Give the two of you a chance. For God's sake, nine years may not make a difference. How will you know if you don't try?

And in the midst of my emotional chaos, another memory surfaced, one of my own mother. She once faced a much more serious problem, took a chance, and won. At the age of 25, with three little babies, she lost her sight and her muscle coordination. She couldn't move. My father took her to the Mayo Clinic.

"You have multiple sclerosis," the doctors told her as she lay paralyzed and blind. "You'll never walk again."

My mother thought that over, and then she made her move: "Bullshit," she said calmly, and she got up and walked out on her own. She walked until she died, and she had five more babies along the way. Our house became a way station for MS patients as doctors sent them over for a good dose of Mom's bullshit theory.

It had taken me way too long, but I could finally see that my situation wasn't that serious. I also had one other thought: Would I be holding back like this if Brant were 35, 45, or even 55? Hell, no. What a bunch of bullshit!

And so what if it didn't work? No guarantees come with any relationship. When I was with him, I felt beautiful and smart, young and alive. That was enough right there.

I walked back to the telephone and dialed Brant's number. When he answered, I took a deep breath and asked him to come for my birthday. He came. And I hope he stays for the rest of my life.

Loving a Younger Man— Can It Really Work?

What happened next is what this book is all about.

Slowly, over the next two years, I began to find out about other women who were married to or dating younger men. What was curious about all of them was that *they didn't want to talk about it* until they learned that I was involved with a younger man also. Then you couldn't shut them up. However, until that moment we all had the same feeling: that each of us was alone, one of the few women involved with younger men. Even more important is the intimidation that many of us feel when it comes to dating, living with, or marrying a younger man. We are afraid of the idea, yet we aren't sure why.

During this time, I had an experience that made me realize how unfair our silence has been to all the millions of women who might really enjoy dating a younger man—or even find a wonderful husband in one. It happened not long after Brant had come to visit. He ended up being offered a job in the city where I lived. Not only did he make major changes in his life by finding a job that made it possible for him to be near me, but that summer we drove north with my children to introduce him to my family. We had begun to think seriously of marriage.

Shortly after we arrived, my father was in a terrible car accident. At the hospital to visit Dad, I ran into an old, old friend with whom I had grown up. We had lived in the same neighborhood, and I knew his family well. Hastily, in the hospital corridor, we caught up with each other's lives. I told him of my divorce and said that I hoped to marry again soon. He congratulated me.

"Well . . . ," I hedged, "it's kind of unusual . . . he's nine years younger than I am." Why did I say that? For one thing, I said it all the time. I was so afraid that people might gossip behind my back that I made a point of putting the facts on the table myself.

But my friend just smiled and gave me a hug. "Hey," he said, "it's a deep, dark family secret, but Mom is 12 years older than Dad. She'd kill me if she knew I told you. Really, don't worry. Ages don't make a difference. Good luck."

He walked off, leaving me standing with my mouth open. I never would have guessed that woman was older than her husband! She didn't *look* older. I had always considered the family to be especially attractive and interesting, with brothers and sisters and parents who seemed to have a lot of fun together.

I wish my friend's mother hadn't hidden that 12-year difference all those years. All of a sudden—perhaps because she was a part of the town and the people that shaped my young life—I didn't feel so alone anymore. If I had known it before, I might never have hesitated when I first felt myself falling in love with Brant. One thing I know now—I want to be sure other women don't hesitate.

After that brief encounter, I began actively to seek out more women like me. At the same time, a curious thing happened. More and more women started to ask me about my own relationship. They wanted to know if it worked and why it worked and to see if it might work for them. I kept saying, "Sure, give him a chance. It's great for us."

Slowly, my worry that people would think something was really wrong with me or abnormal about Brant and me as a

Preface

couple, or that they would make us pay for this in some un-
imagined but embarrassingly public way, was proven quite
unfounded. Well, with one exception. My former husband
did try to tell old friends that I ran off with a 19-year-old
lifeguard. The tactic backfired. Most of them called me immediately, titillated, and demanded the truth, which I gave
them. Several then invited us to dinner so they could survey
the situation, and they discovered how much they, too, enjoyed Brant's wit and intelligence. Our friendships with these
couples have flourished since.

On the other hand, even as I learned how wrong I was in
second-guessing other people, I had to face other, unexpected
problems that occurred between us.

Brant had never had a child. Was I willing to go through
that again if having a child was important to him? The first
time I tried to bring up the subject of late babies with my
gynecologist, I burst into tears because I wasn't ready to be
a mother again. Today I feel differently, but now I seem unable to get pregnant. How will this affect our life together?

And our experience with the "blended family," in which
you attempt to merge your new partner into the home you
share with children from your previous marriage, was perfectly miserable at times. It was enormously difficult for Brant
to adapt to three adolescents barging into his bedroom, using
his records and books without asking, demanding my attention when he needed it, too.

So it hasn't been easy, getting our life together under way.
Often it was tempting to pawn off our personal failures on the
age difference. We had to pull back and remember that no
household exists in which all things work smoothly. But you
can see the kinds of questions that need answering. That's
why this book is about our joys and our difficulties—what the
real problems are that couples like us must face and how they
might be solved.

Why Is This Book Needed?

I was asked that numerous times—although never by a woman in love with a younger man. I think I can answer that best if I tell you about something that happened to me.

When I first began work on *Loving a Younger Man*, I found myself hesitant to discuss it with people I did not know well. Several times I heard myself say, "Oh, I have a rather silly book project I'm involved with. . . ."

A rather silly book project? This is a book about one of the most important parts of my own life—my love for my husband. What was I saying? Why was I saying it? Where did this sneaky sense of embarrassment come from? After all, the very reason I had convinced a publisher that the book was needed was to eradicate the embarrassment and the snickers, to clear up all the misunderstandings.

I had a difficult time answering myself until I realized how many times—because I am a woman—I have a tendency to discount my feelings and ideas. And when I look at our societal disregard for women as they age, which is something I have become more acutely aware of while working on this book, the problem is clear: we don't think of ourselves as *important* people with *important* concerns.

I have since stopped making any remarks pertinent to this book that have the word *silly* in them. If *Loving a Younger Man* makes a singular statement, it is this: you are a valuable human being, and I am a valuable human being, and we both deserve to love and be loved.

After all, men of all ages think of themselves as important. They make people take them seriously. And what we are really talking about in this book is women's right to do something men have always done—choose the person we love from the ranks of possible mates of all ages. Men have long been able to date and marry women much younger than they are. It's time for women to be allowed to do the same without a hint of stigma or taboo.

The Best Marriages
in the World

Did I say I was silly in the first line of this book? I take that back. I feel much wiser these days, particularly since I met and talked with the 40 people (24 of them as couples) who shared their stories with me for this book.

What an independent, energetic, courageous crowd. Seldom have I met more imaginative, bright, hardworking, and physically attractive people. And I don't mean a superficial beauty. Whether they were age 20 or 80, energy and youth radiated from their faces. These are people who know the secret of eternal youth: keeping busy, very busy.

They are people who have faced painfully difficult decisions, survived traumatic life experiences, and still bring a positive, healthy attitude to everything they do. They are dedicated to continuing to learn and to grow and to maintaining the best marriages in the world.

Their names and occupations have been changed to protect their privacy. Each came to my attention through a friend or colleague who knew that I was writing this book. The 10 couples I chose to interview in depth come from different parts of the country and different types of communities: North, South, East, West; urban, suburban, and rural. Many other people were also gracious enough to share with me in detail their innermost fears and joys, their hopes and their disappointments. Family members and friends of the couples studied, interested outsiders, and many women who have considered these relationships for themselves sat down with me to discuss different aspects of the topic.

The couples' age differences range from as little as 6 years to as much as 23 years. Women in their twenties are rarely attracted to men who are more than 4 to 8 years younger. Women in their thirties and forties may be with men who are more than 15 years younger. The gap was similar among women in their fifties and sixties, though these are also the age groups in which an age difference of 20 years or more might be found. These patterns, of course, repeat the age gaps frequently found in couples where the man is older than the woman.

I interviewed couples who have been together for periods ranging from 3 years to 20 years. Most are married; a few are getting married soon, dating steadily, or have just begun relationships and are stumbling through all the confusion and doubt that everyone faces at first.

As I searched through the transcripts that I made of our conversations, examining and analyzing what works and what doesn't work in these relationships, I discovered something deeply personal. I learned that there is a part of me in each of these lives—that my worries, my small terrors, and my happiness are duplicated in their experiences. I faced the same fears that each "older woman" faced. The old taboos have hurt me as much as they have others. At the same time, to emerge from the difficulties with a solid, warm, and loving marriage—similar in spirit to the ones I've discovered and share with you here—gives this new awareness a special meaning. No wonder I feel very close to each person in this book.

I'd like to begin with a quote from a philosopher whose work I admired when I was 18. Only now do I realize that I had only the slightest understanding of the true meaning of his words:

In the midst of winter I finally learned that there was in me an invincible summer.

—Camus

Acknowledgments

As I wrote this book, I was guided by the efforts of many. First and foremost, I was guided by the lives of the women and men I interviewed, who must remain anonymous but who trusted me with their most intimate joys and fears. The stories of these kind, courageous people have changed my life, and I have done my very best to see that they change yours. Their generosity in sharing their stories reflects their generosity toward each other. To them I offer my deepest gratitude.

The two women who first taught me about independence—Alice McBride Kirsch and Catherine Higgins Kirsch—have influenced every page I have written. Some of my most valuable resources, particularly recent writings on women's development that provided essential documentation, were brought to my attention by my daughter Nicole Melcher. Yet none of this would have been possible without the unfailing support of Elizabeth and Joe Houston, parents of my husband Brant. They raised their son to love and cherish those qualities that ensure freedom and respect for all people, which is why we are together today. And to Brant I am indebted for his unflagging good humor when deadlines postponed normal family life. But most of all, I deeply appreciate his willingness to let me share with readers those incidents in our life

Acknowledgments

together that ground this book in reality and experience. He has been the source of my inspiration.

Stacy Prince, my editor and head coach, has provided remarkable insight, guidance, and buoyant good spirits throughout. She has brought a unique energy and enthusiasm to our work together. Through each stage of research, writing, and editing, we have been aided and abetted most ably by Deborah Brody.

My agent, Martha Millard, not only made it possible for me to write about this subject immediately upon my urge to do so, but also put me in touch with excellent sources. Gail Steinberg, a senior producer for "Donahue," deserves special thanks, as her perceptive questions were the catalyst that led to this book. I also want to thank the following people for their recommendations of contacts and other resources that have been invaluable in the preparation of this book: Mary Pradt, Carole Chouinard, Lynda Klug, Judith Cooke, Linda Woodsmall, Bill Oliver, Gary Larson, Diane Galante, and Melanie Kirsch.

A special thanks to photographer Todd Smith for his marvelous photo for the book jacket; and my thanks, too, to Sherry Sullivan, who carefully and speedily transcribed many hours of tapes and took the extra time to provide her insightful comments.

Finally, I must thank all the women who have gone before me to fight the battles of the women's movement. It is their work that has made my work possible.

Introduction

*A new study reports that college-educated women who are
still single at the age of 35 have only a 5 percent chance of
ever getting married . . . the dire statistics confirmed what
everybody suspected all along: that many women who seemed
to have it all—good looks and good jobs, advanced degrees
and high salaries—will never have mates.*

—*Newsweek*
June 2, 1986

That *Newsweek* article, and many others like it, caused a
media blitz that had women all over the United States be-
moaning their fate. After years of struggling to make it in a
"man's" world, we had to face incontrovertible, scientific
proof of what our mothers had been saying all along: if you
wait too long, all the good men will be gone. The bottom
line? Any woman brazen enough to go out there and make it
on her own is going to stay that way—on her own.

So the unspoken fear shared by many single women, a fear
that many had almost succeeded in keeping in the backs of
their minds, was now an undeniable reality. Biology may not
be destiny anymore, but good luck trying to have it all.

1

There were, of course, a few sane, balanced articles that put the study that engendered the discussion, "Marriage Patterns in the United States," into perspective. But they were mostly lost in the shuffle, as headlines like "The Marriage Crunch" ricocheted across the country's magazine covers and boomed out at us from television sets. We became even more obsessed with the "biological time clock" and complained to each other about the horrible shortage of men.

But what most of us didn't notice, and what most reporters neglected to point out, is that the news isn't all that alarming; there isn't a *man* shortage, simply an *older* man shortage!

It's easy to see why the study struck fear into the hearts of millions. Traditionally, women marry men who are two to three years older. In recent years, however, as the members of the baby boom generation reached marriageable age, the number of women in the marriage pool far outdistanced the number of eligible, slightly older men. Then why—and how—are more people than ever getting married? (How many of us *haven't* been to a wedding in the last two years?)

The answer is good news for women who found last year's magazine articles scary. In fact, it's good news for all of us.

The Best-Kept Secret

Would you like a couple of statistics that will knock your socks off?

Of 2,400,000 weddings that took place in 1985 (the most recent figures available) and analyzed by the National Center for Health Statistics, more than 30 percent of the women aged 25 to 34 married younger men. Of the women aged 35 to 44, nearly 40 percent married younger men. And it doesn't stop there. Women in the older age groups also married younger men at a rate well over 30 percent.

A recent article In *Parade Magazine*, citing statistics provided by Barbara Foley Wilson, an analyst at the National Center for Health Statistics, said, "There were 159,000 marriages in 1985 in which the bride was at least five years older than the bridegroom. That represented 6.6 percent of all marriages that year. In 1970, by comparison, only 3.7 percent of our brides were five years or more older than their husbands. That's a 67 percent increase in 14 years.''

Do you know what else these figures mean? They prove that *over a third of us are marrying younger men*. Did you know that?

I didn't. At the time that I married a younger man, I thought I was a singular statistic—a solitary number that would reduce some statistician in the bowels of the U.S. Bureau of the Census to giggles. I was wrong. Millions of women around us are marrying younger men. In other words, that alarm over a diminishing marriage pool of older men really doesn't count for much.

But let's not stop there. Let's take a look at the women who don't marry, but choose to live with a man instead.

In 1985, of 255,000 women aged 35 to 44 polled by the Census Bureau, 32 percent were living with younger men (up from 18 percent in 1980). Of 199,000 women aged 45 to 64, 23 percent were living with younger men. And of the younger women, aged 25 to 34, while a smaller percentage were with younger men, an astonishing 65 percent were living with men their own age rather than the more traditional older men.

If I had been aware that 40 percent of the women my age were marrying younger men these days, I would have been much less reluctant to do it myself. I would not have put off each new stage of my relationship by thinking that it was out of the ordinary.

I asked several women in love with younger men what they thought of the statistics. ''Are you kidding?'' said one. ''If so many women are doing this, that makes me feel much better about my boyfriend. He's five years younger than I am, and I've been too embarrassed to mention it. Not anymore. Numbers like that make me look like one of the lucky ones, don't they?''

The numbers I found only proved what I suspected was happening. My first clue that more and more women were involved with younger men came from remarks such as the following.

"A great thing happened the other day," said Stephanie, a petite, attractive, and very energetic natural blonde who went back to school in her late thirties and now has a career as a record producer. "I went out to lunch with two women friends of mine, and we discovered we're all dating younger men. I'm 43, one of my friends is 37, and the other one is 32. I was dating the oldest man—he's 30. Of the men they're dating, one is 27 and the other is 25."

These comments go hand in hand with what psychologist Herbert Freudenberger said in a *Picture Week* article: "Six to eight years ago, when the man shortage began, women laughed about making it with a younger man. Then five years ago, it became more serious. More recently, they have begun to marry."

I wonder why the statistics were so hard to find. I can't believe no one else has asked for them, yet I seemed to be the first to plague the people at the Census Bureau for these data. Is it because no one cares or because it just isn't important that women know about this major change in our patterns of love and marriage? I don't know the answer to that. It may be that many of the women who have married younger men married men only a year or two younger, so nothing seemed different, and no one asked. But I am very glad that we found these numbers, because they show that women are working around social taboos that have traditionally made marriage to a younger man (even a man just a few years younger) unlikely. The fact is, these statistics may change someone's life. They make reality out of our dream of freedom to choose whomever we want to love.

Freedom and Equal Partnerships

From a sociological perspective, the fact that women are feeling freer to marry younger men makes sense. In recent years, our attitudes have changed and become more like men's in many ways. According to Suzanne M. Bianchi's book, *American Women in Transition* (New York: Russell Sage Foundation, 1986), we now nearly match the percentages of men who feel that a career is a primary life goal and that family life is the top life goal. We are much closer to mirroring men's attitudes toward premarital sex as greater numbers of us both approve of and engage in premarital sex. Furthermore, we are tending to marry at nearly the same ages as men do; our median age at first marriage has risen, and we are marrying during a seven-year age span similar to men's—they marry between the ages of 22 and 29, while we generally marry for the first time between 20 and 27.

Today's American woman has proven she is willing to battle for new options. Here is an impressive list of choices—all of them forcing society to change—that she has won since the women's movement began in the late 1960s:

- the opportunity to be an independent, self-sufficient human being who can support herself, no longer seeking personal identity and expression through a man
- the opportunity to achieve whatever education level she needs in order to compete with men in the labor force
- the opportunity to enter the labor force early and stay late so that she, too, may qualify for the raises, promotions, and other rewards once the exclusive province of men.
- the opportunity to enter professions and occupations once open to "men only," such as medicine, law, business, and engineering
- the opportunity, because she has increased her control over her economic status, to exercise more control over her personal and family life

More women than ever have taken charge of every element of their professional and personal lives, managing to achieve equality with their male peers in nearly every aspect. Older woman/younger man relationships reflect women's new willingness to apply to their personal lives the attitudes and self-confidence they have learned from making it in the work-

5

place. Women are exercising their right to choose the men they love from a marriage pool of older *and* younger men—a pool that is identical, age-wise, to the one our male peers have always had the freedom to choose from.

This equality doesn't end in the choosing of a mate, however. As I researched this phenomenon, I discovered something I thought was unique to my own marriage: these unions are equal partnerships, right down the line, from sex to stocks and bonds. I found that the overwhelming majority of women in love with younger men are working women who, on the average, pay 50 percent of household expenses. Because both partners generally contribute equal shares to the financial support of the household, I found that decisions are considered mutually, children cared for by both, and houses cleaned (or the cleaning paid for) by both.

And if that sounds too dry and calculating, I rush to add that they are men and women who know how to be each other's best friends. Beyond the passion of sex, they love to talk together, walk hand in hand in the breeze, and share the small pleasures of life. And central to every relationship, said each couple interviewed, was respect for each other as individuals. This mutual respect is a tenet of *any* good relationship. And it may be easier, as we'll see in the following chapters, for women to have equal partnerships with men younger than they are.

The Power of Social Norms

Even though the numbers finally indicate that more women are choosing their partners from the ranks of younger men, I found very few who feel comfortable with that choice. I suspect that's one reason those statistics were hard to find: women haven't asked to know more about themselves because they have a secret fear they are doing something wrong. I felt that way. And I never expected to find myself reflected in such numbers—I was so sure I was alone.

Why? Because I have been so keenly aware of a social attitude, a social norm, critical of women like me.

Society frowns on women loving younger men. Call it an outdated attitude. Call it a tired, silly taboo. Call it unfair. It may be gradually fading, but it's here. And we must deal with it in order to defeat it.

To do that we first have to realize that a desire for romantic relationships and marriage still fuels our lives as contemporary women even though we are simultaneously reaching out for independence and self-sufficiency. All the recent studies on women's development and behavior patterns show that one thing has not changed: marriage and motherhood are still vitally important to young women today. Over 90 percent of American women marry by age 30. But one desire does not have to be exclusive of the other. In fact, our emergence as women who have many options to choose from should make our lives better in every respect.

So where does it come from—that feeling that when we date or fall in love with a younger man we're doing something wrong?

From men. More specifically, from men in authority. Our fathers, our teachers, our bosses, our shrinks. We are just now emerging from years and years of social conditioning in which men have been our leaders and the social "judges" of our culture. What we chose to do with our lives had to fit the mold men had created. As female babies, we were reared to live our lives, make our choices, in the circumscribed arena they allowed us.

This is not news to all of you who are interested in women's issues. Being the "good wife" during critical years of change, however, I missed the feminist revolution in all its complexity. For example, I did not know until I recently read Carol Gilligan's *In a Different Voice* that not only were our early, influential social scientists exclusively male, but they based their behavior models, which became *our* behavior models, not on men and women as different kinds of individuals with different developmental patterns leading to different behavior patterns and expectations, but only on the men they studied.

7

"Psychologists have tended to regard male behavior as the 'norm,' " said Gilligan, "and female behavior as some kind of deviation from that norm . . . thus when women do not conform to the standards of psychological expectation, the conclusion has generally been that something is wrong with the women."

In essence, if our round pegs don't fit their square holes, we are in trouble—we are deviant; we are wrong.

All of this is slowly changing, of course. But what's distressing is that, as women, many of us still feel we should conform to men's psychological expectations. We feel wrong if we do not choose (now that we've got the choice) to accept what men expect of us; we risk losing the men, for one thing, and, beyond that, there are still strong psychological and social pressures to conform to the traditional mode. And traditional men do not expect women to want younger guys.

Think back to that "marriage crunch" story and its thesis that all current data prove a working woman's marriage options diminish dramatically after her 35th birthday. That was an excellent example of the power of social norms. Few questioned the reliability of that conclusion. Following a traditional way of thinking, people assumed it was correct.

To their credit, a couple of writers and reporters tried to publish a dissenting opinion. One reason for all the attention paid to the "marriage crunch" story, several pointed out, was that male-dominated society was censoring independent, working women for forcing their way into the workplace. All those articles were a message from the guys that "you can't have it all." You'll notice that no one put *that* opinion on the front page!

It is important to point out that no one is "to blame" here. The taboo against women marrying younger men is a social norm of long standing that is internalized within each of us. Until recently, there has been no avoiding it: social norms have discouraged the marriage of older women to younger men no matter what the age difference. Two years or 20—if the woman is *any* number of years older than a man, she is an oddball, flaunting tradition. Because women themselves have internalized many of the negative attitudes that keep them from getting what they want and deserve, we've got to change the way we think, too.

Time for Women to Adopt One More Male Attitude

"It's imperative to tell women that it's not their fault," Ann Swidler of Stanford University recently said in a paper presented to the American Sociological Association. ". . . They have gotten better [with age] but they've got a bad market situation." The article reported that four sociologists and two psychologists "found that there is no shortage of men in the marriage market, only a practice of men marrying, and re-marrying, women who are younger than they, mostly to impress other men." The fact is that, for whatever reason, men have not thought twice about entering into relationships with younger women. And women have not thought twice about it either—until recently.

"At first, I didn't understand the game," said one woman who is 42 years old. "All the men I used to date are suddenly dating younger women. But I'm supposed to be locked into older guys or ones my own age? I just said the hell with it. If some jerk I went to high school with can divorce his wife and marry a woman 10 years younger, so can I. I work hard; I make money. I'm raising my kids by myself. And, goddamit, my boyfriend turns 30 tomorrow."

Another woman agrees but explains, "I think it's more than just an age issue. All the rules are changing on us. Especially with the high divorce rate and the reduced alimony and child support that you get these days. I have to work to support myself and give my children the kind of life I want them to have. I have to live with all the same pressures that a man in my office has. So my feeling is, if I am willing to pay the price, then maybe I should get the prize.

"Let me put it this way. I'm supposed to run my division like I'm an entrepreneur, right? That takes good old-fashioned rebel spirit and a lot of innovative thinking. So I'm just applying those principles to my personal life: I'm going to take this supposed man shortage and turn it into a bonanza. Who says I have to date a 55-year-old? I feel 40. I'll date a 40-year-old, thank you.''

Judging by the women I know, most of us want it all—family *and* career. I firmly believe that, in order to achieve that, we must adopt the attitude these women have—the traditional male attitude toward relationships—and recognize that a spouse can be found among those millions of people younger than we are.

Time to Talk

Two things have prevented women from being comfortable with an older woman/younger man relationship, even as more and more women are rebelling against old attitudes by getting into this kind of relationship in the first place. The first of these is acquiescence to the norm; the second is a lack of support and communication.

As I mentioned earlier, the power of the social norm is amazing—it can cause independent, successful women to feel guilty about something that should be the most wonderful thing in the world: love. More than the *fact* of what they are doing, these women are bothered by the *embarrassment:* what other people will think.

What is the embarrassment all about?

Let me tell you from my own experience, because every woman I talk to asks me the same questions I once asked myself. We're talking about anxiety of the first order. I'm going to translate each question into the embarrassment factor involved.

Question: Won't I look older than him?

Translation: Gee, how embarrassing. Everyone will notice us, and maybe they'll think I'm his mother or his older sister. And what about when my face caves in—can he cope with my wrinkles?

10

Question: Will I be able to keep up with him in bed?

Translation: Oh, God, what if I go through menopause when I'm 50 and he's only 40? Will it hurt when we have sex, and will I have the courage to tell him? Is that when he'll leave me for a younger woman?

Question: What if he wants to have children?

Translation: Will my teenagers die if their friends find out they have an older mom who is pregnant? What will the people in my office think—maternity leave at 45?

Question: If I'm only nine years younger than his mother, what will she think of me?

Translation: How on earth do I face his parents? They must be appalled that he is with a woman my age. I'd be upset if *my* son brought home a 40-year-old.

Question: How do I prepare my friends and my family for this? I'm not sure they can handle it.

Translation: They will think I'm desperate or weird, and I don't think I can handle it.

Question: How do I tell my coworkers?

Translation: There goes all my status as a good decision maker. They're going to think I'm just a silly female.

And so it goes, whether you are 22 or 62 and your man is 19 or 51. The questions are basically the same, and the embarrassment is acute.

Having first acknowledged our right to have a relationship with a younger man, we must recognize and understand the social attitudes that work invisibly against us. By naming this embarrassment, we rob it of some of its power to hurt us. I will deal with each area of embarrassment in this book; you'll have a chance to find out from me and from other men and women some of the ways we cope with the problem. In addition, you'll learn how quickly these embarrassment issues disappear as very real, age-related issues come up. Some of the questions that these men and women must face—whether or not to have children, for example—are both real problems

11

and potentially embarrassing. But, as you'll see, couples often find some "embarrassing" situations amusing, serving to bring them even closer.

For the most part, we have no control over what other people think and say about us; our only control is in how we react to it. But the second factor, the lack of support and communication on the older woman/younger man issue, *is* something we can change.

It seems that women have been very secretive about their relationships with younger men. Some deny it to themselves for a long time. Others "neglect" to mention their lovers' ages to their friends. Even those who are forthcoming about the age of their lovers often won't discuss their problems with their friends, for fear of getting an "I told you it wouldn't work" response.

Part of the problem is that, though women "share their innermost feelings" with their good friends, there are still things women are afraid to discuss with each other. If we discuss sex too openly, we might be labeled as sexually aggressive (and women, as much as men, have bought into the notion that women aren't supposed to be that way). Or we might fear smirks or frowns, not from strangers, but from good friends who might be uncomfortable with our new loves.

Well, we *are* sexually aggressive. Sex is as important to women as it is to men, when we don't work so hard at repressing our natural instincts. And I still feel anger at myself for letting my fear and embarrassment hurt me in a way that is quite sad. I let it rob me of my exuberance over the wonder of our love. I let it stop me from feeling really good about us early in our relationship. Rather than wave my good fortune like a banner to the men and women around me, the way I might have announced a new love with an older man, I presented it shyly, with an apology.

The irony is that, had we all been talking openly all along rather than loving younger men in secret, there probably wouldn't be a need for this book. I firmly believe the best way to effect a positive change is to begin talking about it openly and honestly. This is how we will make these relationships better understood and more acceptable.

Some Bad Statistics, or Good Reasons to Consider a Younger Man

In case you're still waffling, wondering whether this idea of relationships with younger men is or isn't a good idea, here is a sobering list of statistics. Read these and you'll know how alarming the situation is for a woman still locked into thinking she can marry only an older man.

- Since 1960, the number of women living alone has more than doubled. The largest percentage increases are among women under 25 and between the ages of 25 and 44.
- Over the last 20 years, the number of women heading households has increased dramatically—from 6.5 million in 1950 to 22.5 million in 1983, with the greatest increase occurring among women under age 35.
- Over the last 10 years, the percentage of women between the ages of 25 and 35 who have never married has more than doubled.
- Single women between the ages of 25 and 35 outnumber men by over 1 million.
- Women are widowed twice as often as men, at younger ages, and spend twice as many years widowed; widowers over age 65 are *eight times* more likely to remarry than widows.
- Women outlive their husbands to greatly outnumber men at older ages.

Several of the above statistics were found in *American Women in Transition* by Suzanne M. Bianchi and Daphne Spain, who pulled the information from the 1980 census, earlier censuses, and subsequent national surveys. Bianchi and Spain outline quite clearly how very different men's marital patterns are from women's: because men do not hesitate to marry younger women, their chances for remarriage are infinitely better.

And, lest you think older woman/younger man relationships belong primarily to one age group, consider that, according to the men and women I interviewed, the following patterns are occurring:

- Women in their twenties are attracted to, living with, or marrying men who are one to eight years younger.
- Women in their thirties and forties are drawn to men as many as 10 to 18 years younger.
- Women in their fifties and sixties show the greatest age differences from their boyfriends or spouses, as there the span between them could be as much as 25 years.

Immediately upon starting my research for this book, I was asked by several young women who were in their mid-twenties if I would be interviewing anyone their age. Even though their boyfriends or husbands were only 2 or 3 years younger, they were as sensitive to the age difference as a woman who is 40 and 12 years older than the man in her life: a younger man is a younger man.

The Younger Man:
A New Kind of Man

There is one final fact that should not be overlooked as we examine the changes taking place in our relationships: more women are attracted to younger men because today's younger man is a new kind of man, a man very different from his father and grandfather.

We will be exploring these differences and why they are occurring. We will be looking closely at this new man's relationship with his mother, not only because women worry that younger men are looking for a mother substitute, but because younger men have grown up differently. They are the sons of the pioneers—the women who felt the first waves of change from the women's movement.

We will see why they are men who are more comfortable with women in the workplace and with women as friends and why they are the first men prepared to accept a woman as an equal partner in love and in life.

To offer an example of why a relationship with a younger man may be better for many women, I should mention the studies, such as the recent survey by *Cosmopolitan* magazine, that indicate that young husbands today agree that both husband and wife should share in child care and in the household work load, whether that means participating actively or helping to pay for the cost. The same survey shows that the older man continues to be much slower to change in these areas. Need I say more? Doesn't this sound exciting?

Does this mean that I advocate a stampede towards younger men? Not exactly. For one thing, not *all* younger men are younger at heart; there will always be men, 25 or 75, who prefer 20-year-old wives and girlfriends or for whom the idea of dating an older woman has no appeal. In addition, even in relationships where there is a strong emotional and sexual base, there are problems, as there are in any relationship. We'll be exploring some of these problems in the following chapters. But I want to trumpet the news that more and more women are finding and enjoying relationships with younger men. I want women to stop hesitating before they accept a date or marriage proposal from a younger man. I want women to know the many exciting reasons why loving a younger man can be the best thing that ever happened to them, because I have a well-informed hunch that almost every woman over the age of reason has turned a good man down—for a date or a love affair or a marriage—just because he was younger. As we become more aware, we will have gained yet another freedom once given only to men.

But it isn't just an issue of freedom. Now that the younger man is willing to share our responsibilities as well as our dreams, value us for our independence and self-sufficiency as well as for our attractiveness and emotional strength—love us for the very same reasons we love him—something else happens. As a man and a woman sharing every aspect of our lives, we may indeed be able to have it all.

1

Brave New Couples: How They Meet

He seemed to have lifted me body and soul out of all my past life. This young man of 26 had taken all my fate, all my destiny into his hands. And we had known each other for barely six weeks. There had been nothing else for me to do but submit.

—Freida Lawrence on falling in love
with D. H. Lawrence
when she was 31 and he was 26

How does a woman meet a younger man? Not by design.

Not one woman I interviewed deliberately set out to meet a younger man. Nor did she meet him in any of the ways, such as singles groups, health clubs, or blind dates, that you traditionally meet people with whom you become romantically involved.

Why? Because few women are thinking of younger men romantically when they first make their acquaintance.

Almost every woman interviewed met the younger man while she was at work or completing her education. The woman and man may work in the same department, share responsibilities on a project, end up on the same seminar panel, or meet when she hires him. In nearly every couple studied, the younger man was first a colleague, then a friend, and then a lover.

Their attraction was immediate and simultaneous: each saw the other as a confident, intelligent, and capable person. Because they viewed each other first as fellow workers and then as friends, the sexual charisma that was to draw them together grew more out of an appreciation of their talents and abilities than out of a superficial assessment of how they looked and acted. The man admires the woman's authority and prestige; he likes how she meets the challenge of the workplace and her even, confident way of handling herself.

The women in these relationships are, characteristically, survivors. More often than not, they have survived a series of severe personal traumas before meeting a younger man. An early divorce, single parenthood, full financial responsibility for young children—with no inherited wealth to help—are not uncommon situations for them to have overcome. It is as if the experience of surviving a major life catastrophe makes the women more willing to risk relationships that are different from the norm, that may appear less likely to succeed. It may be that these women, who have experienced periods of severe hardship, actually want to have a chance at "youth" that they never had. Diane, 45, for example, feels that her marriage to Rob, 33, is all the more appealing because she spent her early adulthood as a surrogate mother to her two younger brothers following her mother's death.

In addition, because these women are happy with their employment, they are slow to remarry, preferring to invest themselves only in what they find truly appealing, even if it is something as different as a younger man. Since most of these women are independent, resourceful, and self-sufficient when they meet younger men, it is no wonder that they are full of the kind of self-confidence and warmth that attracts men—of any age.

Of course, you don't have to be divorced and single-handedly supporting children to fall in love with a younger man. But in our society, because traditionally women have been conditioned to measure themselves by the qualities of the men they marry rather than by what they accomplish on their own, it often takes surviving a personal trauma to give a woman any real sense of self-confidence.

It is to the credit of the younger men, as well, that work friendships—and the resulting love relationships—develop. First of all, and usually by dint of their ages, the men find successful women more appealing than older men do. They have grown up around mothers, sisters, and other women who work, so the working woman is a familiar figure. And, while men the same age or older are rarely considered to be the good communicators that women are, younger men are different—they are able to talk easily with women, to share not only ideas but feelings as well. All of the older woman/ younger man couples I interviewed pointed out their amazing ease of communication.

The pull of an instant, easy friendship occurs as couples meet and get to know one another in a work environment where they are sharing ideas and responsibilities, successes and pressures. They bond quickly and easily because they understand one another, thanks perhaps to the similarity in their work patterns and daily experiences.

Most of the couples I interviewed developed friendships in circumstances requiring especially close contact because they had to cooperate on particular projects. This brought them together on a regular basis and put them in situations where things could go well or poorly. They had an opportunity to observe one another under pressure. I am sure this proximity figured in the development of many of the relationships because it's one of the best ways to get to know someone, to learn that you can trust someone under less-than-ideal circumstances. The only better way to learn about someone is to live with him or her.

Seeing how a person handles frustration, deals with unfair conditions, and gets through "bad days" can tell you more about personality than any number of chatty dates. Anyone in the workplace today who must see a project through from start to finish can tell you that working closely with others is one sure way to find out who is mature, fair, honest, and willing to carry his or her share of the load.

The Unexpected Love Affair

Early on, women accept the admiration and friendship of a younger man, but they are very surprised when this admiration turns to romance. Why? Because they initially react to the men as colleagues. The women tend to talk directly, sharing their ideas and opinions openly and easily. Because they aren't trying to attract a lover, they behave naturally, honestly, sincerely, and without guile or pretense: their guards are down.

That's what amazed me. When Brant first met me, I was at my most outspoken. I felt very comfortable in our alumni group, which was mainly women like me, and I knew a lot about the subject at hand. In fact, I disagreed with him vehemently on several points. Because of that, I expected him not to like me much. I'm used to having men my own age react with some hostility when I talk with authority—or just tune out and ignore what I'm trying to say. Brant didn't do that. He listened; he made it clear he valued my opinion. He still does. Today, when I run into hostile responses from other men, I am genuinely surprised.

Emotionally, the woman in these relationships is on even ground because she does not see the younger man as a serious candidate for marriage; she thinks she has nothing to lose. She is free of the tendency most women admit to having—the tendency to overanalyze their reactions to men who interest them romantically, as well as the tendency to imbue these reactions, or men's reactions to them, with too much meaning. She allows herself to love him and enjoy him without feeling that either one is investing too much of himself or herself in the relationship. Not until after they have established a close sexual and emotional bond does she realize that he isn't necessarily thinking in such temporary terms.

Instead, ignorant that she is capturing his imagination and his heart, her initial response is an almost overwhelming feeling of sexual passion and a thrill with the level of personal intimacy—emotional and intellectual—that she is able to achieve with her new lover.

19

"When I got home after my first few days with Alan, I couldn't stand being away from him," said Stephanie, 43. "We really liked each other, and it wasn't just the sex. I finally managed to wrangle some more work out there by him because I just couldn't stand it; I missed him so. It was like I didn't know what I was doing. My work went to hell; I couldn't carry on a conversation. We're both so happy when we're together. I'm 43, and he's 30, and he makes me feel like I'm a teenager in love all over again. God, I love him."

Because relationships between older women and younger men happen so unexpectedly, the women find themselves feeling freer and more experimental. And because they're not trying to impress anyone, or to "hook" a man, they're happy just being themselves. They enter into the relationships without the female hallmarks of self-doubt and high expectations. No rules exist for behavior between a woman and a younger man, so each couple is free to decide how the relationship between them will develop.

Lynn will never forget how she learned about the absence of those rules. A 37-year-old filmmaker, she was walking with her new lover shortly after they had met while working on a documentary together.

"We were just walking down the street, looking in windows, and I asked him about this one famous director that I really admire. He didn't say anything. Suddenly it dawned on me, maybe he was too young to know this guy's work? So I stopped and asked Dan how old he was.

"When he told me he was 29, I was just knocked out. I couldn't believe it! We kept on walking and ended up in some Mexican place for dinner, but I was still shaking my head. I just couldn't handle it. The ring of '29'—it has a sound you don't want to hear. So I just kept looking at him and looking away because I could not believe it. I had no idea how I was supposed to act! But in retrospect, I think not knowing made it easier to get to know each other—and definitely more fun."

A New Freedom

Without exception, the women are delighted with the first stages of these romances. They find the men to be charming, sexually and emotionally stimulating, and just plain fun to be around. The men make them feel like kids again. And as couples, they act like kids—just happy to be with each other—and downright surprised to be having such a good time.

"I seldom go out with men my own age," said Terri, 44, an attractive woman whose dates with younger men have resulted from business contacts liking her voice on the telephone, as well as from her meetings with men she had to do business with.

"The men my age don't act the way I like. I act young—I like to dance and have a good time. I think young. Maybe I'm not meeting the right guys my age, but they don't seem to have a lot of energy. It's because I really want to have a fun time that I end up with the young guys."

In addition to the freedom of letting go and enjoying themselves, women dating younger men talk about the freedom they feel to be themselves as the relationship gets under way. For one thing, the men they date continue to be accepting of them *as they are*. Second, the women are more sure of themselves than they may have been in earlier relationships because of their age and experience.

Once I started to become involved with Brant, I never did hold back my thoughts and opinions—because I was older than he was. I had experience. What I think and what I have to say is important because it's been developed over time, refined. I will no longer accept censoring from anyone, male or female, of any age, because I have confidence that my 42 years of life experience are to be considered and valued equally. Older men seem to have difficulty with my attitude on this; younger men do not.

I have discovered that my ease in saying exactly what's on my mind was shared by all the women interviewed. They remarked on how they enjoyed the same freedom, the same feeling of having equal input, the same relaxed attitude toward the interpersonal dynamics of their relationships. No one held back from expressing feelings or ideas. And they all considered it a major difference from earlier marriages or relationships in that they were able to confront the younger man more easily, with both the good and the bad, right from the first moment they met. Older men just aren't comfortable—yet—being challenged by women.

"Maybe some younger women today do speak up more quickly about what bothers them," said Elinor, 57, a prominent business executive with more than 20 years of management experience behind her, "but I really couldn't until I was older. I feel strongly that my age gives me this advantage."

The freedom older women feel to be themselves extends to the bedroom as well. "His obvious appreciation and relative lack of experience were very liberating for me," said Andrea, 25, of her 20-year-old lover. "There was a delicious sense of naughtiness in our relationship. I could be the teacher-whore, and he was the most eager and talented student."

Because all the women interviewed had been married before or lived with a man in a previous relationship, each was sexually experienced. Feeling comfortable with her own sexuality and knowing her needs made the prospect of a new and younger sex partner exciting. Because the woman assumes (whether or not it's true) that she is more experienced, she doesn't worry about her performance in bed. In addition, she'll often have sex earlier in the relationship than she might with an older man. Since she has broken one social rule by being attracted to a younger man, she has nothing to lose by breaking another and plunging into a casual relationship that she initially thinks cannot last. She feels free and open and sees no need to censor her behavior. Sexually and emotionally, she is free to choose for herself what direction she wants the love affair to take.

"That made such a difference to me right away," said Ellen, 39, who met David, 25, over a cadaver in their medical school lab. "When I first started to date David, I had to know that I could say 'no,' that I would be able to tell him how I felt—because I had so many mixed feelings about us as a couple. That was the only way I could relax about being with him." She said no to their first date, then changed her mind. Today they are married and expecting a child.

Opposites Attract

Women who find themselves romantically interested in younger men have doubts about their relationships (as we'll see in the next chapter), but, as we've already seen, there are certain elements of the age difference that actually help get the relationship going. While the disparity in age can be a problem, it can also be part of the attraction. In addition to the woman's social and sexual self-confidence, the man's young, fun attitudes, and the fact that there are no rules for this kind of love affair, there may be other elements of the age difference that draw the couples together and enable them to enjoy each other in ways they might not were she not older.

A Second Chance at Love: Doing Things Right This Time Around

"Steve was a beacon in the storm—this wonderful, carefree young guy," says Amanda, 41, who was 35 when she met Steve, then 26. "There I was under the pressure of keeping everything together, like my house, taking care of my kids, and the right thing seemed to be to go with the older guy I was dating. But I kept pulling back and saying to myself, 'No, no, I really want to run away to the country and live in a cabin with no electricity, enjoy the simple things in life.' Steve represented that."

Amanda and Steve are typical of the women and men whose relationships are working extremely well. Previously married, like most of the women I interviewed, Amanda reflects the statistics that show that a woman who is happy in her work is much less likely to remarry quickly after a divorce.

Indeed, she had been on her own for nearly 10 years before meeting Steve. During those years, she became an independent, outgoing, and confident woman with a well-paying job. She is very attractive, and, like most single women in her age group, her dates were well-established older men—until she met the 26-year-old who would change her life.

"I remember meeting Steve," recalls Amanda. "But it was a year before we started going out. I was involved with a very well-to-do older man and living the glamorous life. We did the society circuit, traveled abroad, I wore beautiful clothes. He wanted to marry me.

"But older men come with a lot of baggage—former wives, problems with their kids, mortgages on second homes. The man I had dated before that one was also older and more typical of older men. He was a fuddy-duddy, very complacent, and set in his ways. This older man was pretty young at heart, but I still couldn't deal with all the baggage. He always struck me as fatherly, someone to turn to for security.

"I didn't know it at the time, but I was looking for a way out of that relationship, which was one that most women would die for, that my mother thought I was crazy to leave."

"Amanda had just joined our company when I met her," said Steve, 32, a long-boned man, slender, with dark hair and a calm, open face. He is an architect, prized by his firm, but he is eager to set out on his own.

"The first time I saw her, I thought 'Hmmm, they've got a real one in here now. This one's special.' She had a brightness in her eye, and she radiated warmth. I thought she was about 22. I guess I should have known no one at 22 exudes that kind of self-confidence.

"It was about a year after we met," said Steve, "that Amanda was assigned to work with me on a project. She liked my work, and we began to talk more often. Pretty soon she would stop in my office, and we started talking about our lives. She told me about her relationship with this guy who was 16 years older than she was—how she felt money wasn't everything and things like that.

"I just scratched my head," Steve recalls with a big grin, "because I was very down-and-out at the time, and money sounded great to me. So she was philosophizing, and I was worried about my next buck!

"We kept having these nice conversations. I really enjoyed her glamor, her theatricality—she wore this wild fur. She still has all that, but now I know there's a lot more there than just shine. A lot of depth. She's not a crazy, flashy dame.

"And then one day, she brought in her daughter. She was 13—and was I confused! I couldn't figure out how she could be so young and have a kid that old."

Amanda, meanwhile, found herself growing more attached to her young colleague with his aura of maturity and independence, his talent and career goals firmly focused. Steve exemplified the younger man whose intelligence and physical characteristics attract a woman like Amanda—a woman who can look beyond surface appearances like money and social position because she has had enough experience in life to learn that what counts is not how "successful" we appear but how we think and act and feel.

"In my mind, I was still very involved with this other man," said Amanda. "I've always been with men who are older than I am. But Steve was such a nice guy. He was kind of a hippie type, too, which was very different from the men I dated. I must have been unhappy because I felt like I found solace in his office when we talked.

"On the other hand, I'd talk to him and feel like I made no sense, which was frustrating because I'm an articulate person. What was I trying to tell him? That I was involved with a man who had a lot of money and a lot was going on in my life but I wasn't satisfied? I used to leave Steve's office and say, 'Why did I go in there?'

"So in trying to figure out why I always wanted to talk to him, I started to wonder what he would be like in bed. He was young and cute, and he had a flat belly—that's nice, especially if you've been around a lot of older men. That's different.

"Then something else started to happen. Steve and I started this crazy thing in the company cafeteria, where we would hug each other. It was just one of those crazy little things— but it happened a couple times a day."

25

Steve remembers the hugs. "I don't think either of us thought a lot about it, but there must have been some attraction then. Maybe we didn't recognize it when it was happening. And it was about that time that I found out how old Amanda was. It didn't bother me. Instead, it added a certain intrigue. And it explained a lot about the way she was.

"By this time I had learned what a hard time she'd had in her life, raising two boys by herself and making her own way professionally. Some people take lemons and make lemonade. Amanda makes lemon meringue pie.

"Finally, I decided to ask her out. I felt kind of silly because I was asking her to a rock concert, which seemed like something a kid does. I felt real self-conscious. I was sure she would say 'no' or giggle. Later I found out that she thinks young—she thinks younger than I do. So she accepted, we went, and it was a kick."

"Yeah," said Amanda, "it was uncanny. Steve asked me out just when I'd decided to sever my other relationship. I thought it was kind of cute—he left me a note asking me to a Rolling Stones concert, and it couldn't have come at a better time. I was trying to get away from the older man and all the burdens that go with that, like listening to his hassles with his business and his family.

"It wasn't hot sex I wanted from him—it was 'Get me away from this materialism before I screw up my life.' Materialism and conformity—that's what I was always complaining to him about. I can truly say that money does not buy happiness, and Steve was the way to a cleansing, a relief from all that.

"So when he handed me that note asking me to the rock concert, I said, 'Sure, I'd love to.' And he was so surprised because he thought he was handing this sophisticated woman of the world a note that would make him look like a jerk. And here I thought it was the greatest thing he could offer me. I did not want dinner at the fanciest restaurant in town.

" 'Sure, a rock concert in jeans?' That was our first date. I was 36, and he was 27. Because we had known each other nearly one year by that time, it seemed perfectly natural to sleep with him that night. Believe me, I fell in love with his body, too.

"Here I was, already attracted to this very confident, very mature 27-year-old who was talented and who had a very definite direction to his career. Now I found that the rest of him was terrific, too. I love his flat belly and his taut jawline. But something that's especially nice about Steve is his complete naturalness about sex. He is easy about it, and I find that very different from older men.

"Actually, I don't think you can find many 32-year-old men like Steve, because he is so mature and talented and self-directed. I never think of him as being younger—I feel like we're the same age now. But I fell in love with him because he represented a new way of life to me."

She could have stayed in her relationship with a rich, older man, but she chose Steve, with whom she felt the quality of life would be better. Today, six years later, she knows she was right.

Similar Interests:
The Joy of Sharing

Maureen, 43, fell in love with Garrett, 31, more than 10 years ago. At the time, she was married to another man, and Garrett had no knowledge of how she felt. Nor would he know until 5 years later, long after Maureen's divorce from her first husband.

"We first met because he was a friend of our family's through my husband's position as a lay minister in our church," said Maureen. "But right away, he and I became good friends because we were both passionate Francophiles. He was an art historian and a student of French industrial design, and I was involved with contemporary French art and textile products, particularly pottery and fabrics. When we met, Garrett was completing his doctorate in Franco-American studies just as I was setting up a French import shop and studio. He would often stop by to use some of my materials or books, and he helped me locate suppliers and artisans when he was abroad. I was just 31 at the time, and he was 19.

"What is pretty important, I guess, is that Garrett was an immediate contrast to the man I had married. More specifically, he was a throwback to all the men I had loved in my youth but didn't marry: those sensitive, gentle, artist types that you love but don't marry because in the late '50s and early '60s they didn't fit the profile of the successful businessman, the man who represented security and prestige.

"Instead, I married the archetypal extrovert who had little sensitivity. My husband was an orthopedic surgeon and also a very active lay minister in our church. He loved being looked at as a prominent, established member of the community.

"When I was attracted to him in college, he was an enigma to me. I was very young, and this extroverted personality and this enormous ego intrigued me, I guess. He was a very charismatic man who could talk to anyone. And since I was the more introverted one, creative but with a low sense of self-esteem, I was awed by him. He looked like he could be fun. Also, we had a lot of social, economic, and geographical things in common. We were the same age, from the same upper middle-class community, our families played golf—all the things that look good in the *New York Times* marriage announcements.

"But we weren't the kind of couple that could build a great relationship. We did very little together, partly because our personalities were so different, partly because he thought of my work as some kind of trivial pursuit. Until I met Garrett, I felt like my ideas and goals were *indulged,* not taken seriously.

"It was just as the trouble in our marriage was becoming clear that this nice, sensitive, attractive, talented, intelligent, young, single man gradually began spending more and more time around our house. For me, the conversations with Garrett were so stimulating—about all the things I was most interested in. It was funny—talking to him made me feel so alive, so young and excited again. My business is what brought us together with such excitement because it was new and quite different for our community. We felt like we were so lucky to have found each other because we could do so much for each other. He gave me a lot of help with arts, fabrics, textiles, whatever. And, in return, I often let him use my materials for class assignments.

"My husband wasn't at all interested in what I was doing, so it was terrific to have someone who enjoyed working with me. Garrett was dedicated to helping me get my business off and going. He really understood the kind of blood and guts that it took.

"Right after we met, Garrett became a regular in our household. For two years, he came by nearly every day. He house-sat for us when I made my husband take me to France; he would take my kids hiking; he would come over for dinner. And always we would have these very stimulating conversations about art, about France, about the shop, about his dissertation. . . .

"But at the same time, when you find that you like someone that much, if you are at all in touch with yourself, you can recognize the sexual element—whether he's 19 or 90. So I knew right away I had to deal with that. Even after I decided that the wise way was to suppress it, I experienced a lot of inner conflict.

"I would lie awake at night and wonder what to do with my feelings. Should I look at him objectively and write off how I felt because it was absolutely preposterous? Should I fantasize about what it would be like to sleep with him? Should I tell myself it would never work, so forget it? Should I let him know in some way what I was thinking and see if he was thinking it too?

"All I knew for sure was that I was instantly attracted to him. I loved his ideas, his ways, his wonderful shining youth! In the vernacular: it was great vibes. He was just tremendously appealing to me on all counts, but it took a while for me to allow myself to feel the sexual pull because I didn't consider that open to me. It was his personality that grabbed me right away. He was so sensitive and honest.

"I also felt that he was different, out of step with his peers, because even though he was only 19, he acted older. It was his maturity and his kindness. Most 19-year-olds are tremendously self-centered, but not Garrett. He had the gift of being extraordinarily thoughtful.''

Even though Maureen did not make any overtures toward Garrett, her husband confronted her with the closeness he could see between her and the young man. He accused them of having an affair. Garrett was shocked. Soon after the confrontation, he left the country for two years. During that time, Maureen's marriage ended. She started her life over as a single parent and as the proprietress of her now-successful shop.

Even though her love for Garrett seemed impossible and improbable, she didn't forget him. ''I don't know why,'' remembers Maureen, ''but I had this faith. I always felt like something would work out.'' They kept in touch, and three years after the awful confrontation, Garrett came to visit her in the hospital where she was recuperating from major surgery.

''That's when it became clear to me that his youth was so much a part of why he appealed to me. He hadn't lost his sensitivity and this loving, nurturing side. He offered to help me at home and in the shop right away. We became close friends again. He seemed terribly young, yes, but by this time I was even more impressed with his eye for design. Everything he does, everything we do together, is very visual. And it's remarkable to have a partner who sees through your own eyes, who shares the same quality of vision.

''Today, it's accepted for a man to be more sensually appreciative of the arts, more a part of the whole artistic community. But it's more than that. There are things about Garrett that would have been considered sort of sissylike in a man when I was in high school and college. I don't see it that way, especially after living with my first husband, who was so totally closed off from his feelings or anyone else's. So I feel Garrett's youth makes a big difference that way.

''Another big difference is Garrett's easygoing attitude about life. He is a very well-educated man, he has a well-paying position, yet he knows how to relax and enjoy simple things. Or, because he has such a creative mind, he will suddenly spin off in a new direction, all enthusiastic and excited. That kind of impetuous, impulsive behavior is what I first fell in love with, and he hasn't changed—it's part of his whole pattern of living. He isn't the calculating, control-oriented kind of man that my first husband was.

"I would definitely say Garrett's youth has made it possible for us to be together. He grew up at the right time for a man to be encouraged to be sensitive, to be a little more reserved and softspoken. We're kind of a quiet little couple, really. For me, knowing Garrett has been like finding a long-lost friend even though I wasn't sure why he would be attracted to me. I asked him once why he wasn't more attracted to women his own age, but he said he thought they were full of fluff. They weren't experienced, they weren't wise, they weren't good listeners—all the things I like in *him.*"

When Intellectual Compatibility Meets Great Sex

"I couldn't get over Tom and what he brought to my life," she said. The curly-headed brunette, given ever so slightly to a few extra pounds, chuckles when she thinks back to her first encounter with the young lawyer she later married. "First and foremost, let me say that he has given me back the last decade of my life to live all over again—and that's a priceless gift for me."

Merritt fits the profile of the woman who falls in love with a younger man: previously married, mother of two children in their early teenage years, self-supporting. She is the daughter of two alcoholic parents, so she feels she learned early to deal with stress and uncertainty. She returned to school in her late twenties and had been practicing law for just three years when she met Tom.

"We couldn't have met at a better time in my life," she said. "I was feeling good about myself; I was in great physical shape because I'd been running and exercising. My career was really rolling along.

"When he walked into the little room where our panel was meeting—we were both invited to speak at a conference in San Francisco on environmental law and water issues—I thought 'Oh, jeez, what a cute guy. How come all the young ones look so good?' You know, I just figured I couldn't think about him seriously because he looked about 16.

"Then our panel got going, and he tried to clobber me on a couple points, but I fought back. It was fun. We both knew our stuff. I won a few, he won a few. No one lost. I loved the challenge—it was sexy! Well, he made it sexy. Usually, I get treated two ways by men. The ones who are my age are so far ahead of me professionally, they like to pat me on the head in a very patronizing way. The others are just obnoxious about it. They tell me I work too hard, I'm too *earnest*.

"I'm sure Tom's youth had a lot to do with his immediate response to me—he's open and friendly with all the women he works with, and that's much more true of younger guys. Also, our careers are really at the same stage since I started so late. So when we met, we had had the same exposure to the law, and we were both really excited about the same new stuff. And we knew we were both very smart in the field. Very smart.

"I asked him if he wanted to have a drink later because he had some data I was interested in. We had a drink, then we decided to go to dinner. We found out we both made the same kind of mistakes in our first marriages by marrying people who thought we were a little too intense about ourselves, who didn't understand our need to produce and have somebody willing to hear about it or tell us what they were doing, too.

"We really got along, and I felt like I had found a good buddy. When he told me he was 9 years younger than I—just 26—I thought maybe I liked him so much because he reminded me of my younger brothers, who are great guys.

"So I was reluctant to say goodnight. I had a flight home early the next day. You know, back to all the same old stuff. It was already one in the morning, but I asked him into my room for a nightcap. I knew that was dangerous, but I felt like a kid again. I don't think I really knew what I was doing until I let him kiss me. I *adored* it when he kissed me. It was the nicest kiss I think I'd ever had.

"But then I pulled back. I have never been into one-night

stands. Never. This wasn't really like me at all. But I decided I was a grown woman, and a man my age would do exactly the same without even thinking about it.

"Of course, Tom wanted to sleep with me. At first I held off and said, 'Why don't I just hold you instead?' That went over like a lead balloon—he looked at me like I was nuts. But inside, I was thinking that I should be behaving more like a mother. I suddenly pictured myself as the mother of my son and realized that I would be furious if I found some older woman taking my son into her bed. So I worked on that one for a few minutes. Then he kissed me again—and all I could think was, Well, if my kid learns how to kiss like this, he deserves anything that happens to him. So I decided, hell, who would know? The guy was terrific, the place was terrific, everything was terrific—so I said, 'Okay.'

"Except—and this is important—I wanted to be sure he didn't have any herpes or anything like that, so I asked him if he had had any infections recently. I asked him if he slept around a lot. I was very clear with him and said I did not want to get anything. That surprised him, maybe even hurt his feelings a little, but he handled it. He always tells me that's what he remembers most about that night—I was the first woman ever to ask him that. I think if I were meeting him today, I'd go even further and make him use a condom. But what is important about this is, I know I wouldn't be as open to saying that to a man my own age. Older men are so touchy. It's like they have neurosis after neurosis, and you're always running the risk of hurting their feelings."

Tom is tall and well built, a former college football player. His demeanor is studious and accented by horn-rimmed glasses. But while he looks serious, Tom is an affable man. He laughs easily.

"Merritt took me aback when she asked me if I had herpes," he said with a chuckle. "I never had anyone ask me that before. You're so surprised—I think anyone would give an honest answer out of shock, even though I don't know how she could be sure you're telling the truth."

"Oh, I could tell," said Merritt. "I knew from earlier in the day that I really liked this man. I admired his kind of hard-edged intelligence and his cynicism—traits that come out of a real commitment to being honest to yourself. That's something that separates the men from the boys in our business. Also, while we were commiserating over why our first marriages ended, I sensed a kindness and thoughtfulness in him that made me want to cry. He didn't dump on his first wife; he could see what he did wrong, too. I felt he was mature. I trusted him right away."

"She was so pretty and smart without being obnoxious," said Tom. "She had this very natural, easy way about her—and a lot of style, which I like. She exuded confidence. Later, when I found out how well organized she was, how she knew where she wanted to go with her life, it really made a difference to me, because my first wife had been so confused and frustrated and blamed me for everything she couldn't work out for herself. All the women I was dating were my age, and they were going through that same anxiety. They were competitive and confused at work, and they brought it into the bedroom.

"Merritt was a woman on top of her game—that's different from younger women and damned attractive to me. I guess her age sort of surprised me, but I didn't think about it much—she's the one who worries about that kind of stuff. But I think timing was important—we met at the right time. We were both past all that emotional leave-taking that has to take place after a marriage ends, so we weren't dumping a lot of leftover bad feelings on each other. She was happy, I was happy, and I think we were each destined to sleep with someone soon. I'm glad it was each other."

"What happened next was sort of scandalous," said Merritt. "I'd dated and slept with four men in my entire lifetime, and I thought I knew what the world was about, but. . . . First, let me say that all the older guys I have ever been with really put the pressure on. Sex is like their driving goal. It's been that way since high school. Tom wasn't like that. Sure, he suggested it, but I was doing my best to get the invitation. And then he didn't push me beyond what I wanted. Every step of the way he was so gentle and very, very slow.

"I have to admit that I decided to go ahead and sleep with

him because he was so attractive *and* because he was younger than I. I figured the age difference meant that it couldn't lead to anything, so I wouldn't be trapping myself. Then I thought I could have some fun and be the leader. And I wondered what young guys are like in bed—you can see I was into having a good time that night. It was incredible—I kept thinking it was the kind of sex you have after you've known each other for a long time. But here was this young guy, who has always been open and easy around women, and, boy, did it make a difference!

"I can only compare this to my own experience, but the older guys I've known have always been into aggressive kinds of sexual performance. It's like once the hormones start to flow, you can't stop the train. They are very physical and vocal, with snorts and grunts and a need to offer very obvious evidence of an orgasm. But the pressure is on you, too. You're supposed to respond in all these different ways. . . . Before I met Tom, I had begun to think that sex was the most nerve-wracking experience.

"Suddenly, here was this young guy who was so gentle and quiet. He didn't even come that night. I thought maybe something was the matter. Later he told me he didn't know me well enough to be able to let go. That's sweet and honest. I can't imagine a man my own age first not coming and certainly not opening up to me about it. I thought only women felt that way.

"I've thought about that night a lot, and I think that we had such a wonderful beginning because he sees women differently from the older guys. He is part of a generation where women haven't been forbidden fruit—he lived in coed dorms, and he had less of a stigma about early sex than I did. So Tom is much, much more relaxed around women as friends and as lovers. He's more accepting of the physical side of love from a woman's point of view, and that came through right away that night.

"Unlike older partners I've had who made me feel that sex was the exclusive goal of our lovemaking (one man stated that to me verbally just so I wouldn't misunderstand), that I was desirable only because I was 'a good-looking broad,'

Tom made me feel like I was on a pedestal that night. He made me feel beautiful and wanted and just so very, very special. He made love to the woman in my body and the woman in my head.

"The physical fit between our bodies was unusually comfortable, too. Any woman who has slept with a man knows what I mean when I say that it isn't easy to find another body that fits all your own bones and lumps and spaces. So I was struck when Tom's body fit mine perfectly, kind of like the missing puzzle piece. We both noticed it right away.

"That's another thing: he talked to me all that night. The older men I've known don't do that. It's like they want sex with a woman who has a paper bag on her head. Not Tom. We did everything together, every step of the way. So on the one hand, I opened up that night and let everything happen because I knew we would never see each other again. But in my heart I wanted to have the sun shine on us and the world just happen around us—I didn't want a one-night stand; I wanted a 'forever stand.'

"I went back and forth in my mind, feeling very confused. First I was happy he was so young because then nothing was at stake. Then I was mad because we could never be a couple because I was so much older. I kept thinking, if he were my own age, I could really count on things moving forward. Don't ask me why I kept putting any thought of us down because of the age difference. Today it doesn't make sense, but I didn't know any women with younger men, so I felt like it was kind of goofy."

"If Merritt was confused that night, I sure didn't know it," said Tom. "She was the first woman I've been with who was genuinely comfortable with her sexuality. She knows herself. She was relaxed and sexy, and she made me feel like we were very tuned in to what each of us wanted. I'm used to women who aren't so assured and need all kinds of reinforcement. Younger women wait on you to take charge. Merritt didn't do that, and it was a relief."

"The next morning we had to face these other people at a breakfast meeting out at the airport," said Merritt. "And it was pretty funny, because we were up all night, and, boy, were we wiped out! Now that's a pretty important time, because it's in the light of the next day that you find out if you made a big mistake, right? Well, I walked into the lounge just as Tom did, and he came right over, helped me with my bag, bought me coffee and a newspaper. I was tired, but I felt completely relaxed and happy with him. It was the first time in my life that I understood what it means to have a friend for a lover.

"All the way home on the plane that day, I kept going over every detail of what had happened to me. In fact, I couldn't even go straight home—I drove by a friend's house, and when she came to the door, I just stood there with this foolish grin on my face and announced, 'You are looking at the queen of the one-night stand,' and then I told her all about it. I was so happy, but I was also waiting to see what she would say. Would she think I was terrible?

"She sure didn't. When I was all finished, she told me her new boyfriend was five years younger, so we had a drink and toasted a whole new world of romance!"

Merritt and Tom did get together again. Two years after they met, they were married, and they recently celebrated their fifth anniversary. Although they work for different law firms, they hope to have a joint practice someday.

Power: The Flip Side of the Exquisite Aphrodisiac

Something women frequently say they find attractive in older men is their wisdom and sense of authority. In effect, the same principle works for men and women in older woman/younger man relationships, but this time the woman has the charisma that comes with power.

Elinor is a woman whose professional achievement—and the sense of personal power, maturity, and control that results from that achievement—drew first the attention, and then the love, of a man 18 years her junior.

At 57, Elinor is a woman with a fine, delicate beauty. Her hair, a pale, pale blonde, if not white, is pulled back into a bun, although soft wisps escape around her neck and face. When she smiles, tiny lines crease around her eyes, yet she is fine-boned, and her skin is smooth. She uses little makeup. Elinor radiates a quiet, elegant warmth. Hers is the face of a woman in her fifties, and it is lovely to look upon.

Her companion is a man you would guess to be in his mid-thirties, although he is about to celebrate his 40th birthday. Brad has a European flair, and he dresses stylishly. He appears thoughtful and studious.

She was his boss when "the stars went off." That was nine years ago. They have been together since she was 47 and he was 29.

"I had hired Brad several years earlier," recalled Elinor. "I was running our corporate public relations division, a department formerly run by men, and I hired Brad as a senior associate. I remember that well because I really wanted to hire someone else, but the other candidate's portfolio was much weaker than Brad's, even though the other man was more eager for the job. Brad didn't like the salary I was offering.

"Even though it was clear that Brad was the correct hire—his work was outstanding—he was so surly! In all fairness, I had to acknowledge he was far better qualified and literate, and I needed someone with his particular kind of experience. So I hired him, and we worked near each other for two years before we became friendly."

"That's right," said Brad. "At first I was mad at her all the time because, though she'd hired me, I still felt I had to keep proving myself. She was always very reserved or not available. When a project was going badly, I couldn't just walk in and ask for her help. So I did my thing, and she did hers.

"Finally, she asked me to work on a project with her, and that was the first time I felt that we could be friends. The job required a trip to France, where I got to know her a little better. That was when I learned that she had just had a rough two years, during which her marriage was coming apart. But I learned all this very gradually.

"When we returned to the U.S., however, we started going

38

out after work for drinks. Then she really opened up and told me how miserable she felt about the marriage breaking up. So I started to tell her about my own marriage. For the first time, I realized I was in the same kind of trouble—only I hadn't taken the time to see it before. Meanwhile, my wife told me she was leaving me, so suddenly I was feeling just as bad as Elinor.''

Elinor remembers the time well. She was concerned about Brad because she could see his marital problems coming. ''It was strange,'' she said. ''They didn't act like they were married. For instance, they never did anything together. So I wasn't too surprised when he told me they were breaking up.

''But I never dreamed he would be interested in me—because of the age difference. Brad is not one of the prematurely mature guys. He looks young. He acts young. I don't mean that emotionally, but culturally—particularly when it comes to music. So why would a young man who was so much a part of all the new trends be interested in someone like me?

''At any rate, we were working on this special year-long project that had an international focus, so we had a lot to do together. We worked closely every day, bouncing ideas off one another and chatting after work. I'm sure that the fact that I was now living alone and going through a difficult emotional time was a factor. Brad was a sympathetic listener and gave me some thoughts on all of my problems that really helped.

''Even though I was very aware that he did not like his work situation at first, I always liked him. I liked his manner, his professionalism. I could see that, in a very low-key way, he was a giving kind of person. He always helped people in the office. If someone needed to know how to use the computer system, Brad would take the time to teach them. He helped people out, and I liked that. I still like it. He was a fine colleague, and he has done very well over this last decade because he's good and he's fair and he's very sensitive to people.

''When we first started to talk, I discovered that he enjoyed writing poetry and that journalism was his first love. I loved that combination. So there were lots of things about him that I really liked, but I never thought about it in romantic terms.''

Brad was thinking differently, however.

"During those drinks that we had after office hours, I remember her saying things that really impressed me," he said.

"She said she wasn't going to live life with all these compromises, meaning that she preferred to end her marriage rather than stay in it when it was clearly over. And she was very assertive when she made decisions. Elinor doesn't take a lot of shit from people. She just goes ahead and makes up her mind. As they say in New Hampshire, she has to 'live free or die.' I was pretty impressed when I could hear her say something and watch her go right out and do it. Wow! Wasn't like my life at all.

"I think what made the strongest impression on me was a time when she said you have to live with emotional honesty or you're not living at all. I took that to be a sign of maturity. By that time, I knew that Elinor had lived in an orphanage when she was a little kid and had worked her way up in the world from nothing to this job, which placed her in a pretty small percentage of top women executives in the country.

"But I was impressed to hear her talk about living with emotional honesty because I could see she meant it: she'd had all this experience, grown up a hard way, had these two marriages that she wasn't afraid to leave when they weren't working—she wasn't fooling around. I, on the other hand, was fooling around.

"The dramatic moment came when we had our office Christmas party and Elinor and I were dancing together. We had been hanging around together all the time anyway, so I danced her into this dark room and kissed her . . . and the stars went off.

"I really surprised myself. All this time I had been repressing my feelings, thinking, She's my boss, and it's not quite right. Even though I knew I was attracted to her, I was worried because of our office situation. I'd seen enough copies of *Cosmopolitan* in the doctor's office to know they always tell the girls not to fall in love with their bosses because they'll end up creating a big mess and losing their jobs. Their colleagues will hate them. That was my worry—not the age difference.

"In fact, I wasn't even conscious of the age difference until we started sleeping together and I asked about birth control. Elinor said she was past the point of having babies. That surprised me. I guess that was the first time I thought about age."

Shortly after the fateful Christmas party, Elinor and Brad attended a business conference together. During that time, they found that they weren't just attracted to one another—they wanted to be together on a more permanent basis.

"I realize now that what drew Brad to me was that I was living life on an honest, if risky, level. I have the ability to acknowledge and understand my feelings, to act on my instinct because I have learned that I'm usually right. That's something that comes with age and experience. And I think he had a sense that he was missing out on a lot because he wasn't doing that, especially because he could see the changes I was going through during this very emotional time in my life. So the conference was a time when we were able to begin to sort out our feelings toward each other."

Power is a heady aphrodisiac, and Elinor is proof that it works for women. Her professional achievements, her power, her history as a fighter and a survivor, her self-confidence, and prestige make her a charismatic, fascinating woman. Lucky the man she chooses—whatever age he may be.

Happy Couples Are All Alike

In any relationship, dozens of factors affect how the couple feels about each other: looks, shared interests, intellectual compatibility, and so on. As we've seen—and will continue to see—age is an important factor, but it is not the only one. It is refreshing to see that in older woman/younger man love affairs, as in any other, the attraction can be as basic as sex, looks, or just plain personality.

41

Stephanie, who was 43 when she fell in love with 30-year-old Alan, was attracted to him immediately.

"I was the associate producer on a music video being filmed on location," recalls Stephanie, "when I met Alan as I was checking in the production staff." She is a slim woman of medium height, a dynamo of energy with a square-shaped face under a mop of wildly curly blonde hair. She has two children in college and one graduating from high school. Her first marriage ended several years ago.

"He was the last person to check in, and when he walked up, I thought, There's somebody I could really be interested in. He was cute, kind of nasty-looking, with shades and a beard. I remember thinking, Okay, I'm gonna be in trouble here. Turns out he had the same reaction to me."

Stephanie had made rules for herself at work: never have a love affair during a production, never become involved with someone who wasn't at the same management level or higher than she, and, on a more personal level, "never sleep with anyone younger, thinner or prettier than I am." With Alan, who was a technician and definitely below her status on the production, she broke every rule.

"I had this big argument with myself as I kept working with him and feeling this pull toward him. It had everything to do with life being short, and here was the first man in years that I was really drawn to.

"Finally, we had been working together in the field for several days, and I decided to spend a little time with him. I didn't think he'd taken much notice of me. When you're on production, you look like shit. You wear your worst clothes, and if you put any makeup on in the morning, it's gone by 10:00, and there isn't any time to repair. So I was just plain old me out there working hard. But I arranged for us to have to drive to a different shoot together in the same car. It was a four-hour drive, and my heart was going 'ka-pow, ka-pow.'

"He and I ended up in the back seat, and we started writing notes to each other on a pad. It was incredibly fun—like being in high school. In one of the notes, I asked him how old his mother is, and he said, '52.' Then he said, 'Let's make love.' So there I am thinking his mother is only 9 years older than I am and wondering how I would handle my son with a woman like me—while all I want to do is jump into bed with this guy!

"In my note, I asked him how old he thought I was—I knew he was only 30—and he said, '33 or 34.' That's when I told him I was 43. I asked him if that made a difference. He said he'd think about it for 30 seconds . . . and then he said he couldn't see why it should.

"I said, 'I know it does, but I don't know why yet.' "

That night Alan went to Stephanie's room, but she made it clear to him that it was a mistake for them to get involved while on a location shoot—she didn't want to upset the rest of the crew; she didn't want to be distracted. The next night, however, she dumped all her self-imposed rules and slept with him.

Since then, they have been lovers. Even though they live in different parts of the country, both have been able to schedule assignments so they can be together. We will explore many of Stephanie's feelings about the future of this relationship later. However, she is very clear on why she was attracted to Alan.

"There's some good stuff about men who are 30," she said. "They have a kind of sensitivity I don't find in men my own age or older. It comes out of the post-hippie era, and it's an attitude toward life and toward women that men in their forties don't understand. But it's one of the things that draws me to Alan. He is very open and very warm—unlike anybody I have ever met."

Rob, 33, married Diane, 45, five years ago and is sure that her personality would have attracted him whatever her age.

They met through Diane's younger brother, who was one of Rob's best friends. Because of her heavy travel schedule, Diane was looking for someone to live in her apartment while she was gone. Rob agreed to do that and to make repairs to her kitchen in return for a discount on the rent. They soon found themselves working on the apartment together over the weekends.

Diane was openly dating an older man, so she was quite surprised when Rob asked her out. At first, she balked. But after a few days of thinking it over, she agreed to go out for dinner. It didn't take long for them to fall in love.

"It was her personality," said Rob, recalling that initial attraction. "She was really quite a person, quite interesting. I think Diane's unique: she's one of the few people I've ever known who's always on and interested in just about everything. We spent a lot of time together when I was renovating the kitchen in her apartment, so I don't think my interest in her was that big a shock. But she kept pulling back because of the age thing. We were finally able to resolve her feelings about that after some long, long talks.

"The chemistry between Diane and me is basic. I've been around lots of younger women, but Diane is special. She's a secure, energetic woman who knows what she wants and what she likes. She has a tough job, which she does very well. She knows she's good, and her confidence radiates. I find *that* very attractive.

"The amazing thing is we really spend every free moment together, and there is never enough time. You would think that, being together eight years, we would be used to one another by now. But our lives are so fast-paced, we have to work hard to grab time together. I like that, too. Time flies, and we always have plenty to talk about. That's one thing about Diane—she's never boring!"

If Rob always has plenty to share with Diane, that isn't surprising. Friendship and a habit of constant communication are two of the most prevalent characteristics of these relationships and of any good relationship.

With Ellen and David, 39 and 25 respectively, the attraction was a common interest—medicine—and ideological compatibility. They began studying together soon after having met in medical school over four years ago. Within weeks, they had to contend with the fact that even though Ellen was 35 and David just 21 at the time, their mutual interest in medicine had broadened to include each other.

"I guess there were some things that I liked about him right away," said Ellen, a tall, willowy, black-haired woman. "He had a stronger science background, so he was very valuable to me as a study partner, helping me through certain phases of the course that we were in at the time. Then we got to know more about each other because we liked to sit around and talk after the study period was over.''

"It's pretty intangible as far as exactly what attracted me to Ellen,'' said David. He is slender like his wife but firmer in his manner, while she is softspoken and gentle. They share many mutual interests, and Ellen strongly supports David's plan to become a politically active physician, an advocate for minority patients.

"I think that in a lot of ways we discovered early on that we agree on things that both of us think about, such as politics. We had a lot to talk about, and we still do. We're never at a loss for words.''

This mutual professional support and conversation, this kind of constant communication, is especially characteristic of the friendships between younger men and older women that develop into love relationships, yet it is the kind of communication that can spur a mutual attraction between *any* man and woman.

What draws these couples together, then, is basically what draws any two people together—chemistry. These couples just happen to be ones in which the woman is older. While the age difference is hard to ignore, it's also hard to ignore the pounding heart and tingling excitement of falling in love.

2

Say Yes, Say No:
The Hesitation Waltz

It's the '80s, and there are no rules.
— Dan, 30, telling Lynn, 37,
why she should go out with him

If a woman is surprised, flattered, and happy when a professional relationship with a younger man begins to turn personal, the intensity of her pleasure is soon tempered with fear: a fear of abandonment, of looking foolish, an ambivalent feeling toward making a commitment because the odds seem stacked against them as a couple. She faces a series of complex concerns that range from feelings of losing her attractiveness to misgivings about her sexuality to worry about what colleagues and friends will think.

After the first heady weeks of romance, woman after woman begins to look for faults in her new and different relationship. Suddenly afraid that it's wrong, she wants to determine for herself why it won't work before she discovers she is head-over-heels in love and is rejected because of her age. And why not? It's natural to want to avoid being hurt.

Most of these women have a difficult time explaining just why the age difference haunts them, but they force themselves to go through a stage of severe self-criticism as if to mutilate their relationship before others can do it for them. Fortunately, most fail at this destructive tactic.

I wish I had had the courage to steam ahead and not worry about the age difference between me and Brant. But in 1982, I felt alone in my position as an "older woman." None of my good friends were dating younger men—at least none that I was aware of.

Also, I was very confused about all the issues that our age difference seemed to raise. Should I seriously commit to a man who, if society's logic prevailed, might be attracted to a younger woman in a few years? Would the day come, further down the road, when a flash of reality would expose his immaturity—immaturity that I had been too love-blind to see?

And so, like 75 percent of the women interviewed, I shuffled back and forth, refusing to commit to having this kind and generous man in my life. Every day was a struggle. I found myself doing a kind of emotional two-step: one day I would be willing to take another step forward in our relationship, yet the very next day I would pull back, convinced that, even though life with Brant seemed wonderful, I shouldn't risk too much of my hopes and dreams because the nine years between us would keep us from being happy much longer.

I danced this crazy dance that I later found is typical of women whose delightful "interludes" with younger men turn serious. Even though we have no good reason to, we hesitate to commit. And nothing is more difficult in these relationships than that very first stage of commitment—the decision to go ahead and date a younger man, to decide to see him and only him on a regular basis.

What happened inside me as I wavered on the edge of making just that decision is this:

First, I managed to put off acknowledging how much I really wanted our relationship to continue.

Second, I made a constant effort to find reasons to get out of the relationship—I was always on guard for the slightest evidence of immature behavior, of an unreasonable demand.

Third, I openly pulled back from stating that I would make

a commitment when he said he was ready for that and he had to have it from me.

Fourth, even after I did commit, the feeling was always with me that "it can't last."

Stop This Relationship; I Want to Get Off!

From the very beginning of a relationship to the wedding day and, sadly, sometimes beyond, women face serious doubts and fears about loving younger men. They are confused, unsure of what they want—if they want anything at all—from these love affairs.

Ellen, 39, had been friends with David, 25, for quite a while but sensed the friendship could turn more serious.

"One day we made plans to go to a movie together. That's when I started getting really nervous. I was a little nervous before then, but when we decided to go to the movie, I got real nervous—because I felt something might happen and I thought that our age difference would make it awkward.

"So the morning we were supposed to go I told him that I didn't think we should. My saying that was a little presumptuous on my part because nothing had really happened, but I went ahead and said that I felt we shouldn't go out together, that we were going to have to be together in class for four years and if there was a possibility that we could become involved—well, I was concerned about that. I couldn't say exactly why, but I told David it bothered me.

"I was really surprised when he said, 'Okay.' Just like that—'Okay.' Then he said he had other female friends that he could go to the movies with and implied that he wasn't planning on a relationship, just a friendship like ones he had with lots of women his own age. When he saw I felt more comfortable knowing that, he asked me if, given it was just a friendly thing, I still wanted to go to the movies. And I said, 'Okay.' So I felt very relieved because I said no to a date but yes to a friendship.

"Then," Ellen laughs as she tells the story, "we went to

the movie, and I took his hand in the middle of it. I did that! Can you believe it? He was totally confused: first, I'm telling him one thing, and then I'm doing exactly the opposite.

"Why did I do that? It was being able to say no and not have him get angry. I was able to feel comfortable voicing my doubts. His response was so nonpressured—letting me know that however I wanted to be with him was fine. And that's when I started to fall in love."

Diane was 36 when Rob, 24, unexpectedly escalated their casual friendship by declaring his interest in her.

"It was just like a bad movie," said Diane. "Out of nowhere he said, 'I am just really falling in love with you.' And that had never occurred to me. It really had not. I just said, ''Hey, I'm real flattered, but that just can't happen.'

"And he was really cool. He said, 'I can change a whole lot about myself, but I can't change how old I am, and I'm not asking you to get married. I'm suggesting that we date. And I'm not asking that we make love today; whatever happens, happens.' That seemed to make sense.

"But he really caught me by surprise. We were doing plumbing together and stuff, and I wasn't having that much fun. So it was really evolutionary and over a period of time. That had never happened to me before quite in that way. There was a sweetness about it that was very attractive. So I said, 'Let me think about it.'

"The fact that he was younger really bothered me. And I told him that: 'You're my youngest brother's younger friend. And you have a girlfriend, and I've got somebody I'm dating. . . .' I thought about it for five days. Then I called him on a Thursday and said, 'I think you're absolutely right, Rob.' And he said, 'Fine. Why don't we just have supper?'

"So I felt it was my decision. This had never occurred to me before. The man I had previously dated for years and years was nine years older than I. But I really felt going out with Rob was my decision."

Diane finally went to dinner—after resisting for five days. Joanne resisted for six months.

"I was 33 when I met Hans," she recalled. "He was only 23, and we met when we were dancing for the same troupe.

Although we were instantly drawn to each other, I was sure that it couldn't last. When you're a dancer, you know, you appear to be very young. I was tremendously self-conscious about the difference in our ages, so I was convinced our little affair couldn't last.

"We had one month together when we were very close, but then we both had to travel. So we were apart for a good six months. I was sure that the separation would prove I was right, but when we got back together, nothing had changed. He said he wanted to marry me, and I laughed. I hurt his feelings. Finally, I agreed, but it was another year before we were able to marry."

Lillian, 72, married to John, 57, tried to discourage their relationship early on because she felt, even though she found him very attractive, that things were too serious. "We met at a party," she said, "and got to talking and arranged to have a drink the next day. He kind of sprang at the whole thing and decided he wanted to pursue this. And I, aware that he was younger, was kind of distant.

"He called me several times, and I sort of put him off. I never tell anyone my age, and I didn't want to get into it with him. Finally, I invited him over, and I tried to cool his feelings toward me—because of the age thing. We were sitting at my apartment that night, and he said, 'Why won't you take me seriously? Why do you keep jumping and pushing me away?'

"I was interested in having sex with him, but I didn't want to make anything of it. It was like a little adventure that I couldn't treat seriously. But he really liked me. He asked me again, 'Why are you pushing me away?' So I finally said, 'You're too young. I guess the age difference sort of embarrasses me.'

"So he said, 'If it doesn't matter to me, why does it matter to you?' I thought about that. I remember his words so distinctly. And I thought of how unhappy I had been so often and how many lonely years I'd had without meeting a nice person. There was a long silence while all this went through my mind. And I remembered how I had said in talking to a woman friend of mine that if the gods ever threw a good man in my path, I wasn't going to spurn him. So I said, 'You're right, you're absolutely right.' And that was it.

"Then we went through all the business of 'In 10 years I'll be this and you'll be that, and in 20 years'—all that nonsense that people go in for. And then I thought to myself how I'd had three or four relationships besides my first marriage, which broke up in 1959. This was now 1971. So I'd spent a good number of years alone. And who ever knows what is going to happen to them or how long we'll last? So why was I thinking, In 20 years I'll be this? Who knows? I might be dead. He might be dead. Who can tell? And I decided to forget it, and I did. I don't even think about it anymore, and I don't think he does, either."

Voices of Reason

Men in love with older women tend to react to the age issue very differently from their lovers. Though they are just as aware of the gap as their partners are, they dismiss it quite easily as irrelevant.

"Every once in a while I think about the future and how time flies after you hit 30," said Rob, 33, married to Diane, 45. "My parents are already 65, and in only 10 years Diane will be 55. When you think in those terms, it's scary, but then I have to say that Diane may be 45, but she doesn't have the personality of a typical 45-year-old. So I feel secure about us. If we haven't gotten bogged down yet, why should we ever?

"But while the 12 years between us is a big shock to some people, for me it was an instant nonissue. I dated a couple of women four or five years older than I was way back in college, and age was never an issue for me then, either. If I noticed anything, it was that older women have their lives together more than someone who is younger. Like Diane, they're more mature and aren't involved in some identity cri sis about where their career is at. It's a more mature outlook on life, and I find that attractive. Too many games go with dating immature women.''

Paul, 24, concurs. ''I got so tired of women my own age. I had to do it all: plan the date, steer the conversation, practically tuck her in at night and turn out the lights. And if I didn't call her, she'd complain—but she'd never call me. Dating an older woman has been very different. She takes as much responsibility for our getting along as I do. And it's great to be with a smart woman—finally, I have somebody to really bounce ideas off of. Whatever I put out, I get back from her. This is the kind of woman I've been looking for.''

These men are actually quite surprised by the women's sudden self-critical, self-destructive behavior; they simply cannot understand why their partners would fear continuing the relationship. They state again and again how sexy and attractive they find the older women's confidence and self-sufficiency. They talk easily about how comfortable it is to be with a woman who knows her own emotional and sexual needs, what a relief it is to be with a woman who is not threatened by a man's professional success because she has her own.

These are typically men who were raised *not* to expect to control a relationship and women too experienced even to toy with the idea of sublimating their own desires for the sake of a man. Thus, the men do not feel as if they are responsible for every aspect of a relationship, from asking for dates to guiding conversations to seeing that the sex is good. A younger man feels the older woman is with him every step of the way, because she knows what life is all about, she understands work pressures, she knows when it's time to take it easy. And most of all, she makes intelligence sexy.

So the man is quite surprised when the moment for commitment arrives and she pulls back from him and from making plans for their future together. Here is the woman who turns him on because she is his equal, a woman so interesting and exciting that he quickly decides he wants to spend his life with her, suddenly behaving in a way that betrays everything she is. Each man asks the same question with the same puzzlement: why does a woman who has achieved so much suddenly lack the confidence to consummate this love with a long-term commitment?

Being a Good Girl

I did not understand exactly why I felt so unsure about my younger lover until I began work on this book. Then, at last, the puzzle pieces began to fall into place.

When I met Brant, I was out there struggling to be an independent person with a good career and financial responsibilities, but I was still listening to some powerful voices from the past.

It is interesting that time and time again it was the women in the relationships with younger men who worried—the men did not. Why? Because as women we are raised to listen to and follow the rules. We are taught to worry about what others think. On the other hand, our men are raised to be independent, to trust their own instincts, and to follow the rules *when the rules work for them*. We may be older, but we haven't been out there as independent individuals as long as the younger men have—that's what makes the difference; that's why they see nothing wrong in the relationships.

But when we chose to become self-sufficient economically, we also chose the role of the rule maker. And that has taken some time to adjust to. No wonder deep down inside we still experience the old pull that if we don't do things the way they've always been done, we must be doing something wrong.

Although others view me as a "strong" woman, I felt torn about Brant. I saw myself as a risk taker, a woman who follows her own instincts. Then why did I have such difficulty? The answer is that, when it comes to thumbing my nose at society in matters as serious as life and death (which is what love and happiness are very much a part of), I'm as weak as everyone else.

I now believe that the doubt, guilt, and fear that I felt when I fell in love with Brant—and that Diane felt with Rob, and

Joanne with Hans, and Lillian with John—has to do mostly with the mixed messages we received from men, society, our parents: it's okay to succeed in a man's world, but don't go too far. Go into politics, but don't expect to be president. Work long, hard hours, but don't expect to be paid a salary equal to a man's. Be wise, powerful, and strong, but don't ever lose that feminine charm.

To give you an example of how easy it is for women to get mixed messages, I'd like to tell you a story about my mother. She was a remarkable woman, a very attractive woman, who possessed a quick, bright wit. She loved people, and they loved her for her generosity as a listener and her eagerness to talk and to laugh. And she was unusual because she was renowned for her spontaneous and often raucous sense of humor. She could tell a joke or funny story better than any man I've ever heard.

At her funeral, when most would have delivered a solemn tribute, our priest decided instead to tell Mom's best jokes to the people gathered—at least one was a little off-color for those hallowed walls. We ended up rolling in the aisles when we should have been weeping.

That tells you the kind of woman she was—funny and very outgoing. I have known very few women in my life who are as articulate and unafraid as my mother was to take center stage in mixed company. But by social standards, she wasn't very ladylike. So my mother was my first feminist teacher, showing me by example that a woman could speak up and speak out.

On the other hand, she was an exceptionally traditional wife and mother. She bore eight children, and she stayed home to care for us, to care for my father, to run the household. Most of the time.

At other times, she terrified me with her anger over this part of her life. She railed at us, her children, telling us we were the reason she wasn't the woman she might have been. I know she talked about that at especially difficult times in her life, but as a young girl I could see only her disappointment—not all the good things that she might temper her remarks with if I could talk to her today. I never forgot the anger and the disappointment I heard in her voice.

So I grew up watching my mother do one thing but say another. And during my teenage years, even as I grew more and more like her—willing to express my opinions, eager to talk up in a crowd—sometimes she was proud of me, and other times it made her angry. More than once, she chastised me, saying, "You always do it wrong." It was one of those remarks we find ourselves saying to our own kids, like "Wipe that look off your face." When you are a teenager, you really don't know what that look is that's driving your parents and teachers crazy. And that was my confusion then: *what* did I always do wrong?

Many years later, when I met Brant and began to push the limits of what is acceptable behavior for a woman of my age, all my mother's messages reverberated in my head. Because I had suddenly stepped into a territory with no firm guidelines to follow, I wondered, was I doing it wrong again?

I know many women today who are fighting this battle in other areas. They try to be the traditional wife and mother while fulfilling their goals to become independent and accomplished people. They, too, feel confused and frustrated.

I watched this happen recently to a good friend who is employed in a part-time management position. Her husband refused to help with child care when her sitter canceled hours before a meeting at which she was to make a presentation. Even though it would not have been a major inconvenience in his own work schedule, he refused on principle to help with child care, stating firmly that he would *never* leave his office during work hours for such a reason. My friend was furious and said to her husband, who is an admirer of motivational behavior experts, "It's tough to soar like an eagle when you've got three dead weights tied to your legs."

My friend's meeting was critical to her job, but her husband does not consider her work equal in value to his own. He can ask her to sacrifice all for the purposes of his career, but he is unwilling to return the favor. It is no coincidence that this man is in his mid-forties, which means he is one of the generation of men who do not yet seem to believe that marriage is supposed to be an equal partnership.

The point here is not that, as women, we've been given a bum rap by society. Feminists have been pointing that out for years, and, as noted in the introduction, we've made great strides toward equality in the last decades. Rather, my point is that, as intelligent, motivated women, we've got to stop letting other people—or social expectations—tell us what to do. As hard as it is, we've got to accept the fact that we did receive mixed messages, then chose the messages that make the most sense to us from the perspective of our needs today and move on.

A major part of this acceptance is dealing with our greatest fear of all: the fear of abandonment. As children, we were taught to need a man to take care of us—economically and emotionally. We had to be very, very good in order to attract our "Prince Charming." Furthermore, we were taught that to be without him would be to place ourselves—and our children—at enormous risk. That is why divorce seems so terrifying to many of us that one woman, who has survived two divorces, recently described both experiences as "going into the wilderness, frightened and alone." We fear abandonment because we fear being wholly independent. We aren't sure we can take care of ourselves.

Thus, even as I talked with women about various reasons why they hesitated before committing themselves to their relationships with younger men, it became clear that all our worries boil down to that basic fear of abandonment: a fear of risking our self-esteem, of giving all we have to give—only to be left. Each of us, in our private way, had to deal with that.

I'm not sure how every woman resolves that. It's a problem you face regardless of the age of your lover, but it's more difficult for the woman who loves a younger man because she has no role models or guidelines to give her any clues to what might happen. In the end, I dealt with my fear by telling myself that, if things didn't work for Brant and me, if I ended up alone again, I would have my work and my children and some very special memories.

My thoughts on the fear of abandonment are echoed much more eloquently by Michelle, a 43-year-old scientist who married a man 16 years younger than she.

Just as I was leaving her home after our interview, she stopped me at the door to say, "I forgot to tell you that it doesn't scare me to death if this doesn't work out. I was alone after my divorce, and I survived. I can do it again. I love this man, and I know that I am giving our marriage everything I can to make it work. But if it doesn't work, I can live with that."

And then she said, "We have no guarantees for any relationship with a man of any age. Do we?" No, of course not. So why all the worry over relationships with younger men? The point to keep in focus is that these relationships will succeed or fail for the same reasons couples of all age groups make or don't make it. The real reasons are complex and intertwined with the interpersonal psychology of the two people involved.

Getting over the Hurdle

In the long run, it was my recognition of Brant's willingness to share dreams and responsibilities that helped me through my hesitation. It's true that I hesitated for a long time, but what made me change my mind was knowing that Brant wasn't offering me just love and understanding—he was offering me an equal partnership in our life together.

I feel a gift of that magnitude is worth the effort to help others win it, too. And that's what makes it important to name the terrors that I have learned are most likely to frighten us about these relationships. You will find them discussed on every page of this book: fear of aging and not knowing if change in our physical appearance will mean a loss of sex appeal, if that in turn will threaten our sexuality and loosen the bonds that brought us together; fear of reactions from family and friends; fear of his need to have a child; fear of a loss of personal power and independence; fear of a clash of needs and hopes.

Among all the men and women I interviewed, I found only a few who were not still dealing with *some* of the issues that worry older woman/younger man couples: children, finances, family reactions. (Then again, most same-age couples often face variations on these themes.) But almost all older woman/younger man couples must work together to resolve their conflict over commitment relatively early in the relationship.

Many women cope with the age issue as I did, by setting a limit on how long they will allow themselves to enjoy the affair. Stephanie, an intense 43-year-old with a music video production career in full swing, is trying out what I call the "One-Month Plan."

She stumbled into an affair with 30-year-old Alan, and she feels on the ropes emotionally. Nevertheless, she doesn't trivialize her worries. She confronts what bothers her most and deals with each issue in a direct, if painful, way.

"I really worry about us and how long this can last," she said. "I want it to last. He makes me so happy.

"First I wondered what my friends would say, but then I found out they were all dating younger men. Interesting thing is, each of us assumes these affairs will be short-term. Is that because no one is willing to commit? I don't know where that assumption comes from exactly, but it bothers me.

"At first I thought I would take this one day at a time, but that seems pretty shallow. So here is how I handle it. Whenever I can, I try to line up some work close to Alan or vice versa. So far we have been able to see each other for four or five days every month. Once I have that time set aside, I consider myself committed for a month. Sometimes I've been able to resolve some serious matter during that month.

"For example, I told my former husband about Alan right away. Even though we have been divorced for six years, we've had a habit of doing things together with the children, and that's going to have to change. Even without Alan, that has to change. But my ex was really hurt. He told me that the youth of my escort bothered him. At first, I listened to him. Was I humiliating myself? But this former husband of mine happens to be dating younger women himself! So I let him be hurt. I told him I didn't believe in double standards.

"Another of my biggest worries was how my kids would take my being with a guy who looks a lot younger and who is so different from their father. So I invited Alan to visit for a weekend at my house. The kids—two are in college, and one is a senior in high school—were real upset, but they told me later that it wouldn't matter who it was. They don't want to see another man replacing their dad. So Alan's age isn't the issue."

Now Stephanie worries about the vast difference in lifestyles between her and Alan and the fact that they live in different parts of the country and she doesn't want to give up her job. "When he comes to see me in New York, I realize the chasm between us," she said. "It isn't just that I come out of a whole frantic crowd that always has to eat at the trendiest restaurants—I am quite willing to live without that—but Alan is so much simpler about the way he lives. I'm always on the go, while he likes to take it easy. I love it, but I'm not sure I want that all the time."

As Stephanie notes, lifestyle is much more of an issue for her and Alan than age. By talking about her situation—to her former husband, to her children, and to her friends—she has been able to separate the important issues from the less important ones like age.

More common than the "One-Month plan" is the "One-Year plan," to which many women in love with younger men subscribe.

"That's all I ask, just one year with you, and I'll be happy," was what I said to Brant. I am 42, he is 33, and I said that seven years ago.

"I didn't worry too much about my future with Brad," said Elinor. "I just figured it could only last a year." She is 57, he is 39, and she said that nine years ago.

"Well, I thought it was so absurd that this man was interested in me and even wanted to marry me that I convinced myself it would all be over in a year," said Joanne. She is 53, Hans is 43, and she said that 20 years ago.

We all said essentially the same thing. What we were trying

to do was bracket out a period of time during which we would allow ourselves to invest every emotion, every effort, in the relationship but protect ourselves from our fear of abandonment by second-guessing the end of the affair. So we decided to commit for *one year*.

During that year we planned to sort out the following:

First, we would see if we were strong enough to bear up under an anticipated barrage of criticism from family and friends. We girded our loins for battle.

Second, we would test our man's emotional maturity.

"I was watching Brad for signs of immature behavior," said Elinor, "and I saw some. But I also realized I've seen worse behavior in men much older than Brad—particularly in the man I married the first time. Age has nothing to do with maturity—I know that from experience. And I must admit I'm immature myself sometimes. I think all of us can go from being adults to being children instantly if the situation presents itself."

I, too, was on the lookout for signs of immaturity. It was my most significant concern about Brant—or so I thought. As it turns out, *I* am the one who acts like a little kid—at bill-paying time. And I know why. It's because my father thought he was doing me a favor when he shielded me from learning about money when I was a girl. In fact, he crippled me, but I'm getting over it. Meanwhile, Brant has to suffer with my immature emotional conflict over money. So all it took were a couple of major fights over finances to straighten me out on the tradeoffs that would be necessary if I wanted the relationship to work—which I did! And I reminded myself that I fell in love with this man because he is so youthful in his ways and his thinking—that's something I dearly love and hope he never loses. The child in both of us is an essential part of our relationship.

The "One-Year plan" worked extremely well for me because it offered me plenty of breathing space in order to watch, wait, and see if my worst fears might be realized. When they weren't after about six months, I found myself hoping my "year" wouldn't end too soon. Suddenly, everything flip-flopped for me, and I realized I didn't want just one year; I wanted a *long-term commitment*. But getting over that initial hurdle of finding some psychological space ("one year") for coping with all the worries freed me to be able to assess the reality of our situation and then move ahead with the relationship, after feeling I had had time to think clearly.

Not all of the women, of course, set a specific time frame for themselves, but there is a tendency for these women to wait before making an impetuous decision they might later regret.

In the meantime, many women find rationalization a good way to cope with doubts they have about the longevity of the affair. If it's not enough simply to say, "I'm seeing this guy because he's great, and we're great together," we can pull out one of two excellent rationalizations for choosing a younger man: women live longer than men by an average of seven years, so it makes sense biologically; or we share the same religion, politics, or love of birds.

Each is a perfectly sound reason; if it works for you, use it. The first, the biological reasoning, has been proven. Since 80 percent of the elderly now living alone are women, the inequity of men marrying younger while women have not is obvious.

And when a woman rationalizes her relationship because of a sharing of a deep interest such as religion or politics or a love of the outdoors, again the logic is there. If two people share interests, it makes sense for them to be together.

Luckily, our instincts in this instance serve us well; the wait-and-see approach worked for me and for most of the women I interviewed.

We were able to accept our lovers and let our relationships develop. At the end of a year each of us was surprised to find that we felt closer than ever to the men we loved. During that year we also discovered that many of our fears were groundless: families and friends were not critical ogres, we hadn't lost our looks or our man, younger women had not raided our love nests, our kids were coping, our work was better than ever, we felt absolutely terrific, and we were willing to commit for at least another year!

And the men? They had these quizzical expressions on their

faces when I asked. One year wasn't the issue for them, since they thought from the very beginning that they were talking about a partnership for life.

When Age Isn't Really the Issue

I think it is vitally important for a woman to be able to recognize when she is holding back from a relationship with a younger man for reasons that have nothing to do with age, *yet she blames age for their incompatibility*. Sometimes we fool ourselves.

Terri is a stunning-looking woman who has made a name for herself in the garment industry. "Sure I'll talk to you," she said, laughing when I called. "I've got one thing to say— never date a younger man. Never. Never. I've dated nobody but younger men, and I can tell you it doesn't work."

I was intrigued. So we met. And for three hours I listened to a litany of failed love affairs. She entered a long relationship with one man with whom she fell in love after a long telephone courtship, but he turned out to be 14 years younger and immature. Her neighbor was smitten and wanted to marry her, but he was 12 years younger and immature. Her current lover is rich and cute and wants to take care of her forever and ever, but he is 28 and immature. My God, I thought, this blows all my theories out of the water. And I rose to leave.

But Terri sat there. "I shouldn't tell you this," she said. "I haven't told anyone about this. But if you have another minute. . . ." I had two more hours.

And during those two hours I learned about the man Terri fell hard for when she was 30 and he was 20. "I loved that man," she said finally. "Denny was my best friend and the best lover I've ever had. But I was married, and I had two little babies, and I felt so terrible about our affair. We met working on a fashion show together. He was just real sweet and liked to work with me on stuff. I was married to a man who was going out on me—that old story. Our marriage ended five years later, but it was too late. Denny had moved to Atlanta, met a nice girl, and gotten married.

"I should have left my crazy husband for him. I loved Denny, and age never made one bit of difference to me. He never let it make a difference. Whenever I would bring it up, he'd just say, 'Love a person as he is. Expect to be treated well, but other than that, let the other person be whoever he is and love him for that.' I'd marry Denny today if I could."

We went back then, Terri and I, and sorted through all those other men. They were attracted to her because she is lovely and dynamic. The man on the telephone wasn't right because she just didn't like his looks and his ways. The neighbor was very sweet but just not the kind of personality she most enjoys. The reasons the relationships did not work had nothing to do with age: she was still in love with Denny. What Terri was finally willing to admit was that her relationships failed for other reasons. Her feelings of low self-esteem, her insecurities, had prevented her from having a satisfying life with Denny. And her personal taste made her other love options unappealing. Age had never been the real issue! In fact, she continues to date younger men.

There are other issues, many of them valid, that women must explore in deciding whether or not to commit to a younger man.

One issue that surfaces repeatedly is a woman's bad experience in an earlier marriage.

"Ugh, no way I want that again," was Amanda's first response when Steve asked her to marry him. She was 37 and he was 28 when Steve proposed to her. Two years later, she accepted his offer. "Steve asked me for a long time—two years—before I finally said yes," recalls Amanda. "I wanted to be sure that I married for love, for the right reasons, and not because someone was going to take care of me. The only way I would marry again was if I was financially independent myself. I had many opportunities to remarry before Steve, but I turned them down because I had to feel I wasn't jeopardizing my independence. I have never been able to comprehend the role of a woman dependent on her husband, and I couldn't marry a man who expected that.

"It also made a difference to me that Steve had been married before, so he knew what marriage was like. For me, it had been awful. He had had some similar experiences. So we both knew the kind of marriage we *didn't* want. But when I resisted marriage at first, I knew that it wasn't because of the age thing."

Maureen, 43, married to Garrett, 31, felt the same way that Amanda did—she had been burned once in a bad marriage and was fiercely protective of her hard-won independence.

"Marriage had left a bad taste in my mouth," she said. "And I wasn't dying to get married again. We married only because of my children. Since they lived with me, we couldn't sleep together otherwise. I still yearn for some of the luxuries of my single days, like just being a private person.

"I had to make it clear to Garrett that he wasn't the rescuer here. He was not going to 'bail me out' of singleness, as if it were a bad experience, because I didn't view it as that. He was going to enhance what already was."

Lillian, 72, married to John, 57, resisted for a different reason. Like Stephanie, who has similar reservations about her lover Alan, Lillian experienced doubts about the successful merger of their two very different personal styles.

"If anything stood between John and me," she said, "it was our backgrounds. He's not a person who values culture or the arts the way I do. Our styles are quite different. I've learned a lot from getting married a second time. When you're very young and you marry, you don't think much about style because you are still becoming a person. But when you make a late second marriage, you are who you are, and you don't give an inch.

"However, I had to look hard at what does work between John and me. We love our farm, and we take care of it ourselves. We're vegetarians, and we raise all our own food. We do lots and lots of work together, a lot of it physical. That's as important to me as the cultural and artistic and literary things. It's kind of 50-50. So 50 percent of what I'm interested in I share with John. The other we share a little bit.

"Because of that, I didn't particularly want to get married.

John really pressed for it, maybe because he has a certain kind of business mind, and he likes things neat and tidy. So we did apply for a marriage license. You have 30 days to act on a license, and we got married on the 29th day!''

Lillian helped justify her marriage to John (despite concerns over lifestyle differences) by rationalizing that it would make things more comfortable for her socially.

"Two very odd reasons finally persuaded me to go ahead. One was that my office was a very conventional one, as were John's parents, and it was awkward to be living together and hiding that fact when people telephoned me at home. The other reason was that I still used my first husband's name, and I really wanted to get rid of it. So that's how I decided.''

Another valid reason for putting off marriage is the challenge of the blended family. However, few couples recognize how difficult this can be, and, valid though the reason is, it is not often a main reason that a woman postpones her commitment to marriage. It is a "Catch-22" for many couples because it is a potential problem area that should be explored before marriage, even though it is tough to do so. Most of the women interviewed who had children living with them were very hesitant to establish an intimate relationship without the sanction of marriage because they did not want to offer a bad example to their children. On the other hand, how do you determine how well your potential marriage partner and your children will coexist without testing a live-in arrangement first? No easy solution exists to this problem.

Yet another problem causing women to hesitate before making a long-term commitment is when they do not want to *have* a child and the younger men do. Most often, it is the woman who resists marriage to a younger man because she knows he is interested in having children but she may have had one or more in an earlier marriage and feels the child-rearing years are behind her. (We will discuss these child-related issues further in Chapter 8.)

One last reason that women hesitate before making a commitment to a younger man might surprise some people: money. Ironically, it's not the problem you'd expect; it's not that the men are uncomfortable with the woman's (typically) significantly larger salary. Instead, it's that the woman, usually supporting herself as well as a child or two, does not want the increased financial burden of supporting a man who, because he is young, is making very little money to begin with. But we'll examine this interesting phenomenon in greater detail in Chapter 6.

However, some women do persist in naming the age difference as the reason they avoid a long-term commitment to a younger man, when in reality they may have a fear of loving *any* man. Others simply lose interest in a man the moment that he becomes interested in her. I talked with several women who date younger men because they like the idea of forbidden fruit. Once the man is taken with them, they drop him for another. I recommend professional help for a woman who finds herself in such a pattern. Still other women like to set themselves up for failure, and choosing a younger man provides a handy excuse to blame the relationship's failure on reasons other than their own inability to sustain a relationship.

My interviews have taught me to view those who "protest too much," those who insist that it is *always* unwise to date a younger man, with a dim eye. A confident, secure woman will not deride the man because of his age. Rather, she will confront her insecurity over the age difference and question how she can cope. She will be willing to shoulder some of the responsibility for the making or the breaking of the relationship.

If you are considering a relationship with a younger man, I would encourage you to be honest with yourself about your fears. Love with a younger man, or any man, is too wonderful to risk losing because you have not come to terms with your own needs and fears.

Are women doomed to forever dance the hesitation waltz?

Hardly. The evidence is growing that relationships with younger men are becoming more common and more accepted—even more accepted by the women involved, who are the ones who worry most. With over a third of all women over age 25 marrying younger men these days, it's hard to believe that women in the next generations will worry about the age difference as much as we do.

Younger women are our best proof that this is changing. I have found numerous couples over the last six months in which the woman, who is in her late twenties and as much as eight years older than her fiancé or husband, is not in the least concerned with the age difference.

"My daughter is getting married this month," one proud mother told me. "She met her husband-to-be in graduate studies at Stanford. We didn't know until last week that he is seven years younger. They didn't think it was important, so they never mentioned it. We think he's perfect for her."

But the kicker comes from my own daughter. She is 21, a senior in college. I asked her if she was aware of women on campus dating younger men.

"Really, Mom," she said with the look of tired resignation she gets when I ask what she considers to be silly questions, "first of all, very few people pay attention to who dates whom. I happen to know a senior woman who dates a freshman but only because he lives in my dorm. Nobody cares. Really, nobody even thinks about it."

And for those of us who *do* notice age differences, it is important to realize, as Dan, 30, told Lynn, 37, that we live in a time when strong, independent people can easily ignore societal taboos: "It's the '80s, and there are no rules." What better time to fall in love with a younger man?

3

Family, Friend, or Foe?
How Do I Tell Them
About Us?

When you'll be 30, she will be an old hag.
> —Albert Einstein's mother, talking about
> his first wife, who was four years older

*I decided after going through a real push-pull of commitment
to Garrett that the only way to make our relationship work
was to put us first and everyone else last. I had to focus on
what was good and right between us. I had to blank out what
other people thought and go with my instinct. I made up my
mind to hold on to my fantasy.*
> —Maureen, 43, on her decision
> to be with Garrett, 31

*I never think about differences in ages, any more than about
the opinion of imbeciles.*
> —comment by Colette's 50-year-old
> heroine in *Break of Day*

"Nice to meet you, Brant—but, Vicki, you look old enough
to be his mother! Don't people ask if you're his mother?"
So said one of my sisters as I introduced her to Brant for

the first time. With a sister to make a remark like that, who needs an enemy?

But while her response caught me off-guard, it didn't upset me. This particular sister is legendary for her lack of tact. As a result, her words don't carry the sting they might. But her remark is an example of the kind of reaction that I was afraid of when Brant and I first, tentatively, began to tell our friends and our families about us. I felt very self-conscious and worried that people would assume we fit the stereotype of the woman with a younger man: she is in it for sex; he is looking for a mother.

Making the decision to declare our love for a younger man, and thereby to express our intention to continue with the relationship, puts us in the vulnerable position of being open to approval or rejection by our family and friends. I know several women who have turned down dates with younger men; with reactions like that of Pauline Einstein to her son Albert's proposed marriage, it is easy to understand why.

After all, I remember my own reaction to my observation of an episode between a much older woman and a young artist that I knew. It happened at a reception given for the artist. I saw the woman put her arm around him and ask him to go out with her in a way that made her infatuation with him obvious. On the one hand, I felt embarrassed for her. On the other hand, I knew what attracted her because it attracted me, too.

The man was in his late twenties and the woman about 45. She was a bright, well-educated woman and very elegant. He had given a wonderful talk—one that was inspiring and brought back memories of childhood and love and whimsy. When you spoke with him one on one, he had an open, intuitive manner that made it easy to like him and to feel as though you were able to communicate accurately and share your ideas.

Today I understand how the woman I watched that night might have fallen in love—the youth and creativity inside her must have recognized a kindred spirit—and I am ashamed of the embarrassment I felt for her. That night, I thought it was ridiculous for them to be together, though I wouldn't have thought twice if it had been an older man asking out a young female artist.

So if I had hesitated longer than usual before telling people—longer than a woman with a boyfriend who is her age or older might wait before announcing that it is a serious relationship—it was because I wanted to be sure I had the confidence and the energy to explain our relationship, to defend it if I had to, to make people whose opinion mattered to me understand.

As it happened, I worried needlessly for the most part. The people whom we care about accepted us as a couple far more easily than I ever imagined they would—not necessarily without explanation, but easily. That includes families, friends, my children, and people with whom we both work. They accepted us graciously. There were a few nay-sayers, people who were not happy for us, but they were indeed the exceptions to the rule.

It seems that the older woman/younger man taboo has lost much of its punch when it comes to the people who care about you. Those couples that anticipated a lot of negative reactions were usually pleasantly surprised by friends and family who understood and accepted the new relationship. And those few who did meet some real resistance found that it's just not that difficult, in our society, to stay together in spite of it.

Today, seven years after I told my family and friends about Brant, I never worry about the opinion of others. I have learned there's no need to. But when Brant and I were taking the first steps toward making a serious commitment to one another, my worry over what others would think of the nine-year difference in our ages consumed me—and I have learned that my feelings are typical of women in my position.

Swallowing Hard
and Telling Friends

Most of the women I interviewed went to friends—before going to their families—for approval of the new relationships. I sense that this is because we judge our friends, whom we have chosen, to be most like us. While we spend most of our lives separating ourselves from our families, we want to get closer to our friends. Telling those friends, whose opinions matter to us more than anyone else's, is a big step. What if they don't approve?

The first friend to whom I turned was Anne, a woman who had known me well for over 15 years. She'd shared my triumphs and my disasters, my strengths and my shortcomings. Especially my shortcomings.

She wasted no time getting to the point after she had met and spent some time with Brant.

"Do you know what you're doing?" Anne asked me in a tone that implied, "Have you got your head screwed on straight?" "This guy is good and kind and sincere. He's sensitive, and he cares so much for you. Do you realize how badly you might hurt him? He means business. . . ."

Anne confronted me with the stereotypes: first, she was sure that this relationship was just a fling, a short-term love affair. Several women interviewed have experienced the same response from friends—they think the relationship sounds great, but they immediately assume it's short-term. It did not occur to Anne to ask me if I was thinking of us as a couple that might be together for years. Brant, never anticipating her assumption that it was just a fling, had been open about his serious interest in me. That alarmed her. Second, she also assumed there could be no future between us because of the age difference. Her concern for Brant was immediate because she foresaw certain doom for us as a couple and wondered why I was leading him on.

Even though her response was frustrating, because I had to deal with reactions that wouldn't have been there if I'd been involved with a man my own age, it was valuable. It occurred *because she met and liked a man that I also liked very much*. That meant Brant as a person had her respect, her approval. Her reaction to Brant validated my own assessment of him.

Let me say right now that it would be terrific if I could say that I didn't need outside validation like this; it would be terrific if I had been secure in my own opinion. But I did not yet have that confidence in my own judgment. I used to feel that this was a major flaw in my character until I learned that this is part of our psychological development pattern—a deeply ingrained behavioral need foisted on us by society the day we're born and subtly reinforced in millions of ways as we grow up. It's a fact: women are conditioned to seek approval. We are changing this as we become more independent in our work life and more self-sufficient financially, but most of us still seek that approving nod to tell us that we are doing the right thing. Men, on the other hand, are conditioned to stand alone, to feel comfortable making decisions independently. That's why I went to my closest friends for approval, but Brant did not. However, that did not mean his friends weren't ready to check us out.

In fact, the first time that I met several of his oldest and best friends socially, friends who were his age and had known him since junior high school days, one took me aside to say, "We all know how Brant feels about you, and we're worried. We don't want to see him hurt. Are you taking him seriously?"

That took me aback. What I could hear behind his carefully chosen words was "This is real life, lady; this isn't fun and games. If you think you're just fooling around, you'd better think again." In essence, Brant's friend stopped just short of threatening to break both my legs if I turned out to be playing with Brant's emotions. The specter of the old stereotype had raised its ugly head as he assumed I was just an older woman out for a good time. He took Brant's intentions seriously, but not mine. Essentially, whether I was dealing with my friend or Brant's friend, the fact remained that I was the older woman, and I was the one who had to prove the old stereotype wrong.

Because I judge people by the quality of their friendships, and I think it's unusual for a man to have such strong friendships as Brant clearly shared with these people, I wasn't upset by the challenge. These bright, sensitive, gentle friends were willing to question me because of their affection for and commitment to Brant. That they recognized him as someone so valuable, so worth their efforts to understand and protect, gave me one more reason to love him.

"I don't know what's going to happen," I replied to his friend. "But I certainly am not just fooling around. I have children, a reputation—my own world is being rocked by this. . . . I have no intention of hurting anyone, and I don't want to be hurt either."

They seemed so quick to assume I was the female equivalent of a Don Juan preying on a young lover. They made me anxious to prove to everyone that I was serious about Brant. The stereotype made me feel cheapened, but that, in turn, heightened my resolve to prove to myself and to them the value of my feelings about Brant.

I wondered, too, if this meant that his friends would always be suspicious of me.

Then, a few days later, just as I was beginning to feel that maybe I was too old and too out of synch with his contemporaries for us to be together, another friend of Brant's relieved the pressure.

"So," this jolly fellow said within two minutes of meeting me, "what do you think of Brant's taste in music?"

If anything is distinctive about Brant, it's his deep interest in all kinds of music, from the latest rockabilly-punk synthesizer sequence to the Rolling Stones to Mozart. Some people live in the fast lane; Brant lives at an incredible decibel level. He's a rock critic, so it pays off, but it's an experience nevertheless.

"I like it . . . I guess," I said a little hesitantly, because I really didn't know yet. My ears were lagging behind the rest of my neurological system, which had already fallen hard for him. "He's always playing stuff I've never heard before," I added, hoping I wouldn't have to confess that I had been scrambling to erase 20 years of ignorance of new music ever since I met Brant.

"You're not alone. *No one* has ever heard some of the music he plays," laughed the friend, tickled and satisfied with my confusion. "Nobody can keep up with him." So my answer was correct: I admitted bewilderment, it was legitimate, and I was accepted. Whew!

Of course, Brant wasn't interested in what other people were thinking, so he wasn't seeking outside approval.

Right after I made the decision that I wanted to try for one year with Brant, I told just two more of my closest friends about us. Both are women who share an outlook on the world similar to my own, as we are all eager to combine a high-powered career with a satisfying personal life.

The first, Julie, listened to my story with her mouth hanging open, but not because my news was unusual. Quite the contrary: she was stunned because I was the second woman in less than a week to tell her I was seeing a younger man. She had just heard from another old friend who had begun to date a man 12 years younger.

"I'm envious," she said without skipping a beat. "The younger men sound much more interesting than some of these aging 40-year-olds the rest of us are stuck with. I mean, I love my husband, but he has some ways that drive me crazy. Not only are you two [meaning her friend and me] real survivors, but now you've found these charming, sensitive men. It must be wonderful to have a man put you on a pedestal like that."

Then I came at the issue from a different direction and asked Julie what she would think if a son of *hers* became involved with an older woman.

"First of all," she said, "if the woman were 5 years older, right around that number, I wouldn't even think about it because I don't consider that a significant difference in any way. When you get to 10 years, then I might be bothered. What would bother me most is a woman I don't like. Age has nothing to do with it. If I don't like a woman, *that's* what would worry me."

Julie's response meant a lot to me. Not only did she accept

my choice; she encouraged it. And the fact that she knew about another woman's success with a younger man helped me feel more confident, which was good, because I was about to get clobbered with the stereotype again.

The second friend I approached, Chris, may be a very bright woman, but that didn't stop her from asking me a ridiculous question that showed me just how ingrained a stereotype can be: "I know the sex is great, Vicki," she said, "but what else is there?"

Right. What else is there? The stereotype holds that an older man brings wisdom, prestige, and financial security to a relationship; therefore, the *only* benefit a younger man can possibly offer is good sex.

I thought about getting huffy, but I cooled down and very reasonably countered by asking her, "Have you seen any evidence of nymphomania on my part in the 10 years that you've known me? Any evidence that I am interested in men only for sex?" That didn't really answer her question, so I asked her to see what she thought after getting to know Brant better.

Which she did, and her question was answered not by my defensive listing of all the reasons I was falling in love, but by who Brant is. Once she met him, she knew I was attracted to him because he has many of the same qualities that are true of all of my friends, male and female: intelligence, kindness, curiosity, ambition, a strong sense of outrage against inequities in the world, and an enduring interest in other people.

One old friend, however, a man who is a year older than I am and has known me since childhood, went out of his way to be deliberately rude to Brant and to tell me he was "disappointed in the age of my escort."

From the time we were kids, social acceptance has meant a great deal to this person. He has always been quick to alert me to the ways of the "upper class"—the right schools, the "in" clubs, the accoutrements of the aristocracy. He encouraged me, when my first marriage ended, to seek out a wealthy investment banker, someone older and well established. Need

I say more when I tell you that for him my marriage to Brant was the exact opposite of a class act?

And a woman friend who made my acquaintance during the prosperous years of my first marriage, the wife of a multimillionaire and a woman finely tuned to the essence of propriety—a woman who had graced me with social invitations up to the time of my divorce—dropped me like a hot potato when Brant appeared on the scene. Again, it was made clear that I was violating the social norms of the upper middle class.

To both that man and that woman, a younger man is fine as a companion for dinner or the theater, even acceptable as a casual bed partner, but not as a serious contender for a long-term relationship. That, my dears, is just not done.

So while I may have lost two friends stuck with some social attitudes that harken back to the fuddy-duddy '50s, in their places are new people, bright and intelligent people, people without pretense—people who are truly "class acts."

The women I interviewed all went to their friends for approval, with much the same results. They found their friends supportive for the most part, with only a few negative reactions.

Donna, 65, was teaching when she met Eric, 42. They got to know each other over the next few years, as Eric would periodically sign up for her courses. Eventually, they became friends and began to attend lectures together. One night, Eric invited Donna to join him on a three-week vacation—he wanted to rent a van and drive across Canada. Each day's direction would be decided by how they felt that morning, with nothing planned ahead of time.

At first Donna was thrilled with the idea. As she had gotten to know Eric, she had come to like him as a close friend. Now, however, she realized her feelings were stronger than that. Her conflict over their age difference was deeply personal but also tied to what others would think.

"Instantly, I was worried. Was this okay? Were we allowed? I knew I was talking about love and sex, not friendship any longer. So I went to four different colleagues who were good friends. I asked them if they thought I was doing something wrong.

"And each one said no, that even if we had met in the classroom, this was a relationship that developed outside of class. Plus, we're adults. When I pointed out the age difference, saying that I was 61 and Eric was only 38, they would just laugh and say, 'Go for it.' So I really did not make my decision to take the trip until I had some approval from people who respected me and could help me feel okay about Eric and me."

With approval in hand, Donna and Eric set out on their trip. That trip was four years ago, and they have just celebrated their third wedding anniversary.

"I never worry about age," said Eric, "or what people think. What bothers me is that Donna will die before I do, and I don't want to think about my future without her."

It was from a slightly different point of view that Lynn, 37, was able to reassess the future of her relationship with Dan, 30, whom she had begun to date thinking he was only a year or two younger. When she discovered there was a seven-year gap, she was taken aback and discussed the age difference with friends to see what they thought.

"Most of them said right away not to bother, not to worry, who cares, it doesn't matter. That was easy for them to say, because all their husbands are four years older, and they have the perfect structure. The only person whose comments really made a difference to me was a woman who is a film editor and works with me. She has a lover who is 13 years younger—she is 41 and he is 28.

"We were having lunch one day, and I told her I was thinking of a documentary on older women with younger men, and she said, 'I have always thought that would be a good idea.' She told me more about her own experience. Finally, it dawned on me that these age differences are more common than I thought.

"But she was the only person who really helped me understand. She's a very attractive woman—very energetic. She's thin and dresses nicely and has all this curly blonde hair. You just want to be her friend. But she's shy about her lover, even though you can tell she's very flattered. She said it makes her feel very womanly and very much in love.

"Regardless of age, she's in love with this man, and it shows. So I got to thinking about that. I decided to forget about numbers, about ages, and think more about how I feel. I'm getting away from my sensitivity to age and focusing on how Dan supports me—how I've never been so enjoyed and supported like this by anyone in my life."

And so, with her friend as a much-needed role model to give her the confidence that her new relationship was not wrong, Lynn continued to see Dan. They are now considering marriage—and the only roadblock is that she loves living in Washington and he refuses to give up San Francisco. Age is not the big issue.

Like Lynn and Donna, Lillian, 72, also turned to a friend who was a coworker for support and approval of her relationship with 57-year-old John.

Before her retirement, Lillian was a top executive in her manufacturing company; she has been featured in national magazines as one of America's most prominent female executives. So even with the power of the boardroom behind her, she was still sensitive to public opinion.

"But I had this wonderful friend in the office, and she was one of the first people I told about John," said Lillian. "Right away I said, 'Jan, there's only one thing I think about, and that's that he's a lot younger than I.' It's one of the few times I've talked with anyone about it. And she said, 'That's great. He'll keep you young.' So I felt much better."

Two women reported initial negative reactions.

Ellen, 39, met David, 25, shortly after both had started medical school. "It was September when we started seeing each other," she recalls, "and by October we were really getting together. I think our classmates thought it was rather strange and odd, and they all gossiped about it. When we were married right after Christmas, the class got together and bought us a gift, but I found out later that one of the students organized it because she felt people were reacting negatively and she wanted to make a statement that supported us.

"It makes me laugh now when I think that people might have been critical. I wonder if they were jealous or something. But I felt very defensive at first, and we didn't tell anyone we were married. I'd wear my ring at home and take it off walking up the stairs to class."

Ellen wonders if the other students reacted out of jealousy, since the pressures of medical school make having the built-in support of a mate very appealing, but it's more likely that they felt awkward because the situation was unfamiliar and they simply didn't know the appropriate response to make at the time. She acknowledged that, later, their fellow students treated them just like any other couple.

Michelle, 43, married to Henry, 27, had an initially negative response that turned quite positive with time. She and Henry did not feel that age was the main problem for them—they were more concerned over the difference in their religions, and that was the issue they concentrated on resolving.

"When I told my rabbi that Henry was going to convert, he really flipped," said Michelle. "He's a very traditional man, about 65 years old. And he was so upset. He said, 'Is Henry younger than you are?' I said, 'Yes.' 'How much?' he asked, and I told him, 'Ten years.' That wasn't true, but I knew 16 years would push him over the edge."

"He said, 'That's ridiculous. That's terrible. Those marriages never work.' And all kinds of stuff like that. Then he got to know Henry, and now he's enormously warm to both of us.

"He and his wife had us to dinner recently. Afterward, he said to his son, who is a very good friend of ours, 'Boy, that Henry is such a nice boy, but what are they going to do when Michelle is 50 and Henry is 40?' "

Michelle laughs. "That's the only negative we've heard. Henry's friends have been very supportive—they are people of all ages who've been sensitive to some of the problems he might encounter, mainly because of my family."

Henry agrees. "They've reacted two ways generally: one, people were very excited and interested and happy for us; and two, since Michelle has two teenage girls, they were concerned about my life changing—did *I* know what I was getting myself into?''

I spoke with a close woman friend of Michelle's who remembers when she first learned that Michelle was likely to marry a man much younger than she. Her reaction to the match was overwhelmingly positive.

''Michelle is a very interesting, very dynamic woman,'' said her friend, who has known her personally and professionally for over 10 years. ''When I met her, she was married to a socially prominent, wealthy man—a marriage many women would suffer through even if they were unhappy in order to keep the money and the prestige. It was the country-house-with-a-swimming-pool-and-a-Mercedes-and-the-country-club set. That made no difference to Michelle.

''I know she was living on less than $20,000 a year right after she divorced that guy. She had moved her girls and herself into a tiny, but darling, little house, and I never saw anyone so matter-of-fact about a huge change in lifestyle like that. She had begun to get national recognition for a series of scientific papers that she'd published—so even though she and the girls were living on tuna fish, they seemed happy. I know things were very hard for her because she took a night job as a cocktail waitress to make ends meet. At one point, she was even going to sell vacuum cleaners door-to-door if she had to. This is a woman who is probably one of the most brilliant minds in her field, working until midnight to make two-buck tips so she can live her life the way she wants to.

''So when I found out there was a younger guy in the picture, all I could think was 'My God, I hope he can hold his own against a woman that strong.' Then I met Henry—and he sure does! In fact, I don't think I've ever met another man who's her match intellectually the way Henry is. They keep each other on their toes—and that's what makes Michelle tick. I think she and Henry might be different ages chronologically, but they've got the same-age metabolism and energy level. With those two working in the same field, I'm placing bets that a few years from now we'll see some dynamite research out of that brain trust. Talk about a think tank—those two are well matched!"

Amanda, 41, reported a warm and positive response to Steve, 32, and their relationship from one of her dearest friends, an older man in his fifties who was very familiar with her reluctance to marry again.

"I had introduced Steve to Charles," said Amanda, "and after Steve walked away, Charles turned to me and simply said, 'You're going to marry that man.' That's all he said. That was Charles's way of instantly accepting Steve—and Charles knew that I still thought I would never marry anyone again.

"But the fact that my older friend accepted Steve made such a difference to me. Steve is very well educated, very well informed, and it also developed that Charles accepted him—both of us—into his social circle. Today we are all very close friends."

As I mentioned, few of the younger men appeared to be at all concerned about friends' approval or disapproval. Rob, 33, married to Diane, 45, made a typical statement when he said, "Our relationship made a difference to several of my friends. They married, moved to the suburbs, and live a very different kind of life. So we don't see those people anymore. However, that's more a difference because they want to live outside the city and I like this pace—I don't think it is wholly an age thing."

Elinor, 57, and Brad, 39, who have been together for 9 years, have developed a wonderful philosophy about friends. Elinor has moments of anger over the stereotype, but they've ended up working it out very well.

"Every once in a while it goes through my mind that, if our ages were reversed, nobody would think twice about it. A 57-year-old man and a 39-year-old woman doesn't seem strange.

"Sometimes, I'll find myself in a group of people, most of whom are Brad's age, and I'll suddenly pull back and look around me. I don't think of my own age most of the time, so I'll wonder if they look at me and think, What is she doing here?

"I remember one funny time when Brad and I were having people over, and he had invited an old boss of his, whom I'd never met. You know how you develop an image of someone—especially when words like *boss* are used? Well, I had this preconception of this very talented man I'd heard so much about. So when I opened the door and saw a guy who looked like a freckle-faced teenager, we both did a double take! That was really funny. Neither of us was what the other was expecting."

"I'm interested in a wider frame of reference," said Brad, explaining their friendships. "Elinor knows all these people, and I know others, and we manage to blend them together. That's why I don't worry about age, because as long as we're contributing things to each other's lives, it doesn't seem to be pertinent.

"We have these parties often, and I can look around and see people of virtually all ages represented. Memorial Day we had a party at our country place, and there were people there Elinor's age, my age, one guy brought his mother who was 88, we had kids and teenagers—it was great. That's what we do instead of having children—we have a family of friends."

And so it goes. Each couple experienced very similar reactions from friends. Most good friends show an immediate curiosity about the relationship, which some, but not all, first assume is primarily sexual and likely to be short-term. However, on becoming better acquainted with the man, the woman's friends accept the relationship the same as they would any other. The man is less concerned with friends' reactions, but those who seek approval find it easily. Few friends focus on the age difference after the initial introduction.

The Toughest Critics: Our Families

Oh, how I worried about meeting Brant's parents. I tortured myself with the thought that they might be mortified by my age and the fact that three children were involved. Disapproval by my own family I could handle, but his? I could not imagine what they would think. He is their only child. I am nine years older than Brant and nine years younger than his parents.

Brant, of course, was concerned about family acceptance just as I was. Anyone who loves and respects his or her relatives cares about what they think. But, as I pointed out earlier, the person who worries most over family acceptance of the relationship is usually the woman. However, she is not worried as much about acceptance from her own family as she is about the reaction from the family of the younger man. This was true of every woman interviewed.

An old image from the past haunted me as I worried about meeting Brant's parents: my parents speaking in hushed tones about the horrible situation facing close friends of theirs whose son had fallen in love with a divorcée. She was much older than their son and had three children! Now I was guilty of the same scandalous behavior. I wanted to run away and never have to confront these good, unsuspecting people.

Finally, I met the man who would become my father-in-law. I don't think he even noticed that I was older. He welcomed me into his family and has always made me feel like I was the logical, natural choice for his son. From that first moment he was warm and friendly.

And my mother-in-law! She gave her approval before she met me. "Oh," she said to Brant on the telephone when he supplied some biographical details, including age and number of children, "how flattering to have an older woman who has done so much be interested in you. That must make you feel good."

Later, when I was working on this book, I asked her myself what her early feelings were. "I was relieved," she said. "Ever since he was little, Brant wanted brothers and sisters. That didn't work out for us. So when he told me that you had three children, I thought, Good, now he has the family he's always wanted.

"Otherwise, his father and I were talking about you two just the other day. We think you are one of the most compatible couples we know, because you both do the same kind of work. You understand each other so well.''

Brant's parents judged me as a whole person and not as a stereotype. And I am pleased to report that my family, with the exception of my one mouthy sister, did exactly the same.

My father did make one remark shortly after he met Brant. Pulling me aside, he whispered, ''Why don't you think about coloring the gray in your hair?'' That was it. And that came from his own sense of vanity. All the men in my family have very dark hair, which turns prematurely white in their early forties, and I inherited that gene. Furthermore, at the time that he met Brant, my dad, widowed two years earlier, had just married a woman who was 17 years younger than he was. So I am sure he was very aware that any criticism from him about the age difference might be met with some outright hostility from me—as in, ''Oh yeah? Sez who?''

My sisters and brothers—I am the oldest of eight—may have been curious, but with that one exception they never said anything critical. The one sister who thought I looked older has since apologized. Everyone has been quick to accept us as a couple who are very much a part of our close extended family.

My grandparents, whose opinions matter more to me than anyone's, have been especially open and accepting.

Right after their first long chat with Brant, my grandfather told me, ''That's quite a bright young man there. I like him. I never liked your first husband much, you know. I didn't like the way he talked to you at the bridge table.''

To my grandparents, a man who treated me well and made me happy was right for me, whatever his age. So much for the stereotype of older people as old-fashioned!

With only one exception, all the couples interviewed said their families accepted their relationships just as easily. I think a major reason for that acceptance is that we are talking about adult relationships and not young kids. Older parents have learned to respect their adult children in other areas of their lives, such as careers or raising children. Respect for the way those responsibilities have been carried out extends to the arena of relationships. They have witnessed earlier choices made by the man or woman and learned to have confidence in those choices.

Typically, there *is* a comment or two (like my sister's), but once parents, siblings, or grandparents meet the new partner, most of the doubt disappears.

The mother of Amanda, 41, had to have had some interesting thoughts as she watched her single-parent daughter turn down a wealthy man who wanted to marry her in favor of a much younger man (Steve, 32) who could not provide the same kind of luxurious lifestyle.

"I think her perspective at the time was that I was crazy," said Amanda. "Here I had this older guy who wanted to give me everything, and she couldn't understand why I wouldn't marry him. He was a great guy; she really liked him. She thought I was temporarily insane.

"But the only remark she made was right after I started dating Steve—and I want to point out that she only said it once and my mother never said anything *once*—but she said to me, 'Use your head. As you get older, you're going to look like his mother.' "

If it isn't the sex angle, it's the mom motif!

"I think it's testimony to Steve that she never once said that again. And I knew it was just a crazy comment because I know I don't look my age, and I certainly don't look like Steve's mother."

Amanda went on to deal with reactions from Steve's family. "Only his grandmother said something—and she asked me how much older I was. Just knowing the age difference seemed to satisfy her.

"Steve's parents were great. I think part of their acceptance of me was that, even before we met, they noticed a change in Steve, who had been kind of a hippie type. He cut his hair; he changed the way he was dressing. So I think they were already of the opinion that 'whoever this Amanda is, she's okay. These are good changes.'

"I got to know them over a period of several years and spent many holidays with them. During that time, they made it clear that they loved my two girls. They always gave them gifts or invited them over to spend the night.

"When Steve and I finally decided to get married, we invited them over for dinner. We served champagne, and they are so used to Steve winning awards for his architectural designs, they were sure that was the occasion. When we raised our glasses, and Steve said, 'Amanda and I are going to be married,' his mother was so surprised and so happy she started to cry. My in-laws are wonderful people."

I think it is touching that, no matter what our ages, we do remain sensitive to our parents' reactions. What happened to Lillian, 72 (married to John, 57), is both illuminating and humorous.

"When my mother learned Lillian was retiring, she was very curious and made about a dozen attempts to find out exactly how old Lillian was," said John. "But I never told her. To this day I think everyone in my family thinks she's about 3 or 4, maybe even 5, years older. I don't think anybody realizes she's 72."

"His parents were one reason we finally got married," recalls Lillian. "They were very uncomfortable with our sleeping together, and if we visited, they put us in separate bedrooms. Here I was, 66 years old, and John would sneak into my room in the middle of the night. I said, 'For God's sake, John, we're never going to stay here again—this is mortifying!'"

They did stay there again, but as a married couple. John's parents liked and approved of Lillian even though his mother was always curious about her age. I think it's important not to resent that curiosity, whether it comes from parents or friends or outsiders. We are all children at heart, and if we encourage our children's curiosity because we know that's how they learn about the world, we should understand that the same principle works for adults.

However, that doesn't mean you have to tell everything. In fact, Lillian *never* tells her age.

"Absolutely not," she said, though she did divulge it to me knowing that she would remain anonymous. "The reason is I don't like to be categorized, not even by myself. So 20 years ago I stopped celebrating birthdays, and I pay no attention to my age.

"It scares me to think about it because you tend to box yourself in with expectations of how people in different age brackets behave. Say 'age 60' or 'age 70' or 'age 80' and see how people suddenly react because they have preconceived ideas about age and how you behave if you're a certain age. It's just like trying to break away from the old ideas about older women and younger men—we don't need that kind of categorizing!"

And she's right. Furthermore, Lillian looks like she's in her fifties, but it isn't a cosmetic youth—she has a craggy, lined face that is alive with energy and humor. Her attitude toward life shines through and makes her appear 20 years younger. I stopped telling my own age the day after I met Lillian!

Not surprisingly, women who are significantly older than their boyfriends are the women most worried about parental reaction from *his* family. However, that fear appears unjustified. All of the much older women interviewed have had very warm and welcoming responses from the parents of the man involved.

"My family disapproved of my leaving my first wife to go live with Elinor—but that was before they met her," said Brad, 39 (living with Elinor, 57). "Once they met Elinor, it was much better. She relates to them a lot more than my first wife ever did, and they like that."

"Brad's parents are very decent people, just about 10 years older than I am," said Elinor. "I feel awkward about that at times, although we get along very well. That's one of the real positive things about my relationship with Brad—I feel I've been a good influence on his relationship with his parents. My own cousin made a couple of little cracks at first, but after she met Brad, she liked him. She's never said anything since."

Very often, the parents' experience in their own relationship serves as a major influence on their reaction to their son's or daughter's alliance. If the parents have had an unconventional situation, they are likely to be quite open about a similar pattern in their children. Good examples are both Michelle's and Henry's parents. In fact, the age difference was easily accepted, and parental concern was greatest over the difference in religion between the two.

"I met Henry's parents for the first time right after we became engaged," said Michelle, 43 (married to Henry, 27), "so the two of us as a couple was a *fait accompli*. And that was okay. His parents were very accepting. They didn't know how old I was and figured I was about 38. Meanwhile, my mother didn't know how old Henry was and figured him for about 30. So both families lopped three or four years off on either side for each of us—and no one has ever told them otherwise.

"My mom said she thought it might be hard for him to handle the kids and all, but she was more worried about our religious difference and the fact that I might steal his identity in some way. Since she was widowed a long time ago and has dated many men much younger than she, she didn't mention my age. For her the issue was that I am Jewish and Henry was not."

Henry had a similar response from his family. "My mother married fairly late, had her own career, and has always made more money than my father," said Henry, "so there were many things that helped them deal with the issues in my marriage. I am sure their relationship worked to open my mind to marrying somebody who was older than I, too.

"For them the major issue was that I might change my religion for Michelle—that was the difficult part."

Henry did change his religion, and family feelings were tense for a while, but that has changed, and the couple enjoys warm relations with his parents today.

I should mention the one couple interviewed that faced serious resistance from both sets of parents. As you will see, the issues were not only age, but the fact that Ellen, 39, and David, 25, as medical students, were already trying to cope with the educational and financial strains of medical school. The parents could not help viewing their unconventional marriage as likely to add even more pressure. And even these parents seem to be coming around.

"We decided to get married because David was living at his parents', and my young son lived with me, so it was really awkward if we wanted to be together," said Ellen of their wedding, which occurred less than six months after they had met. The reason for deciding to marry so soon was thus two-fold: confidence in their feelings for each other and Ellen's reluctance to have a live-in relationship when a young child was present.

"When we set the date, we didn't know if either set of parents would attend. My parents had seen David only once, when he walked me to the car during one of their visits. They knew what he looked like and his biographical data, but they didn't really know him. They thought he was an acquaintance.

"When I was home for Christmas break two months before the wedding, I told them about us. My father said, 'There's no way you can marry this guy!'

"But we went ahead and sent out invitations. We had very little money, so all we had after the ceremony was champagne and cake at a friend's house with about 20 people. My mother wanted to come, but my father didn't. My mother had always been fairly supportive—she thought David and me being together was okay. It was my father who complained about things.

"But she talked him into coming, and they contributed to the wedding and brought all kinds of goodies. After I got over my nerves, it turned out to be a fun affair. So it all worked out fine. Just the other day my mother told me she was very glad she had come to my wedding—that was nice to hear."

"My parents were very, very angry at first," said David. "We argued back and forth, but I didn't think they presented me with issues that were relevant. A lot of their anger had to do with taboos.

"On the other hand, I think there are legitimate concerns. For example, are you going to be forced into having children in the next couple years when you won't even have a job? Will your career have to be put on the back burner? Because of our marriage, my career has been affected. My study time has been hindered, but career isn't my only focus in life. I know several physicians who live for only one thing, and I would hate to live like that. So there are a lot of nitty-gritty considerations when you marry someone older, but my parents didn't think about those.

"I don't believe they were fully aware that they were never very big on any of their children getting married anyway. Age of spouse had nothing to do with that. They thought we should concern ourselves more with our careers—that that's the most important thing.

"You can understand that when you know that they grew up very poor and really had to struggle because they got married very young. My dad told me he's held as many as three jobs while going to school at the same time.

"Even though they didn't give this as a reason, I think more of the anger had to come from the fact that this came at a bad time for me financially. I had had to stop working to go to medical school, and I was living at home to save money.

"But it made me angry when they said, 'You are dependent on us, and you will live a certain way.' That was the straw that broke the camel's back. I wasn't going to put up with that.

"So I was very angry when I told them Ellen and I were going to be married, and I said, 'Look, it's already too late. You can't do anything about it.' Some angry words were exchanged, and we didn't talk for about a month.

"But we made our peace just before the wedding ceremony. I still didn't think they were going to come, because we had had a death in the family, but they arranged all their plans so they could be with us. My mother and Ellen met for the first time that day.

"I don't think we have any problems with them now. They talk to Ellen just like they do me. In fact, I came home the other day, and my father was talking to her on the phone. I think we both get treated equally. Like one of their kids. So it's worked out okay.

"My parents have come to see that she's a person, I'm a person, and age doesn't make a damn bit of difference."

It is now three years since all the turmoil. Ellen and David have been offered the residencies that they most wanted, so their medical careers are still on track. Confident that their career goals can be meshed with their hopes to have a family before Ellen's age makes it difficult to conceive, they were pleased to discover they are expecting a child of their own soon.

In spite of all the good news, Ellen's father still has a few reservations over his daughter's marriage. "I got over the shock gradually. I had met David and thought he was just a pal, so I was dismayed when she said she wanted to marry him. I wondered why they had to marry—couldn't they just live together?

"Today, I feel it's fine, but every once in a while I wonder if the boom will lower and if the age difference won't be a problem as the years go by."

He told me that another one of his early concerns had been Ellen's finances and whether her marriage would put more strain on her parents since they were helping her pay for school. Since deciding that Ellen's marriage is working well, her parents have continued to offer their support.

Her mother, meanwhile, told me firmly that she has had no doubts about Ellen's relationship from the very beginning: "I'm just delighted about the whole thing. They are very good for each other and very happy."

In sharp contrast to her enthusiasm, David's mother said, "I was very, very bitter at the beginning. I made a much bigger fuss than my husband, but I was initially pretty upset. David used to date these cute, bouncy, ambitious little girls— and then he married an older woman. I just couldn't understand.

" 'I'm worried as to what's going to happen in the future,' I told Ellen when I met her. I like Ellen, but I felt I had to tell her I thought she was too old for my son, and I found it very upsetting.

"At first, I had to ask, 'Why does he need such an older lady? Is this because he needs a mother somehow? How is this going to affect him down the road?'

"But things are changing. I've mellowed. I like Ellen very much, and I've decided to give myself and this girl a chance.

We get to see them only once a week—I would like to see them more often.''

It's clear that Ellen's father and David's mother were motivated by a deep love and concern for their children. Each one responded harshly to the news of the relationship *before getting to know the new person*. Each responded on the basis of the old stereotypes: the father felt that men are not interested in older women for the long term; the mother felt that her son must be looking for a mother substitute. Even though she did not say so specifically, it was apparent that David's mother was also concerned that his interest in an older woman reflected on her in some way. This is true, in fact, and it is something we will explore in more detail in Chapter 9.

It is also interesting to note that, like the women who hesitate to commit, many parents blame age for what are really other worries—financial, religious, familial. Both parents begin to see, over time, that their new in-laws do not fit those old images. Family feelings are rekindled, and the new couple is accepted for the man and woman they are. Respect is mutual.

My favorite example of parental support and approval came from Joanne, who was 33 when she met and fell in love with a fellow who was 10 years younger. She resisted at first, sure that the age difference would make a difference, and when it didn't, she decided to marry Hans. When I asked Joanne what her mother said about her marrying a younger man, she replied softly as if to chastise herself for her groundless concern, ''My mother never said anything.''

The Kid Factor

Although kids are family, they get their own section in this chapter for several reasons. First, if *they* don't approve of a parent's new relationship, they can cause real problems because, in most cases, their parents have to live with them. Second, parents are trying to raise their kids and provide good role models as adults, not merely coexist with them. That brings up other issues—namely, sex. And third, kids are less likely than older relatives to keep silent; if they're unhappy, they'll tell you one way or another. Their unhappiness, if it isn't dealt with straightforwardly, can do more to sabotage the relationship than most parents first imagine.

For those reasons, it was very important to me that my three children accept Brant. As a parent, I believe in being open and direct with my kids, but I do not take direction from them on how to run my own life. Given that, I was anxious to know how they felt, but I was ready to recognize that any negative feelings might have to be worked out over a long period of time.

As you'll see in Chapter 8, we did encounter some problems, less in approval of my relationship than in the actual process of "blending" Brant into our family unit, but basically, the kids were open to Brant from the beginning.

They watched and evaluated. Ryan, my youngest, was 6 at the time. Brant was gentle and sweet with him, and they hit it off right away. My daughter, Nicole, who was 14, remained aloof at first. She may have resented Brant's taking her father's place, but she says today, "I didn't think about whether I liked him or not. It's your life. I didn't think it was any of my business."

It's my son Steve, who was 13 then and has just turned 20, who most clearly articulates his feelings toward Brant.

"I've always had the idea that marrying someone younger is better because it's someone I can relate to more easily," he said. "It was a kick for my friends, too, because in the areas of music and sports we really get along. Brant lets me borrow his records and tapes, which is great. Most middle-aged parents are so unhip that to find somebody in the category of parent who isn't a complete space-off is kind of a relief."

I wondered if Steve had ever felt embarrassed because I look older than Brant.

"People notice," he said, "but it's always positive, so it never bothered me. Like if you're both together, and people ask 'Who's that?' and I say, 'It's my stepdad,' they'll say,

'Oh, wow, how old is he?' So I guess if you're someone sensitive to people noticing, that could be a problem, but I get a kick out of it. The way I figure—the more attention I get, the better. So it's cool because it's out of the ordinary.''

Worry over her children's reactions was the initial stumbling block in the development of the relationship between 43-year-old Stephanie and 30-year-old Alan. Stephanie's children are aged 21, 19, and 14, two of them away at school. Stephanie has been divorced from their father for six years, but, before Alan, she had not entered into any relationship since the marriage ended.

"I didn't realize how hard this would be on my kids until I mentioned it to my daughter, who is a junior in college," she said. "When I told her I met someone on location and would be going out with him, she was real interested. She asked if I was sleeping with him.

"I figured she's 20 and we've always spoken directly about sex and stuff, so I'd answer her in an intelligent, adult fashion. So I said, 'Yes, I am.' With that, she burst into tears.

" 'When were you going to tell me?' she sobbed.

" 'I'm telling you now,' I said. 'It's not something you call up and announce with bells and whistles.' So she was very upset; her brothers became very upset.

"What's happening now is I want Alan to come and stay at my house when he's in town to finish the sound work on the new video. And I see no reason why he shouldn't. But I'm fighting all these battles—no one wants him there. Even my ex, who's dating a woman 15 years younger, is coming around here, playing the hurt innocent.

"Right now, I'm trusting that my children, including the 14-year-old, will have enough brains and enough manners at this point in their lives to at least not be rude. They may not. But, you know something? I don't care anymore.

"I went to a shrink. I said, 'I have this problem. I want this man to come stay at my house, and my kids are giving me a bad time.'

"The doctor said, 'Whose house is it?'

"And I said, 'You're right; it's my house.'

"So I'm doing this one step at a time. Alan's coming out

here, and he's going to stay at my house. If my kids hate it, what can I do? What difference does it make?

"Alan really cares about me—am I going to shut him out of my life for another two years with my children living at home? This is a problem I've always had anyway. I've always felt pulled in all these directions, like everyone wants 100 percent of my attention always. I'm in a position now where there is someone I would like to give my attention to. It's an amazing thing to me to have someone like Alan who wants to kiss me all the time. So am I going to tell him to go because of my kids? What am I? A jerk?"

Stephanie didn't tell him to go. Alan did come and stay at her home, and her children did get upset.

"It was interesting," said Stephanie afterward. "My 14-year-old was barely civil. My daughter, who is just 20, told me Alan looks just like one of our relatives that I know she doesn't like. Of course, she said, 'I didn't think you would date anyone who would look like that.' That was it.

"Meanwhile, Alan and I had a good time—not the best time, because I was so tense, but it didn't throw a wet blanket on our relationship. And after he left, both of my older kids told me that it didn't make any difference how old he was; they don't want me to replace their dad. They will have the same hostile reaction to anyone."

It's interesting that Stephanie sought professional help to gain approval for her relationship since her children were so opposed to it. Another woman I interviewed did the same. Michelle, 43 (married to Henry, 27), sought family counseling help because of the children, too, but more because of the problems of the blended family. I think it is important to stress that there is nothing wrong with a woman seeking the support and approval from a health professional that she needs before committing to a relationship with a younger man. Do whatever helps.

Sometimes, kids can have a real impact on the direction a relationship takes. Says Maureen, 43, of her children's response to Garrett, 31, "For my children, Garrett's change from friend to lover was difficult. It wasn't the age difference, but the move from being family friend to Mom's boyfriend and now stepdad. I think any family would have a hard time with that change. At first I dragged my feet on marriage, since I'd had such a bad experience, but Garrett and I wanted to live together.

"That was hard because I didn't want him just to move in. His family lives close by, and that would have been difficult for them. Plus I was very hesitant about having anyone living in with the children present. For a while we continued to see each other but not live together because I just wasn't ready to commit. For one thing, I liked how self-sufficient I'd become. My shop was thriving; I could take care of myself, my home, my children, the dogs."

Maureen, like most of us, was trying to resolve several issues at once. They ranged from her need to present a positive image for her children to her desire to respect the sensibilities of Garrett's parents, both while balancing her own need for independence. Of them all, the children presented the most significant problem.

"I had trouble reconciling the children with a live-in situation," said Maureen. "I didn't want to be that role model—the single mom who has her sleep-over boyfriend every weekend. All my single friends were doing it, but it didn't feel right to me. Also, my children were 11 and 13, which are critical ages. Absolutely the worst. So living together was never an option. We had a very comfortable four-days-a-week relationship. We would share meals, go out, but we would not sleep together as far as the children knew."

How did she resolve this? There is only one answer, and it's one many of us choose even though we might prefer to wait a little longer—she got married. She felt, as did I and the others I interviewed, that we are committed to presenting our children with a socially approved family setting rather than violating one more social standard and living without marriage.

Luckily, but not atypically, their families reacted positively to Maureen and Garrett's decision to marry.

"As we started seeing each other regularly and got closer to getting married, his family accepted me very easily," said Maureen. "I had known them before my divorce. They are very unpretentious people, and I'm quite fond of them and their lifestyle. I think they would be good friends even if they were only seven or eight years older than I am, but they aren't; they're my parents' contemporaries. So I can relate to them easily as older parents.

"Because of my early relationship with Garrett through our work together, I had become a fixture at their house as much as he was at mine during those first years. That meant I was first accepted as his friend, which made my relationship with Garrett more easily accepted later.

"Then, right after we got married, my daughter asked me, 'Mom, did you realize that when you were going to your junior prom, Garrett was falling off his tricycle?'

"She wasn't being negative; she was making it funny. She was letting me know that she was aware of our age difference and that she approved. 'When you were a mother with two children, he was graduating from sixth grade, Mom. Would you have looked at him in sixth grade, Mother?' When you put it that way, it is pretty funny.

"I told her, 'Yes, I think he's adorable. Look at his baby pictures. I definitely would have looked at him.' Other than that little bit of kidding, my children have said nothing about our age difference."

Children can be not only supportive, but even wiser than their parent.

Terri is a 44-year-old executive who has had long-term relationships with several men 10 to 12 years younger than she. As I pointed out in Chapter 2, she has refused numerous offers of marriage from these men, ostensibly because of the age difference but really because she was still in love with somebody else.

Whatever the real reason, she tells her daughter that the relationships do not work because of the age difference.

"My daughter is 15 years old, and she thinks I'm totally ridiculous about the age thing," said Terri. "She loved one of my boyfriends very much and told me she wanted me to marry him. She said to me, 'Mom, if you love somebody, and that person is 10 years younger than you—or 12 or 15— if they love you and you love them, then that is what makes a difference. Even if your face changes, your insides won't change.' "

More children of women and men interviewed for *Loving a Younger Man* feel the way Terri's daughter does than feel hostility toward their mother's sweetheart.

George is 77 years old. He met and married his late wife, Marie, when she was 65 and he was 50. Six children from her first marriage were still living when she died at age 92.

"We had 28 wonderful years together," said George, "but when Marie died, I said to one of her daughters, 'I guess that takes me out of the family. . . .'

"And my stepdaughter said, 'After being Grandpa for 28 years? I should say not!' So I still have contact with all of them."

Happy endings like George's lend hope to situations like the one faced by Stephanie. Also helpful is the fact that, as we've seen here and you'll see in Chapter 8, age is rarely the reason for kids' open hostility.

Outsiders—
The Icing on the Cake

For most women I talked to, the opinions of outsiders matter little once family and friends offer their approval. Curiously, yet happily, no one seemed particularly concerned about being the object of prurient gossip. Nevertheless, it is reassuring to have some idea of general public response to couples when the age difference is physically apparent. After all, people *do* notice, but rarely are they unkind.

"After we were married, there were a number of times when people said something about my mother," said George. "I always corrected them and said, 'That's not my mother; that's my wife.' Then they would apologize and feel a little embarrassed, but that's all there was to it."

Ellen, 39 (married to David, 25), laughs when she tells the story of the photographer for their family portrait who suggested David move closer in by saying, "Ask your older son. . . ."

"Then, recently, we were at a neighbor's, and this elderly gentleman wanted to meet my husband," said Ellen, "so I pointed David out to him. 'Oh, isn't that your son?' he said. Sometimes I make a point of saying, 'This is my husband' so people know the relationship. I'm always more embarrassed for them than for myself." Ellen looks older than David, partly because she is a few inches taller. However, after five minutes into a conversation with them you forget there is an age difference.

"I don't notice anything socially," said David when asked if he was aware of the confusion. "I think if you're going to worry about the age difference, you shouldn't get married. I don't even think about it. People at my stepson's school know I'm his dad, and they're used to it. I run his scout troop and have a number of people under me that I'm always telling what to do. These other parents are a good 10 or more years older than I am, but they don't seem to have any qualms about it. We all work quite well together."

Elinor, 57, is used to people noticing the age difference between her and Brad, 39. "Mostly it's strangers like doormen ('your son is waiting upstairs') or cleaning ladies. Our age difference is pretty obvious. I've had only one negative experience, and that was a neighbor who isn't a very nice person. A few years ago, we had a young Japanese friend staying with us, and when she saw the three of us together in the elevator, she said, 'Do you live with your two sons?' I said, 'Yeah, one's Japanese, and one's not.' I let her figure it out."

Brant and I have had one unpleasant experience. We were having dinner at an expensive restaurant on Cape Cod, and I was showing him a new batch of photos that I had taken of my children. Seated next to us was an older couple, the man in his late fifties or so. When they stood up to leave, he leaned over and rather nastily said to us, "Show him pictures of your grandchildren next time." Brant can look very young at times, and the fellow's tone made it clear he thought the situation was appalling.

When we were first together, I was mistaken for his mother on a number of occasions, mainly because my dark brown

99

hair has turned nearly all white across the front and top of my head. Since I've colored my hair, I haven't had anyone mistake me for Brant's mother. And I like myself without all the white, which is more important.

So when it comes to the opinions of outsiders, most women with younger men either don't care, view the mistake with a sense of humor, prevent the mistake by announcing the relationship themselves, or do what I did and make some small cosmetic change that makes the difference less obvious.

The Dynamics of Worry

Now you know that I didn't escape the concerns that every woman who considers a younger man is likely to face as she decides to commit herself to the relationship. Having survived that period, however, and having spoken to many couples who have gone through it, I am more able to pinpoint the reasons for our anxiety and what we can do to stop worrying.

We agonize over what others will think of our new loves for four different, yet interwoven, reasons: personal vulnerability, our lack of control over the attitudes of the people around us, our compassion and respect for the men we love, and our own sense of self-esteem.

Let's look briefly at each of those.

First, we feel vulnerable to being categorized by the stereotypes that people bring to unions like ours. It's disheartening for two reasons: one, men rarely have to endure the negative, demeaning aspect of the stereotype when they have a relationship with a younger woman, so why should we? Two, having to deal with the stereotype means that a relationship and its value are subordinate to that stereotype. The old image comes first, and it is up to you to demonstrate the fact that the stereotype isn't right, a variation on the ''guilty 'til proven innocent'' theme. Dealing with misunderstandings and false assumptions costs you energy you would prefer to direct to other parts of your life.

But this expenditure of time and energy is, as any woman in this kind of relationship will tell you, well worth it! Every time you see a friend relax because he or she understands your decision, you know it's worth it. Every time you greet the person you love and know that now you both fit more easily into the world around you, it's worth it. Before you ask people to be generous in accepting you, you must be generous yourself and show them why they should.

And when you are feeling at your most vulnerable, remember this: the seemingly rude or inappropriate remarks are made not because people want to hurt you, but because they are confronted by an unfamiliar variation—the relationship between a woman and a younger man does not fit into predictable molds. Five to 10 years from now, it will, but these are the years of change. Today, people still don't know what an appropriate reaction is. Oddly enough, they are even more disconcerted when the unfamiliar seems so correct, as our relationships do if you look at them logically. So, does that mean something is wrong with the traditional type of couple? Does it mean they are missing something themselves? If what they see in your relationship seems so right, is what has gone before somehow wrong?

Of course not, but seeing the new relationships between women and younger men makes people uncomfortable as they consider all these questions; hence the inappropriate behavior. It is the same thing that greets newly divorced people— friends don't mean to be rude or cruel; they just don't know the right thing to do or say. And even though divorce has become a fact of life and easier for people to handle, public opinion lags behind the times a bit. But most important, that public opinion is not stopping unhappy couples from starting over with someone else.

A second reason for worry is that our lack of control over what people say is distressing. As a society, we talk, we gossip—we tell our friends, our children, and our relatives the good news and the bad news of everyday life. Women, especially, are comfortable in the role of "the talker." We are not, however, comfortable when we are the subject of the talk.

Because we know how news travels, how words can heal or wound, we are acutely conscious of the fact that the moment news of our relationship gets out, the facts are subject to manipulation according to different points of view. We can't control how *our* news is presented, and we worry that only the stereotype is being passed along, gossiped about. Is there anything we can do to gain more control over "our story"?

Yes and no. Already, by confronting our friends with our news in a positive, frank way, we are showing them that the old ways are wrong.

And by being honest and straightforward, we show that we are women thrilled with something new and exciting: a relationship that is an equal partnership, a relationship that is a logical outcome of our new roles as independent, self-sufficient working women.

One of my goals in this book is to stress how important it is that those of us who are comfortable talking about ourselves become more outspoken about *why* we fell in love with a younger man. I think it is critical that we tell people we didn't deliberately choose a younger man. Rather, we chose the man who seems most likely to share every aspect of our life: the intimate, the intellectual, the emotional, the professional, the cultural, the financial, and the practical. He just *happens* to be younger.

Soon people will realize that he happens to be younger the same way a former husband, a brother, or a male friend might meet and fall in love with a *woman* who happens to be younger.

For many of us, one way we have resolved that feeling of loss of control over what people are saying has been to state early in a conversation that our boyfriend or husband is younger. We don't do it too blatantly, but we let people know that, yes, this is our partner, and, yes, he is younger. End of conversation.

This is, in fact, a handy tool of communication long utilized by canny public relations people: the quicker you can get factual, controversial information into the open, the sooner the controversial element loses its power to confound or intrigue or hurt.

Diane, 45 (married to Rob, 33), provides a good example of how this works.

"Most people don't notice our age difference even though I think I look much older," she said. "But even if they don't notice, I usually announce it because I would rather address it as a fact than have someone gossip about it. I guess whenever we meet people I kind of like, I put it on the table right away—just to get it out of the way so we can get on with things."

Woman after woman I interviewed discovered this strategy. I think it's a perfectly acceptable way to present ourselves and to gain some control over the passing along of information. That is how we plug the good news into the bad: we make sure the facts are available from the informed source.

And before you sigh and wonder why so much must be made of this, I hasten to assure you that the most sensitive time for anyone is at the beginning of the relationship. After you feel comfortable with a few people, you ease up and don't worry any longer. And, for heaven's sake, if it doesn't bother you that your boyfriend is younger, then don't say it does.

A third reason for our worry is our compassion for our men. I felt that, when the stereotype was applied to me, the logical consequence was that it demeaned Brant. It implied that he was a gigolo. While he, like all the younger men interviewed, couldn't have cared less about others' opinions, I was very sensitive to this. I felt the same anger a woman feels when she knows some jerk is treating her like a sex object and not like a human being. I resolved my feelings of conflict over this by being sure to introduce Brant to any person who I thought might have the wrong idea. Thus, I demonstrated the respect I have for Brant and that I expect others to have.

Finally, for some of us, our self-esteem is threatened when we think about what others may be saying about us. We are proud of our achievements as working women, proud of our newly acquired independence. And to take on the stereotypes associated with a relationship with a younger man threatens our image. How can we look like intelligent decision makers with images of sexually famished, dilettantish, sex-for-money "older women" plastered to us like pages torn from a Frederick's of Hollywood catalogue?

On the other hand, fighting the image is a very small order compared to what we have already accomplished, individually, as we have carved our niches in the workplace. Indeed, it was the self-confidence gained through all the personal and professional experiences of the women interviewed that gave them the courage to pursue the relationships they knew intuitively were right for them. Not one woman interviewed felt that any "image" problem prevailed against her once her friends and co-workers became more familiar with the individual she had chosen for her partner. For example, not long after my marriage to Brant, a position opened up in which I was very interested—it would mesh well with my experience and provide a challenge for me professionally. A lot of other people felt the same way; there were over 100 applicants. After a series of interviews, which I thought had gone very well, I did not receive a job offer. I was very disappointed. I had really wanted that job. Finally, I called the man who had interviewed me, as I needed to pick up my portfolio.

"Well . . . ," he paused when he took my call, "I really want to hire you, but I have one serious reservation. I'm a few years younger than you are, and I'm not sure you could be comfortable working for me. What do you think?"

I asked him how old he was. He is seven years younger than I am. "I think I can answer that pretty easily," I said. "The man I'm married to is nine years younger. . . ."

"You've got the job."

I rush to assure you that all these concerns over what others think of the age difference are not debilitating. Instead, I bring them to your attention so you know it is natural to worry at the very beginning of a relationship with a younger man. The concern really does drop away quickly. Five years into a relationship, every woman interviewed said she no longer thought about the age difference. "I forgot about it," said Amanda, 41 (married to Steve, 32). "We seem like we're the same age always."

Furthermore, since almost every woman has survived a major life trauma such as divorce or the loss of a close family member, she has a perspective on life that includes confidence in her own value judgment. She has learned what is important to her and will consider the opinions of others within a very limited scope. So the more she values her relationship, the less she is inclined to be bothered by social attitudes. But it takes time for the relationship to develop, and it is in the early stages that we are most likely to stop dating the younger man for fear of what others might say. Now you know why that shouldn't happen.

In fact, the main reason for discussing our self-consciousness over the age difference has been to make it possible to move that worry aside so we can focus on the real issues that can be problematic because of an age difference. In reality, I think these concerns will diminish rapidly over the next few years, so that young women who are in their late teens and early twenties today will wonder what all the fuss was about when, 5 or 10 years from now, they choose a younger man without a second thought.

The Only Thing We Have to Fear . . .

It is ironic that at the onset of our relationships we are most worried about the opinions of our families and friends, when the reality is that other problems, such as blending families and finding time to be together, turn out to be the serious ones. Yet we don't think about that until later.

In the long run, all the people who love us accept us. In fact, our concern over censorship of our relationship was self-imposed. The way we imagined people responding to our relationships was totally out of proportion to the reality of their response. Because of our sensitivity to the old attitudes and stereotypes, we allow our imagined reactions to us to sap some of the exuberance of our thrill with our new love.

Couple after couple, woman after woman, told me how the actual responses of acceptance and reassurance soon added another dimension to their relationship: a feeling of such encouragement that a new impetus was added. This is a feeling I experienced, also. Suddenly we find ourselves admired, even applauded, because we are doing something adventurous and right.

It is for many reasons, then, that we should not downplay the importance of friends and family as they relate to the older woman/younger man couple. First, these are people we love and trust, people we count on; they are part of what makes our lives rich and full. Second, we do take our friends' and families' needs and concerns seriously. Many of us got married before we may have really wanted to—because we wanted to avoid giving mixed messages to our children or to prevent embarrassment or discomfort of friends and family.

For many women, the reactions of others become overlapping elements in their decision. But then, few decisions are made in a void. And none of us feels we have made a mistake. Instead, our marriages are working, and those of us who were ''forced'' into them out of consideration for others are relieved. We might have continued to hesitate otherwise, because of the age difference, and possibly have missed out on a successful marriage.

But if the stereotype of the relationship between a woman and a younger man is so prevalent that even the most intelligent and trustworthy of our friends and family are likely to make a comment or two at first, what can be done?

First, we can stop feeling vulnerable. People who make a hurtful remark are rarely trying to hurt us. They are just trying to make sense of a new phenomenon.

Second, we can take control over what people are saying to us and about us by talking openly about our ages—before anyone else can.

Third, we can be thankful for small favors. Even though this is still a predominantly sexist and ageist society (with women suffering the worst of both inequities), at what other time in this millennium have we been able to be as free to do as we please?

Fourth, we can take a positive attitude toward the future of these relationships by agreeing to let them develop week by week, month by month, or year by year.

Fifth, during that time, we can close out the negative by spending time only with those friends and family members who love us and accept us easily.

Sixth, we can refuse to lose sight of the future we can have together—stop thinking about ages (or what other people think about ages) and imagine only the time we can spend together, the enjoyment we can get from each other. If we do that, if we say, "The hell with appearances; this is right for us, so let's stay together," we'll find our lives so full of adventure and excitement and happiness that we won't have the time or energy to be concerned about anybody else's opinion.

This is how most successful, creative people approach the world, regardless of their specific situations. They do what they feel is right for *them*, and they do it *their* way.

And with that good news, I want to close this chapter with a short anecdote about acceptance.

Earlier, I mentioned my grandparents and how their approval of my relationship with Brant mattered a great deal to me. They were my surrogate parents during a time when I was very ill as a child. They loved and supported me even when I was a rebellious, obnoxious teenager and when I was the first person in our family to be divorced.

They are gentle people with a quiet, proper elegance that they have tried hard to instill in me. I think they have succeeded a little bit, but their ways are much softer than mine. And yet, more than anything, I have always wanted them to be proud of me.

Gramps and Grandma seemed to like Brant. It was a quiet approval, and I wondered if it wasn't offered out of polite consideration. Then, two years after we were married, both of us changed jobs, and we moved across the country and into our first house. The day after the moving van had come, leaving boxes and furniture strewn haphazardly through the house, the doorbell rang. A UPS man stood there with a big box.

I was mystified. We hadn't lived here long enough to have ordered anything. The box bore my grandparents' return address, but I couldn't imagine what they'd be sending me. I opened it up. Carefully packed in layers of newsprint were four gray velvet sacks with braided drawstrings. I removed each one gingerly. Tears streamed down my face as I slipped off the velvet to uncover a precious family heirloom from Gramps and Grandma's own marriage—their sterling silver tea service.

On my knees over the box, weeping in the midst of household chaos, I finally got the message. Their acceptance of me over the years—after I made all the big mistakes—was more than unconditional love. It was their way of telling me they believed in *me*. They believed in me when I followed tradition and believed in me when I challenged the old order. They have confidence that, in the end, I always do what is right for myself and for the people I love.

With grandparents like that, who needs anyone else to say yes?

4

Wrinkle Phobia: Must We Buy the Madison Avenue Myth?

I haven't felt like this ever. I've never been made to feel so special. Alan thinks of me as a person who has brains, can think, can take care of herself, and he likes me for all these reasons. Then he has the nerve to tell me that he loves my body. I mean, who are we kidding? That's when I thought of having him committed.

This is an old body that has had three children. And it never really recovered successfully from any of them. It's lumpy and soft. It's comfortable. I've lived in it for 43 years, and it has its share of scars. I need a lot of filtered light. But Alan sees me very differently from how I see myself.

—Stephanie, 43,
on dating Alan, 30

"What on earth does he see in *her?*" "How can he be attracted to *me?*" In all my conversations with women dating or married to younger men, the same topic cropped up early and over and over again: looks. Appearance. Physical attractiveness. It's one of the first things that draw us together as couples, yet it can often be the first cause of worry. It's certainly among the first things we think other people will notice when they meet older woman/younger man couples and one of the first things we expect them to comment on.

I—and the women I interviewed—worried about everything from sagging breasts and flabby thighs to gray hair and wrinkles. We worried about how, as we aged, we would keep the men we loved in our beds and in our lives. We worried about competition from prettier younger women. And we often couldn't figure out why, even now, the men we loved found us attractive.

That women have some very real problems with self-image and body image is no news to anyone who's noticed numerous diet books hitting the best-seller lists or the unending barrage of new "beauty" products or read about the thousands of women who suffer from weight-based eating disorders. But the way women feel about their looks is especially critical to women in love with younger men, for looks-wise, they're starting out "behind" in a race where men have always had the lead. Even women married to men their own age complain that "men get character, and women get old."

I was in excellent shape when I met Brant, so I didn't immediately find fault with my body. I felt confident about my physical condition. I had also learned that I could maintain that condition for another 20 or 30 years if I was willing to work at it.

However, like nearly every woman interviewed for *Loving a Younger Man*, I managed to dredge up some physical shortcoming to torture myself with. In my case, it was the stomach. I was acutely aware of the ugliness of my stomach, which will never recover from bearing three children. It sounds absurd, and it is absurd, but at first I would never let Brant see me completely naked because I was sure the sight of my stretch marks would destroy the total effect of my physical attractiveness.

I began to check out women Brant's age, nine years younger than I. Had they had babies? Since he had known mostly women his own age before me, did that mean he'd never been exposed to such a terrible sight as an older woman's stretch marks? Should I put the skids on our relationship? Better to end it before he saw my stomach and dumped me for a flat one with no marks.

I made a mistake I had been taught to make: I assumed that my sex appeal was wholly a result of my physical appearance. I ignored the fact that my odyssey over the years since my early twenties had produced a new person. My return to school and my slow but steady accumulation of work experience had yielded a woman more productive on a professional level. The steadily accruing balance of independence spilled over into my personal life as I grew more confident and sure of myself. That's where my sex appeal lay, not in my stomach. But I chose to deny that. I remained unforgiving of my abdomen.

And so, when it was clear we were quite serious about each other, I staged for Brant an unveiling of my anatomy, demanding it be observed from all angles so that no ugly surprises were in store for anyone after the marriage license had been signed. It seems ridiculous today, but then I did not doubt that a stretch mark could cancel our relationship.

Brant just looked at me like I was nuts—my stomach had nothing to do with why he loved me, and he said so.

I found it hard to believe at first, but in time I managed to stop worrying about it. Pretty soon I could stand in front of the mirror and accept it as *my* stomach and not *the* stomach. In fact, the very next summer I bought myself a two-piece bathing suit for the first time in years! I inflicted the sight of my stomach on our entire neighborhood pool population, and no one tossed his or her cookies. No one even noticed.

But it was Brant's acceptance of my body and all its flaws that got me over the hurdle of accepting my body myself. His simple, straightforward appraisal of my body as a part of me that he loves, but not the most important part, has allowed me to set aside all the fear that lies behind those words "What happens when I'm 50 and he's 41?"

Today I recognize that we are attractive to each other for the very same reasons: how we think, how we present our thoughts to the world, how successful we are in being true to what we value, and how we go about accomplishing our individual goals. He takes pride in my work and I in his.

At the same time, we are mutually critical when one or the other of us gets out of shape or slightly overweight—not because of physical appearance, but because we know it's a signal something else is wrong. Since we feel our best when we are exercising and eating well, fitness is a sign of physical and emotional health.

What Brant has taught me is that the physical evidence of our age difference doesn't matter if emotionally and intellectually we challenge each other. And that's where we are equally matched. That's what makes it interesting and sexy and exciting to be together.

We all worry about our bodies, and, sadly, most of the women I interviewed, like me, couldn't fully accept their own shapes and sizes until they were sure their bodies wouldn't betray them by turning off the men they loved.

What follows is a litany of concerns expressed at one time or another by women whom younger men find exciting and sexy. Maybe by the end of the list, as I include the younger men's reactions to these worries as well as how some of the women coped, it will be clear how unnecessary it is to waste so much energy worrying about looks; it's time to accept ourselves and adopt a better attitude toward these hardworking, comfortable bodies of ours.

Worry No. 1: What Happens When We Let Numbers Dictate the Image

When Lynn, 37, found out that Dan was 29, she immediately allowed the stereotypes to affect how she would think. As a documentary filmmaker, Lynn is paid well to be very aware of new trends in the country. When it comes to her own life, however, she lives in the Stone Age. "I couldn't believe it. There's some age difference that's manageable in my life, but not that! I just didn't believe it.

"It made me seem so desperate. I think of all the things you read and hear as you turn 35, 36, and 37—you know, dwindling forces, drying up organs. When he said '29,' I thought that would make me look like I was just going after anything I could get my hands on so I wouldn't be part of that left-out group.

"It took me a full day to handle the idea in my mind. I kept thinking it couldn't work because of the way women age—because of what we know about the deterioration and eventual uselessness of our bodies."

Lynn worried about two things: her looks and her sexuality. We'll explore our feelings about our sexuality in the next chapter. However, as we reflect here on our worries over our body image, you will see how closely the two are tied. And so they must be—you need to feel good about your body to be able to feel confident in your sexuality.

"Since dating him and sleeping with him, I look at myself differently," said Lynn. "On the one hand, I feel better about myself, but I'm also more self-conscious right now. I keep looking to see how old I appear. Like, is he going to see me someday and say, 'Ooh, when did *that* happen? I didn't notice her neck isn't smooth.' "

Lynn, like so many of us, counters her initial joy in her new love with an immediate concern about her body. She refuses to accept Dan's approval of her as a sexy, attractive woman. Instead, she asserts that it cannot last because she is chronologically older. And then she does something very typical of women in this situation: she brings up the issue of sexuality as if it, like her body, is likely to self-destruct on some specific date.

"Now I look at a woman who is 65, and I think she can't *be* sexual. Those sorts of thoughts run spontaneously, subconsciously through my mind, and I don't know what to do about it."

So there it is. Lynn expressed exactly what society tells us about a woman and age: to grow old is to lose your beauty and, consequently, to lose your sexuality, your sex appeal. She lets the numbers dictate the image. It's an old trap and one to be avoided.

It's also important to note that the "numbers," like any numbers, can be manipulated in our favor.

David, 25 (married to Ellen, 39), says, "The facts are plain and simple. Women outlive men by at least 8 to 10 years.

Hormonal differences change the cardiovascular system such that men have their heart attacks 10 years before women do. So if you're looking at it from the stance of living your life together and the golden sunset years and all that stuff, you may want to think about having a mate who's going to be alive at that time.

"The only real difference age makes between Ellen and me is the reproductive cycle. I could have waited to have a child, but Ellen can't. So our age difference has made us deal with whether or not we want a family. Otherwise, we're the right ages to be together longer than most couples."

David, as a younger man, makes an excellent point in favor of these relationships. His attitude is one of many that show how the traditional point of view—that "age is the final inequity between the sexes"—is changing. He can see the physiological reasons for women choosing younger men: women age more slowly than men and live longer. So a woman who wants a partner in her later years may actually be *wise* to choose a younger man.

Worry No. 2: Aren't Looks Everything?

Terri, 44, dates many younger men and takes a different angle on the same issue. She is a strikingly beautiful woman who is one of the few women I interviewed who does look much younger than her years would dictate. You would think she'd have nothing to worry about. But she proves that even those women who don't look their age believe the myths surrounding age and its effects on women. She believes men don't look beyond the surface.

"It's not that the men I date are 10 years younger than I that bothers me so much," she said, "but the fact that I don't believe they see the real me, love the real me. I would rather stay by myself, live alone, and never be in love again than be with somebody who doesn't see and love the person behind this face.

"So every time I date a younger man, I think that in 5

years I'll be almost 50 and he'll be only 30 or 35. Am I going to look like this then? Is this all they see? What if, in 5 years, all of a sudden everything falls apart?''

I asked Terri if she had any proof that it would all fall apart. She said no, her mother and her grandmother still look lovely in their old age. Her insecurity reflects how successful the marketers of beauty are in convincing us of our perishability even when we have evidence of the opposite. Terri manages to discount her lovers' interest even though the relationships are ones that have lasted more than a year—plenty of time for a man to find the woman behind the face.

This is true of all the younger men interviewed—they tune into many different aspects of the women they admire. For example, Mick, who at 34 is 6 years younger than his wife, Helen, says, ''Frankly, in the physical sense, I find older women much more attractive than younger women. I like the aura of age. I think the older woman exhibits more character, more experience, more depth, more diversity. I guess I have some difficulty relating to the blonde-haired, cherubic, tight-skinned, naive face of a young girl.

''I don't find that nearly as attractive as the physical presence of an older woman. I'm sure part of this is I'm in a high-pressure job as a trial lawyer and I deal with older men all the time—attorneys, legislators. I like the maturity factor. It has impact. So maybe my work ages me, and I like the same sophistication and awareness in a woman.''

Mick's attitude is similar to that of Henry, 27 (married to Michelle, 43), who met his future wife in an aerobics class.

''Sexual attraction really ends up being your own concept of it,'' said Henry, as he succinctly sums up why the age difference is not a major factor in his attraction to Michelle. ''Men's bodies also, maybe even to a greater extent, change with time. Thirty-five-year-old guys have potbellies from drinking beer. I always feel like I'm not doing the sports I did in high school. I just don't have the time. In many ways, I think women—certainly it's true for Michelle—look awfully good when they're 40, whereas lots of men don't. It doesn't have to do as much with age as the way you treat yourself.''

Worry No. 3:
The Younger Woman Threat

Sharon was 35 when she started to date a 23-year-old fashion photographer who was working in New York City and Los Angeles, the two national headquarters for beautiful, *young* women. She had hired him to shoot photos for a book project she was editing. They were married two years later and have been together now for 8 years. She is now 43, and he is 31. Her fears were directed at the impact the sight of younger, beautiful bodies might have on her lover.

"I'm not unattractive, and I'm very fit," said Sharon, "but Jerry is extraordinarily attractive himself and has access to all these little Malibu beach bunnies. Since he is both a photographer and someone who appreciates beautiful things, at first I found not only his youth somewhat frightening but also his profession, because he was around beautiful models all day, women he certainly has social access to because of his age.

" 'I feel very inhibited because you can have the most beautiful-bodied women anywhere,' I told him when we started sleeping together, and he said to me, 'Looking at a California body is like seeing just another Mercedes. I want more than looks; I want brain power upstairs. It's one thing to have a beautiful woman on your arm at a restaurant; it's another to have to spend four hours with her in the solitude of your home. What are you going to do together?'

"He told me he wasn't attracted to many women his own age because they weren't experienced, they weren't wise, they weren't good listeners.

"Of course, when I look at men my age—especially out on the West Coast—I can understand what he means. You see a lot of immature guys in their forties and fifties, the single Porsche owner with his shirt unbuttoned, salivating around singles bars. You tell me that's attractive?

"But I still worry about my appearance. I work on my fitness. I know I'm in better shape than most women my age, but am I in better shape than a 22-year-old? No. I've got squishy thighs and all that stuff. But it doesn't make a difference to Jerry. He's very accepting.

"I hope this will last. He's so intent on preserving the naturalness of the way we live together. And, yes, there are perfect bodies around us all the time, but you never know how much plastic surgery they've had. Everybody I know—all my friends my age—have had the boob jobs, the tummy tucks and the thigh fat sucked out, all that horrendous stuff.

"But Jerry tells me, 'That's not you. You are what you are, and everyone gets older. Accept it.'

"So I do. This is definitely more my hang-up than his."

Sharon's story should quiet a lot of anxiety for a lot of women. She is a pretty woman, but there are lines on her face. She wears eyeliner to highlight her eyes, her best feature. Her hair hangs to her waist, curly and shiny. She glows with good health.

Her words point out how immaturity can be a greater leveler of human beings than looks—and it isn't defined by chronological age. It is also reassuring to note that a man like Jerry, whose job it is to promote the image of beauty that seduces so many of us, doesn't buy it himself. He knows what a boob job or tummy tuck can do, and he doesn't see it as anything appealing.

Yet, still you hear a lingering note of insecurity in Sharon's voice as she says, "I hope this will last. . . ." She lets herself be haunted—occasionally—by the fears that Jerry's tried so hard to allay.

It is important for women to realize that some men actually find older women more attractive than younger ones. Says Michelle, 43 (married to Henry, 27), "Recently, I've noticed in my face that I've started to look my age, and it makes me kind of sad. I ask Henry, 'Don't you think I look old?' but he doesn't; he is clearly someone who likes unconventional looks. He thinks my mother is beautiful, and she's 73. Last year he wrote me a long letter while I was abroad, telling me how he had spent the whole day looking at older women and deciding that they really are more beautiful and so much more interesting-looking than younger women, especially in their faces."

Elinor, 57, who has lived with Brad, 39, for 9 years, feels that as her relationship with Brad develops, she worries less and less about competition from other women. Yet she is a woman who has had to deal with an age difference that, in terms of body image, could prove insurmountable to a woman mired in old ways of looking at herself.

"I was definitely worried about the physical thing at first," said Elinor. "I wondered, How can this young guy be attracted to me when he obviously could be attracted to young, unwrinkled types? It was an ongoing fear. I'd always feel he was going to look around and see this or that attractive young woman, then look at me and think, Gee, this isn't so great. But over the years, it's become clear that that isn't going to happen.

"Instead, our relationship has deepened. We have differences and fights, sure, but we also have more fun. I realize that's an outcome of having confidence in myself. At this stage of my life, I understand better what I have to give, that I have something besides beauty that he appreciates. For instance, I know that Brad likes the fact that I'm a 'feeling' person, that my emotions are on the surface—I express them.

"So where I was so worried at first that he would be attracted to a much younger woman because I might become less attractive, after we were together awhile, I began to have enough confidence to see that I have been a positive factor in his life and helped him in lots of ways," said Elinor. "And he recognizes that. That's very out on the table between us, but it doesn't totally take care of my worry over the physical side of our relationship.

"I still see myself aging and think, Ooh, that's unattractive. But I haven't felt any criticism from him in the slightest way. I don't know if he represses it; he's an unusually unbigoted guy in lots of ways."

Elinor has a gentle, elegant loveliness, but she also has an edge to her, an aloofness enhanced by her direct gaze and her slightly severe, no-nonsense approach. She is coolly analytical about her work and her personal life. She carries herself with a confidence born of having been in a position of power and authority for the last 20 years of her career.

And she has learned that the way to counter the fear of younger women is to accept her own face, lines and all. She sees beauty in the evidence of her age.

"You may find it odd, but I wear less makeup now than I used to. I use blush and mascara, but when I was 14, I wore pancake foundation! I like the way I look now a lot more, even though you can see my age. The throat goes first. Then you see the lines around the eyes. But there are compensations.

"I feel so much more my own person than I did starting out in this business 30 years ago. Today I see myself in a different perspective. Everybody isn't all that interested in whether you have lines on your throat or not. If you're enthusiastic and really excited about things in your life, what does it matter how smooth your skin is?"

Worry No. 4: Only Beautiful Women Really Attract Younger Men

I think it's important at this time to answer one question that came up numerous times during the interviews for this book. Woman after woman asked me: "Is there a specific type of woman who attracts a younger guy? Is she a woman who looks younger than her age? Is she an unusually attractive woman?"

I am pleased to note that the women were all types, and so were the men. Just as the ages varied from mid-twenties to the eighties, so did hair color, size, shape, and weight. The women were blondes, brunettes and redheads. Some looked much younger than their age; others looked older. They were tall and slender, short and slender, petite and plump, or tall and large-boned.

The same for the men. Some, like Brant, look 5 years younger than their age; others can pass for men 10 and 20 years their senior.

Individually, these people are all very different, and yet they are attractive. What makes them attractive is the enthusiasm and energy in their faces.

119

Diane, 45, and Rob, 33, are a good couple to use as an example of the kind of beauty I'm talking about. They have been together for 9 years and married for 6. Diane is petite and spritely but given to a pleasant, round plumpness. Rob is of medium height and very slender. As a couple, they are very well suited when it comes to energy levels. They move fast, talk fast, and work hard. They make the world spin a lot faster when you are with them, and you walk away from that duo a little out of breath. But no, Diane is not an unusually attractive woman; she is average-looking, like most of us. And I think you would find Rob an average-looking man. For both, however, one thing is true: when they begin to talk, their eyes light up and they are instantly appealing—both physically and sexually.

Or, as the old saying goes, "beauty is in the eye of the beholder." George was 77 when his wife, Marie, died at the age of 92. Their marriage lasted 28 years.

"I never noticed she was failing in any way," said George of his wife's death, which caught him by surprise. "I was too close to her to notice, I guess. You know, it appeared to me that Marie never did get wrinkled. Her skin was always smooth. Well . . . I guess if I look at earlier pictures, then it does look like she wrinkled a little bit—but I never noticed."

George always saw his wife as the woman he loved sharing his life with, not as an object in need of a fresh coat of paint.

Worry No. 5:
What Happens When I Get *Really* Old?

This is the question that is at the heart of all our worry. We can rationalize keeping fit and attractive into our late fifties and even our early sixties, but beyond that it is difficult to imagine maintaining our sex appeal. Why? Because we are conditioned to think of people who reach their later years in very specific and unfairly categorized ways. We equate growing older with a lack of fitness and a decline in our intellectual and emotional capabilities.

We think of a woman in her sixties as someone who is

definitely fading. In her seventies, she will hardly be able to get to the grocery store alone. In her eighties, she will need a wheelchair. And so on. Well, think again. Lillian has a lesson to teach all of us.

At 57, John is a tall, well-built, strikingly handsome man who looks like he stepped out of the pages of the L. L. Bean catalog, fishing rod in hand. Lillian, his wife of 12 years, is 72, but you would guess that she's in her early sixties. She is very tall, strong-boned, with an open, lively, craggy face. Her broad smile and rich, deep laugh make her someone you feel you've known for years even if you've just met. Before she retired from her first career, she was one of the highest-ranking female executives in corporate America.

They each have full-time careers, which they pursue from different locations. Lillian spends weekdays in the city, where she keeps a small apartment. John has an office in the country. On weekends, they relax together at their mountain farm.

"I was taken with Lil when I met her at a dinner party about 13 years ago," recalls John. "Here was this stunning-looking woman who had so much to say. I remember how we connected. One of us mentioned blue jays—we both love the outdoors—and both of us agreed that, if blue jays were uncommon, bird-watchers would drive thousands of miles to see such an attractive bird. But since they're so common, no one gives a damn about blue jays.

"So Lil and I shared a point of view. Later we discovered we felt the same way about dozens of things. So we started seeing each other. But because of the age difference, she fudged things a bit, always referring to herself as 'over 54' when she was actually past 60. She told me how old she really was once we got serious.

"But I have never really had any concern over her age because I've been interested in her as a person. I don't think I'd ever gone with any women that much older than I am. My former wife was a few years younger. I really didn't think much about our ages because Lillian was clearly a healthy, active, nice partner in all ways.

"I think it was important that we lived together a year before we got married. During that year we found many things

121

that we liked or didn't like about each other. Mostly, I found a great majority that I loved and cherished in her.''

Lillian told me that, because she was so uncertain about the 12 years that separated them and because John preferred a very different lifestyle, she resisted the idea of marriage. Then she realized, she told me, "I had once said to a friend that if God ever put a good man in my way, I'd never let him go." Despite her initial doubts, she agreed to marriage and has had no regrets.

She was curious about John's response to my questions about her physical condition, since she considers herself to be in just as good shape as or better shape than he is. I think John did her proud.

"Now that she's 72, I can see that when we go walking she walks a little slower than she did 12 years ago, but she was quite healthy and vigorous then for a woman *my* age," said John. "You should know *I* walk a little slower than I did 12 years ago! Lil keeps herself in good physical condition and always will. She continues to do exercises, walks every day, swims regularly, eats well, and tries to keep her weight down. We both have minor weight problems. She has a back problem, but I do, too.

"We have a difference in our energy levels, but I kind of like it. Lillian is a healthy, vigorous woman, and I love that in her. We both love the outdoors—I think you see that in our faces."

How does it happen, this terrific expression of health and energy? For one thing, Lillian and John have dispensed with any personal concern over age, talk about age—*anything* to do with age—because the kind of categorizing that people do when they begin to think of the numbers, such as "the seventies," leads to negative kinds of expectations that they refuse to allow to affect their lives.

"I make it a point not to talk about age, and I don't like people who do," said Lillian. "If my friends keep saying 'people our age' then I kind of don't see them too often. I really feel it's a downer. In fact, if John says something about it in relation to projected life spans, I always catch him up

122

on it and say, 'Don't assume anything. You don't have a contract on how long you'll live any more than I do.'

"After all, what is 20 years? When you look back, 20 years is nothing. Time flies by. You know that hackneyed statement—'Live each day as if it were the first day of the rest of your life'—it really does make sense.

"For example, I just saw this movie on Picasso. He was painting at the end of his life and he was in his nineties. The most sexy-looking guy I ever saw. He wore short shorts, and the upper part of his body was nude—marvelous, muscular, smooth skin, full of vigor.

"Women are like that, too," said Lillian. "I swim all the time and, my God, the different bodies I see. I see as many young women, old men, young men, who are too fat or beginning to ruin their bodies. Faces age, but even there there's a difference. I think it's psychological: it's all in how you see yourself, the kind of expression you have on your face.

"John keeps telling me I'm beautiful, and I say, 'yes, yes,' and don't pay too much attention to it one way or the other. To him, I'm beautiful. What that means to him, I'm not sure. He really is a very handsome man, but he doesn't know it. I have to cut his beard and tell him when he needs a haircut and go with him to buy clothes. One wouldn't worry about looks with a guy like that for very long," said Lillian as she laughs and laughs, this vibrant, energetic woman with her rough-hewn face and her straight, athletic build.

She and John teach us an important lesson—it isn't how you look but how you live that will determine whether or not you survive as a lover and a loved one. Age doesn't mark your body in some diabolical way that will sabotage your future. You do that kind of damage with your very own mind. Nor does love with a younger lover signal a high-risk affair if you are confident and secure that who you are is not just what you look like.

Why We Worry So Much

We've been taught to worry. Every American woman over the age of 30 is the victim of a long history of emotional blackmail that is emblazoned on our billboards and magazine covers and shouted from every television ad—society's slogan that to be a beautiful and sexy woman is to be *young*.

Think about the following, and you will understand why you worry about your physical attractiveness, why you are convinced you will lose it as you age:

- Over 85 percent of all women seen on television are under age 40, and those over age 40 are presented as the female equivalent of a eunuch.
- Nearly all women's fashion magazines are aimed at the 18- to 34-year-old consumer, even though most of the clothing advertised can be worn by 90 percent of women over age 35.

If you are overly concerned about aging, you are hardly alone:

- The magic age for cosmetics marketers is 35, because studies show at that age women start to feel they must look younger than they are in order to compete for jobs and men.
- A recent study of women's attitudes about beauty showed that women depend on cosmetics for confidence and effectiveness in job interviews or when meeting people at a party.

Men are quick to recognize that advertising and images endlessly repeated in our popular culture affect women's self-esteem more than their own.

Mick, 34 (married to Helen, 40), summed up the expert con job that has been done on us when he said, ''Maybe this sounds sexist, but I think age is more of a female issue than a male issue. I think society has done that and continues to do that with the help of Madison Avenue.

"Look at what's-her-name bent over in her little Calvins. I think a woman's embarrassment over being older than her man has to do with American society's consciousness of the physical body. It's contrived, it's packaged, and it's sold even if that's contrary to NOW and the women's movement.

"Marketers have found a weakness in the female psyche: she wants to be all things forever—sexy, beautiful, all of it— but age doesn't allow that to occur."

And who are the people who develop and manipulate these images designed to make us buy? Mostly men. But they have another consumer in mind at the same time that they set out to make us feel insecure—our male peer. They want to reach him because he is traditionally the consumer with the most control over the dollars. But in order to make him buy, they want to make him feel good about himself. To do that, they show him with a younger woman.

Why? As older men begin to droop physically and lose their vitality either because of fatigue, lack of exercise, or lack of ambition, they project the same negative feelings onto women their own age.

The advertising media capitalize on this. They spend millions to tie self-esteem into body perception. They want us to look to them for reasons to feel good about ourselves/our bodies. Thus, the man is sold a younger woman and the woman is sold the necessity always to try to be a younger woman in order to make him feel good.

Only a man is encouraged to bolster his sense of well-being with a younger partner. And it works! Some men seek out younger women because they want to think young and act young. Some men do so because they want to impress other men with the fact that they are attractive to younger women. Some men consider a beautiful, young female partner to be a "reward" for achieving success. But regardless of the reason a man has for wanting a younger partner, rarely does he waste time worrying about whether his appearance will matter to her. Why? The media don't tell him he has to look good—all he has to offer is his air of assurance, the prestige of his experience, and his financial security.

But if more and more women can achieve the same assurance, prestige, and security, why do we still worry so much? Why do we think it's fine for men to have younger partners but let men continue to tell us—via the media and the social attitudes they encourage—that it is wrong for us to have younger partners?

Two reasons. First, women have only recently reached that stage of financial independence that makes it possible for them to ignore men's opinions and directions. Second, the old ways are deeply ingrained, and many women are still more comfortable taking direction from men. They still buy into the old attitude that says men know better.

When it comes to themselves, men do know better. After all, how does society judge an older man? By his air of confidence, authority, and accomplishment. We find him sexy because of who he is and what he has become. We love the no-nonsense hurry in his walk. The lines that experience and hard work etch across his face are defined as "handsome" and "distinguished." We see in him proof that success and power are real aphrodisiacs. This means an older man is given many reasons to feel good about his body, his work, and himself.

But how do we judge an older woman? Tradition holds that years are hard on her. Age saps her of vitality and beauty. Rather than accept her hard-earned history as it tries to map its way across her forehead, around her eyes, and down her throat, she is pushed by culture and commerce to spend millions to try to erase it. We define her face and body with words like *wrinkles* and *bags*. Even we women try to deny the older woman's existence as we smear bottled youth across our faces.

Worst of all, we women buy into the whole mess. Even now, as more and more women in America are beginning to view themselves differently as they age, we refuse to change our body image, despite the fact that we have changed as *people* and our futures hold something different now that the majority of us are working women.

Standing on the shoulders of those who helped us discover new options for our lives through the women's movement, we are beginning to pluck for ourselves the rewards men have hoarded too long—autonomy, independence, authority, financial security, prestige—and with those treasures has come an enduring aura of sex appeal.

In fact, a great number of us are discovering we have a sexy new image in the eyes of younger men. These men neither know nor care how old we are because they see us differently than we have ever been seen before. They see us in the full measure of who we are, professionally, personally, and physically.

Ironically, we find it tough to believe that a younger man is interested in us, especially if we are over age 30, because we still believe what we have always been told—that a woman loses her sex appeal for men as she ages. So even if we can understand the attraction at the moment, we just don't have faith that it can endure the passage of time.

Unfortunately, even those of us who decide to return the romantic interest expressed by younger men—once we move beyond worrying over what others will think about us as a couple—insist on a period of severe self-criticism and worry over the exact date that our aging physical apparatus will sabotage our sexuality and sex appeal.

The Marlboro Woman

When I was 18, I hadn't yet learned to let the world tell me what to do. I wore a black leather jacket and cowboy boots. I thought I was tough, and I had an image in my mind of the woman I wanted to be: she would hit 35 looking better than ever, with a lean, hard body, sexy in worn Levis and with a history of rugged independence etched into a face darkened by the sun. She wanted a man like her whiskey: expensive, smooth, and tough. She was the Marlboro woman.

I was naive when I was 18 and transposed my self-image-to-be over that man on the magazine page. I was 23 when I discovered she didn't exist. That was when my lean, hard, independent husband, aided and abetted by every popular women's magazine, made it clear that the woman I should become was a soft, lovely, gentle, cosmetically defined show-case for his success. My destiny was to become a totem to *his* achievements.

I was confused. Something about that made me very unhappy—close to suicidal, as a matter of fact. So I decided some change was necessary. I quit smoking. I started running. I got a part-time job. I went back to school one course at a time. Since I had two little babies, I squeezed changing my own life into spare moments of everyone else's. I decided to go for a compromise, some small measure of independence that would place me somewhere between the Marlboro woman and June Cleaver.

A few years later, my father made my quandary even more complex after my mother died. He was in his mid-fifties at the time, an age I consider young, and I encouraged him to begin dating, even suggested several women in his circle of friends.

But the woman he eventually courted was only five years older than I. Though he never said so explicitly, his actions implied that for him the attractive woman was the young woman. He might qualify as a ruggedly handsome older man, but a woman his age, whose face was also creased with the lines of age and experience and exposure to the outdoors, wouldn't be looked on so admiringly. And when, in my 35th year, my father married this woman who was 40, he seemed to underscore the traditional belief: men grow handsome as they age, but women deteriorate. The mature man is prized; the mature woman is sexually disenfranchised.

I was puzzled by my father's marriage. Did this mean he did not find my mother attractive as they grew older together? If he wasn't attracted to women his age, did that foreshadow my fate at age 50?

It wasn't until a few years later that the right questions finally dawned on me: What makes the older man an expert on what is or is not attractive in a woman? Have I been listening to the wrong voices, male voices schooled in outdated attitudes, for opinions by which I will gauge my own sense of self-esteem as I age?

I asked myself those questions just after meeting Brant. I think I had the courage to challenge the traditional perception of an older woman's body because some important changes had taken place in the years since I was 23 and suicidal— since 1968.

The women's movement brought new faces to the forefront of everyday life. I had some new role models, and they weren't glamor queens. Georgia O'Keeffe applied paint to the canvas and never to her face. Her wrinkled, sun-worn visage was an icon to a woman like me. It was in the face of Georgia O'Keeffe that I first saw an image very similar to the woman I envisioned when I was still a teenager, my tough, sexy, independent "Marlboro woman," and I felt new hope. I devoured everything written on her: she was a brilliant success in her work, she lived independently by choice, she made her own fortune, and in my eyes her face affirmed a new standard of beauty.

At last, for me, the image of the older woman began to change. At the same time, more faces of working women— simple, honest, direct, and remarkably unadorned—graced first the pages and then the covers of the popular women's magazines. Even the cosmetics industry moved grudgingly toward a more natural look.

Over the years, I have kept running and exercising because it feels so good. I like doing it. Meanwhile, fitness has become a nationwide trend for both sexes. For a while, I even taught exercise classes.

And, yes, I've reached my forties as a long, lean woman who feels at home in a pair of old, worn Levis. If I'm sexy, that's great—but I'm not trying to be. I'm also beginning to wear the face of my father, to show the lines and creases of good years and rough years. But what about that Marlboro woman and the line about men and whiskey? Well, I've never really liked whiskey, and I'll take my man just the way he is.

Why the Marketing of
Female Youth Will Change

Many women, including me, now see themselves as survivors of the same battlegrounds as the men. We have learned to be team players. We have entered the work force and logged the hours, paid the dues, endured the politics, and brought home the paychecks, as well as the self-confidence of success. If we think we look a little tired and worn from the battle, we're proud of it; it's evidence of hard work and accomplishment.

Very recently, without being fully aware of it, we have begun to drop our critical attitudes toward our faces and our bodies. It's happening because we're meeting other women who are also working hard and achieving—and we like what we see. But that's because we aren't measuring each other the way we used to in high school and even in college. We aren't just paying attention to our faces and our curves—we are judging one another by our level of intelligence, our interpersonal skills, our ambition, our energy level. Even some of our female role models have changed. The glamor girls like Linda Evans and Joan Collins are relegated to the TV soaps as escapist fiction. In real life, we—and our daughters—are inspired by women like U.S. Supreme Court Justice Sandra Day O'Connor, *USA Today* publisher Cathleen P. Black, the Pretenders' lead singer, songwriter, and guitarist Chrissie Hynde, and the many other prominent female businesswomen, lawyers, doctors, professors, and athletes who are frequently featured on the covers of today's popular women's magazines.

We are recognizing how important those qualities that help us succeed in work are, and, because we are proud of these qualities in ourselves, we are becoming more accepting, woman to woman. This increasing acceptance of each other as our own best friends is critical to our individual sense of self-acceptance. As I pointed out earlier, however, these changes aren't necessarily enough to undo years of tradition and youth-based advertising. But money talks, and legions of baby boomers, both male and female, are hitting 40, and are forcing change on the advertising media. We exist in large enough numbers that we speak with a very loud voice when we state that we age differently today and we want our images to reflect our new ways and our new attitudes.

We must be listened to by the advertising media for the simple reason that our buying power is already four times greater than that of the youth market. We are the largest consumer market, and we will stay the largest as we get older and older.

Already, more and more of us are openly declaring our dissatisfaction with current advertising that does not reflect people in our age groups—people over 40. We are carrying healthy bodies and healthy attitudes into our mid-life and later, and we will demand to see this reflected in the sales jobs done on us, or—we won't buy.

Recently, consumer groups have challenged the cosmetics industry to prove that new "antiaging" products for the skin really work. I believe we will see more challenges like this, but they will come slowly. As an expert in public relations, I know that advertisers will not break new ground until they have the numbers, the demographics to prove the market already exists. Advertising never leads; it follows.

In some ways, women must still go it alone as we change the world of hype around us. Those brand managers and copywriters are young men (advertising is still a male-dominated field, and only a few of the people developing major advertising campaigns are female), and we have to tell them what we want.

We've begun to do just that. Our incomes are rising as more and more of us crowd into the boardrooms, supervise the departments, and earn our degrees. One-third of American households are headed by single parents, most of them women. We have become a large consumer group with significant buying power. Now is the time to announce our pride in what we have achieved, to demand that the advertising media show us the way we want to be seen.

We can make this demand because so much of our life is changing, making us stronger, more independent, and more financially secure. We are becoming a market force equal to men. I, for one, want to see the women we have become reflected in the billboards, magazine covers, and television advertising that surround me. And I want this image to change the lives of our daughters and granddaughters.

Women, especially working women, have learned that their physical flaws make little difference out in the world, where the stakes are tied to how smart you are and how well you can manage the environment around you. Stretch mark erasers and false eyelashes are not on the agenda, nor do they lead to raises. Intelligence, capability, skill, and talent are the attributes in demand. It is when a woman is behaving as a working *person* that she is most likely to draw the attention of a man, who values her for all the same qualities that have long been hyped as the top selling points for older men: experience, sophistication, achievement, money. I believe that is why we are seeing such a dramatic increase in the numbers of women between the ages of 35 and 44 who are romantically involved with younger men today.

In fact, I've found that women have begun to look at men differently than they have in the past. No longer is the older man accepted without question as the most desirable partner for love and marriage. If the woman puts time and effort into keeping fit, she fully expects a man to keep fit as well.

I know that over the years I have become acutely aware of men my own age who let their bodies deteriorate, their shoulders sag, and their stomachs protrude. In contrast, I look at Brant, and the sight of him can take my breath away. He stands straight, and his muscles are solid. I love to look at the lines of his legs and his body. I don't expect this to change as he gets older, because he makes it a point, as I do, to stay fit.

And yet, there are women who subscribe to the same unfair attitudes men do, and that's not likely to change. Over and over again, as I researched this book, I came across comments from women on older men. "Why do I want to date an older man?" asked one woman. "Fat, balding, and boring doesn't do much for me."

"An older guy is out of his element," said another. "When

it comes to dating, all he wants is to get you into bed. He has no idea what comes before or after—except TV.''

"I like to look at bodies," said Marsha, 50. "The men my age are kind of sad. I've been told there are great ones out there, but I haven't found one yet. The younger men I date are all physically active—they run, play squash. It's such a treat to look at a healthy body. That's why I work hard on mine."

Amanda was 35 when she was first attracted to Steve. She had previously been dating a man 16 years older than she; Steve was just 26. "I'm sure I'll always love him because there's a lot more than just his body that appeals to me, but the physical thing was a big reason I first fell in love with him. That makes me wonder how I will relate to him as *he* ages. I think it may be more important that Steve keep his looks than that I keep mine. After all, I went after that smooth body muscle, that taut belly and jaw, his supple skin. That's my question—do these younger men ever worry about getting old?"

If Amanda sounds harsh, it's because she's telling it like it is: concern about body image as they age is becoming important to men, too, which is only fair.

One very visible group of women challenging traditional male/female relationships are female celebrities. They have become more open about their relationships with younger men. These include Sigourney Weaver, Mary Tyler Moore, Goldie Hawn, Audrey Hepburn, Olivia Newton-John, Maureen Reagan, Priscilla Presley, Shelley Long, Yoko Ono, Bette Midler, Katherine Helmond, Estelle Parsons, Kate O'Mara, Jane Morgan, Marsha Mason, and Louise Fletcher, to name a few who have been featured in recent news stories with younger boyfriends and husbands.

This is important, because these women establish a certain kind of fantasy image. The celebrity may be richer and prettier than the rest of us, but if she falls in love with a younger man in a very open and public way, it allows the rest of us a chance to observe and think about it, too. After all, she is implying that in her world, where the image is so important, she has confidence in her beauty as an older woman. She is not threatened by the younger new star. She accepts herself.

This also makes it easier for younger men to think about older women. And if popular culture is going to endorse these relationships—which it is doing with lots of titillating but endearing publicity—it gives women loving younger men a good name. After all, all of the celebrities mentioned above are stars who have established positive media images for us, even if they don't exactly reflect real life.

Another area of popular culture where I've observed one small but potent sign of change in the image of the older woman is in the work of best-selling novelist Elmore Leonard. In his book *La Brava*, Leonard introduced a sexy, seductive actress who proved dangerously alluring to the hero—yet she was 12 years his senior!

And so, more and more frequently, we are seeing the image of the older woman presented as a female who is lovely and sexy and, as Elmore Leonard wrote, "the kind of woman who heats up fantasies."

I predict that the days in which the debut of wrinkles meant the exit of sex appeal are waning. Instead, we are on the brink of a new era in which a woman's perception and acceptance of her body image will improve just as her self-esteem becomes more and more a product of her feelings about *everything* she accomplishes.

New Options in Health, Fitness, and Beauty

Nothing has done more to improve the self-image of millions of women today than new patterns in health, fitness, and beauty that have emerged over the last decade. Most of the women involved with younger men told me that, while their pride in their physical fitness is one factor that gives them confidence, it is also something they deliberately look for in a man, whether he is their age, younger, or older.

Over 65 percent of the women I interviewed said they exercise regularly with their younger partner. Of this group, many of the women, ranging in age from 27 to 72, continue to be active in sports such as tennis, racquetball, squash, swimming, windsurfing, and sailing.

"You are what you want to be," said Lillian, 72 (married to John, 57), explaining why physical activity is high on her list of priorities. "You aren't made attractive; you *become* attractive. When you feel good about yourself, you radiate. You make people fall in love with you." Her point? If you want to feel good about your body, it is your own responsibility to see that you keep as fit as you need to in order to be as active as you want to be.

It is the women who take the time to exercise, to take part in athletic activities, who quickly discover that is the ticket to feeling good, feeling comfortable and happy with themselves—and looking terrific no matter how old they are.

An excellent example of this is Elinor, 57 (living with Brad, 39), whose positive perspective on her age and the signs of age in her body and her face did not just "happen." She discovered the importance of athletics in Brad's life and decided to share his enjoyment. Even though she had never been active in sports prior to knowing Brad, she has become an enthusiastic participant, and their sports activities provide a great deal of the pleasure they get from their life together. This means she did not become sports-minded until she was in her late forties, which should inspire any woman who worries that it's too late to begin.

"I was never athletic before we got together," said Elinor, "but Brad keeps his body in excellent shape, and he encourages me. So I learned how to play tennis, which we now play together. We really enjoy cross-country skiing, and that's something we do at our country place. I have discovered I thoroughly enjoy sports, and this has become a very important part of what we do and share regularly."

Brad responds just as enthusiastically, "I think Elinor looks a lot better now than when I met her 10 years ago. Her sense of self has improved, and you can see it in her face. She's much more relaxed. She worried a little at first that she might hurt herself, but she didn't. I think sports have improved her whole outlook on life."

If you need proof that fitness and exercise can improve your looks, Joanne, 53 (married to Hans, 43), succinctly makes the point when she describes how Hans is often mistaken for the older partner in their marriage of 20 years.

"Everyone thinks Hans is older than I am. I am a dancer, and, even though I am 53 now, I have the body of a 30-year-old. Hans stopped exercising 10 years ago. He has a wonderful body, but he doesn't look better than I. And he's the one with white hair! So he may be only 43, but I look younger. I still exercise and dance religiously. I warn Hans, 'If you don't exercise, you will turn to flab.' "

And so the tables have turned. Women are indeed getting older—and better. And who are they really doing all this for? Men? Oh, no. The big difference today is that most women are staying in shape because *they* want to. They feel better when they are in shape, so they are doing it for themselves.

I know because I took up tennis at the age of 26 and continue to play regularly, not only because I enjoy the game and being outdoors, but for another reason. Twenty years ago, when I was a young mother and trying to do some hasty repair work on my physique, which was still suffering from childbirth hangover, I noticed an elderly woman in our neighborhood because she had the best-looking figure. One day I complimented her on her great legs. She told me that her secret was tennis. Since I would like to preserve my own legs and that urge has nothing to do with sex appeal—my legs are as important to me as my eyes because both keep me in the mainstream of life—I decided to make a long-term commitment to tennis. That's how tennis and other sports have become my way of ensuring myself a healthy old age, with or without a man.

My attitudes about makeup are changing, too. As recently as the early '70s, it was practically unthinkable to leave the house without some kind of cosmetic aid. Today we have more options as a "natural look" is in vogue. Unfortunately, however, most of us—along with the rest of society—have a long way to go in this area, because the cosmetics counter is still a dangerous place, a confusing, expensive maelstrom dedicated to telling the contemporary woman that she needs all the help she can get in order to look halfway decent.

Boy, do we get the message. How many of us file in dutifully every season to ask a salesgirl—herself horribly made up in order to demonstrate every product she is selling—to take 30 minutes to teach us the perfect beauty plan? How many of us waste too many hours of our lives discussing under-eye creams guaranteed to remove our bags, silicon gels guaranteed to fill in our wrinkles, and face lifts guaranteed to help us keep our men?

How many of us do this? Tell me who *doesn't*. I've done it for years. In fact, it was costing me several hundred dollars annually. But last fall, something happened that really changed my mind about wearing makeup.

I had arrived late for a television interview. I rushed into the studio, frantic for a mirror since I hadn't had a chance to apply any makeup beforehand. Another woman was already peering into the mirror. As I dumped a collection of battered and greasy jars, pencils, and brushes on the counter, I glanced at her.

Oh no! I winced. Of all the women to have to follow. Standing beside me was Kaylon Pickford, a stunning woman in her mid-fifties, famous as one of America's top "older" models.

Clumsily, I completed my own makeup, and then I introduced myself. As we chatted, I summoned up the courage to ask her if she could recommend a good makeup artist.

"Not really," she said. "I do my own unless it's a modeling assignment, and then the client takes care of it." She looked at me quizzically. "Why? You don't need makeup."

"Oh, I do," I stammered, a list of facial flaws at the ready.

"Nonsense," she said. "The point I'm trying to make on the show today is that women need to redefine beauty. We have to begin to see ourselves as being as attractive in our older years as we are when we're young—what is considered beautiful must change for the older woman.

"Why do we hide our lines? Older isn't ugly. A woman has to learn to see the beauty in her older face, to stay natural and let a good feeling about herself give her a special glow.

"Just touch up your eyes a little," she said to me. "You have lovely skin, and you look like someone with a lot of energy. You look great. Don't worry about it."

She was right. After that conversation, I felt like I'd been released from bondage. I trashed the bottles and creams and brushes and pencils. Today I use makeup only for photo sessions or television. During the day and at work, I use a small amount of eyeliner and a touch of mascara. No lipstick, no blush. I feel like Elinor—I like my face, and I'm liking it better every day.

Natural, Unnatural—
Do It the Way *You* Want It

My one major concession to vanity is my hair. Like 35 percent of the women interviewed, I color my hair, because I am prematurely gray and I happen to prefer my original dark brown color. When I let my hair go gray, I am constantly mistaken for Brant's mother. When I am all brown, no one makes that mistake. Every woman who colors her hair feels the way I do—we like our original hair colors because they make us feel better. Most of my friends tell me I look "distinguished" in my silver-gray mop. That may be. *I* like myself as a brunette. And while Brant prefers my hair long, *I* like it short and zapped with a permanent that gives it a wild curl. That's because I feel full of energy these days, and I like my hair to reflect that. I am making a cosmetic choice because I prefer it myself and not because of any social pressure.

The same is frequently true of other women when it comes to faces and makeup. Eighty percent of the women interviewed said they prefer a more natural look, especially because so many of us work. We don't want to be seen as heavily made-up in the office environment because it gives us a "superficial" appearance. You never see a man with carefully drawn eyeliner on his lids. You don't see him whip out a lipstick tube before a conference. Men are happy with natural faces, and more women have begun to feel that way, too.

Sharon, 43 (married to Jerry, 31), is a good example of how we do this while learning to handle the old standards of cosmetic beauty. She lives in a world filled with perfect female images, since Jerry's work as a fashion photographer exposes him to the loveliest women you can imagine.

"Maybe because of that, Jerry really likes me to look natural," she said. "All I use is moisturizer and a thin, soft pencil line above and below my eyelid. I don't use mascara because I think it's dangerous for your eyes. And before you ever put a foundation on again, look at an older woman who is wearing it. It clogs in your wrinkles; it sits on top of your skin like some kind of paste. I do not understand where an older woman gets the idea it makes her look better—if she will take a real close look at herself, she'll be appalled."

Sharon's dedication to preserving a natural look was echoed by Elinor when she, too, said that she uses less makeup than she ever has, even though she is 57 years old. Seventy-two-year-old Lillian uses no makeup whatsoever—and looks more vibrant and alive than most women you meet.

But for one woman, the facial appearance was something so important to her that she felt a need for plastic surgery. However, it is interesting to see that she did this not because her younger husband wanted her to but because *she* wanted to.

"I had puffs under my eyes," said Donna, 65 (married to Eric, 42), "and I felt like I always looked tired. Eric didn't want me to have the surgery. He said he didn't notice anything. But I did. So I found myself the best plastic surgeon and decided to give myself this treat. It makes me feel terrific to look so relaxed and not like I've been going without sleep. But I didn't feel that I was doing it for Eric. I did it for me."

Her positive feelings about plastic surgery are based on her desire to do something *she wants* for her own satisfaction and comfort, not something she felt compelled to do socially or by her younger husband. This is a healthy reason to pursue such a major cosmetic change. It is interesting to note that all the other women interviewed did not see cosmetic surgery as something they would choose. Most were quite satisfied with their conservative cosmetic approach and were not interested in taking such drastic action.

In fact, the idea of plastic surgery bothered Lillian, 72, who mentioned a friend, just turning 50, who had recently had a face-lift.

"She looks all right," said Lillian, "but she looked all right to me before. I don't see what she gained except a kind of smoothness. I thought she was very good-looking before. It just makes me think we've got a pretty superficial culture—especially in the way we look at people."

Lillian is right. Our culture is superficial in its approach to older women and how they should look as they age. Even women well aware of the power Madison Avenue wields aren't quite immune to it. But as long as we use cosmetics to please ourselves, or to help us achieve professional and personal goals that *we* have chosen, we will use these products and services in healthful ways—exploiting them rather than being exploited by them.

As more and more women attract younger men, yet another door is opening for us. There need be no doubt that, in the words of the famous Clairol campaign, we're not getting older; we're getting better. And confident enough not to need Clairol to tell us that.

5

Sex: the Ecstasy
and the Agony

*We have sex three to four times a week. There's no truth to
the idea that women lose their appeal as they get older. I will
want to have sex with this woman as long as we can walk
around!*

—Ed, 59, married for 15 years
to Carolyn, 74

*Women in their forties and fifties are as robust, as vital, as
sexual as ever before in their lives—perhaps more so. They
are victims of a myth of aging rather than a reality.*

—Erica Jong

Men have kept two big secrets from us over the years. The
first one is that work is a hell of a lot of fun. But the second
secret is even better: *sex* is a hell of a lot of fun—and it gets
better as you get older!

Not only is the older woman more likely than a younger
woman to be an experienced, exciting, and most willing partner in the bedroom, but her age is in her favor when it comes
to sexual enjoyment. The woman who has maintained an active sex life not only continues to be sexually active well into

141

her later decades but *enjoys* it more! Thus it should come as no surprise that, in their love affairs with younger men, many "older" women bloom sexually.

I know that my initial response to Brant was genuine surprise at how the old "guard gates" between the sexes did not exist between us: he did not begin our relationship by treating me like I was a sex object, he did not put pressure on me to perform, he wasn't critical of my body or my concerns, and he was not worried about his own sexuality. His ease with our relationship made me feel much more open and free. As a result, our early sexual encounters, which have become a wonderful cornerstone of our marriage, were blessed from the beginning with an openness, a playfulness, and a level of acceptance that I have since found to be true of all these older woman/younger man relationships.

Older woman/younger man couples exhibit sexual love in its most liberated and equal form. Both the men and the women enter into their love affairs with experience and enthusiasm, each takes a great deal of pleasure in the other, and both make every effort to be sure their partners are happy and feel comfortable as their feelings of sexual intimacy develop.

Why Sex with a Younger Man Is Easier—and More Fun

All of the older woman/younger man relationships studied were distinguished from their onset by spontaneity, a lack of pressure from the man, and a feeling of freedom to thoroughly enjoy one another's bodies.

The women I interviewed recognized the sexual impulse the moment it charged the air between them and the younger men. "The thing that attracted us right from the start was the sexual electricity between us," recalls Steve, who was 26 when he met Amanda, 35. They knew each other—at the office—for over a year before he finally asked her out, although they immediately established an office friendship that had strong sexual overtones. When they did finally date, they made love that first night.

For Steve and Amanda, the spark was there from their earliest conversations. The same was true for most of the couples interviewed.

Michelle, 43 (married to Henry, 27), remembers that moment of recognition vividly. "We talked nonstop from the time we met," she said. "Something happened that first night when he walked me back to my apartment from this aerobics class where we met, and we found out we were working in the same field. I remember thinking, I'm interested in this guy . . . I wonder how old he is. But I decided that he was interesting, and I liked him, and I was going to stop looking for anything serious anyway."

In fact, the first sexual encounters between these men and women were characterized most often by spontaneity. The women weren't afraid of pregnancy (either because they used birth control or because they were past the childbearing age), and while they didn't plan for the relationship to be one of long standing, they decided early on that they were attracted to and wanted to enjoy sex with the younger man. Their partner, on the other hand, flattered that the older woman was interested, was more than ready for the affair: intrigued and ready to play.

And play they do. Mutual enthusiasm and the willingness to try new things are the initial binding glue between all these partners. Stephanie, 43, is very much aware of that in her relationship with 30-year-old Alan. "I really looked forward to seeing him the second time," said Stephanie. "I was scared about it on one hand, and on the other hand I couldn't wait because I knew it was going to be really fun. I have fun with Alan like I haven't had in a long, long time. And he notices everything about me. The other day he said, 'I was thinking about you all day. I love to watch you.' He makes me blush.

"I love to watch him, too. His body, when he gets out of the shower. And also, I think he's a little more adventurous sexually. I may have dirtier thoughts, but he has dirtier actions," said Stephanie, echoing a spirit of playful sensuality that infused many of these relationships early on.

Neurosis appears nonexistent in the bedroom. Some women keep their worries about their bodies, their "camouflage techniques," to themselves (for a while) and jump in to have a good time while it lasts. Others are confident enough not to worry at all.

Steve, 32, bases his feeling that Amanda, 41, is more comfortable with her sexuality, more open and freer than younger women, on his personal experience.

"Amanda was very glamorous and very sure of herself when I met her. I've always had this theory—maybe I read it somewhere—that women don't really warm up or become sexually aware until they're over 30. I believe that. Until then, it seems like they're just sort of experimenting and doing what they *should* and not necessarily what they *want*. They don't know themselves well enough or physically aren't warmed up enough. Men, on the other hand, peak around 30, just when women are getting started. And I always thought the paths should cross at a certain age, so actually this is a very good time—30 for a man and 40 for a woman—for everyone to meet.

"I was married before to a woman who was my age, and I notice a difference in the sexuality. Amanda and I . . . our initial attraction was definitely very sexual. And it still is. It's a very important part of our lives. She just seems to have more enthusiasm, more appreciation than anybody I ever met. She's freer, with fewer inhibitions. She also knows how to make me feel good.

"When we are together, I feel more comfortable than I ever did with younger women. I get more gratification, more feedback. I feel better about it. I feel like when we make love, it's something we do together. I'm not just doing it *to* somebody."

This sense of really connecting through sex was mentioned many times by both the men and the women I spoke with. Michelle, 43, says of her husband, Henry, 27, "We have a wonderful sexual relationship. He had been with women his own age, most of whom were not that sexually experienced. I think I opened him up sexually. And I think that he has this sort of bedrock, sensual nature that I put him in touch with.

"He had had another woman who was also very sensually experienced. This woman was his own age, but there was something not right about how she approached him sexually. She was very demanding and aggressive in a way that he felt many women his age were, but I wasn't. It was like she expected him to be responsible for her satisfaction, and if it didn't work it was his fault. I'm not worried if it doesn't work every time. So we clicked even though it wasn't anything conscious on my part. But I think that, also, he is enormously sexually attractive to me. This is our fifth year together, and I still feel that way."

Most of the women I interviewed felt that their man's more liberated outlook toward sex was a function of his youth; these men differed significantly from older men. For one thing, they grew up in a more sexually relaxed atmosphere, at college in particular. In addition, many had experienced sexual relationships with a number of different women. Thus, they look at the age difference as only one of many factors that they take into consideration—"for 30 seconds," as one man said. And, perhaps most important, they have spent more time with women as *peers* in the classroom and in the work force and tend to be attracted to women who are independent types. Energy attracts them, as do intelligence and competence.

Because of their sexual experience, many have developed fairly relaxed attitudes toward sex, attitudes that distinguish them from men who are older—at least from the standpoint of the women who have known both. A major reason for this is that they learned about sex during the '60s and the '70s, an era of change in which young women were much more accepting of premarital sex than older women were at the same age. This means that younger men have been intimate with women for a (relatively) longer time and in a much more socially relaxed atmosphere than older men. Because sex has been less "forbidden" for these men as they mature, they differ from older men in their more realistic and fair acceptance of their sexual partners.

It is very interesting that three women interviewed said they had wondered for a short time early in their relationships if the younger men they were seeing were gay or bisexual because their sexual behavior patterns were so much less pressured, more low-key, than those of older men the women had slept with. Orgasm was not demanded as evidence of the success of the encounter. The men took a great deal of time with foreplay. The women, in fact, often felt that they made the first move toward sex or made it simultaneously with the man. They definitely did not feel pressured into it.

I think it is very important, however, to realize that every younger man isn't one under the age of 35, because it *is* true that you are only as old as your attitudes. Ed is 59, and his wife, Carolyn, is 74. They have been married for 14 years and met when he was 44 and she was 59. Ed brings many of the best traits of the new "younger man" to their relationship. And together they prove that sex is terrific no matter how old you are.

"Sex has been very important to me ever since I was a youngster," said Ed. "I masturbated when I was a kid, I talked about sex a lot, I've always been fascinated by sex.

"My first marriage lasted many years, but my wife, who was a few years younger, never really enjoyed our sex together. A great deal of that was my fault. I was old-fashioned. I'd get hard, enter her, come, and that was that. I never gave any thought to her satisfaction. We never talked about it. I really feel bad about that today.

"After my marriage ended, I had a number of affairs. Several women I slept with were just super in bed. I began to learn what sex was supposed to be for *both* people. So when I met Carolyn, it was terribly important to me to be able to start over as a new, fresh individual.

"From the very first time we slept together, I was determined to hold back and let her take her time to become aroused. By this time, I had learned how to wait, how to avoid coming too soon. I suspect she thought I was impotent at first.

"What has meant a lot to me is that, even though she has known many men, she told me she had never reached orgasm before. She enjoyed sex, but she had never climaxed. She has with me. During the years we've been together, she has reached orgasm dozens of times. She tells me that ours is the best sexual relationship she has ever had.''

Ed is one of the few men who felt comfortable sharing the intimate details of his sex life with me for this book, but he talks easily about it since he recognized years ago how important honesty and openness are to his happiness and the happiness of the woman he loves.

One final characteristic, important in these days of AIDS and other sexually transmitted diseases, is the ease with which the women were able to *discuss* sex early in their first encounters. ''Let's be blunt,'' said Merritt, 42, after she had been sleeping with Tom, 33, for three months. ''How can I possibly be intimidated by a guy nine years younger than I am? That's exactly why I didn't hesitate to ask him whom he'd been sleeping with. I wanted to know if he had girlfriends with yeast infections, herpes, anything. I told him nicely but firmly that I'm also worried about that.

''Later I learned that during the last 20 years he's slept with about 30 women. During my lifetime, I've slept with 4 men. That's a big difference, and it makes asking health questions very important. However, I think it's the older men who are more likely to have been with callgirls and prostitutes, which I think is more frightening. But I asked my question in a caring way because I felt he had the right to ask me the same question. The weird thing is I don't think I'd ask an older man quite as easily. They are so much more difficult to deal with sexually. Instead, I think I'd put off starting a relationship until I felt I really knew him well.''

The Short-Lived Worry over What He Will Think of Her Body

While, as noted earlier, the women tend to put aside their fears of not having a perfect body *at first,* many admit it soon becomes their major concern in the early stages of a sexual relationship with a younger man.

''The only thing that got in the way of making love with Eric was my own head, when I realized that he could not see me as a young, beautiful thing,'' said Donna, 65, of her sexual relationship with Eric, 42. After they first had sex, she said, ''I looked hard at my wrinkles.'' She tried to see herself as he must see her, and she worried that her appearance as an older woman would turn him off.

Diane, 45, had the same fear. She met her husband, Rob, 33, nine years ago when she was 36 and he was 24. He is slender, of medium height, and dark-haired with a pleasant, open face. He's the kind of man who would be very attractive to younger women, and it is understandable that an older woman might be concerned about his comparing her body to that of a younger woman.

Diane is a short, buxom woman, given to a slight plumpness even though her figure is basically firm and fit. She has a round face and alert, inquisitive eyes that reflect her overflowing energy. But her body is typical of most women over the age of 18: not perfect. Her male counterpart would be a short, stocky, muscular man—someone you wouldn't be surprised to see with a slender model on his arm. Would a woman be turned off by the body of the man I just described? Of course not. And that is true of our older woman/younger man couples, too. The men simply don't judge the women's sexual appeal by traditional standards of beauty. They love these women's bodies for all the complex reasons that women love men's bodies—which cannot be carefully categorized by size, shape, and weight.

Rob, for example, adores Diane's breasts.

''I was worried about my body first,'' she said, remembering her thoughts when she first started sleeping with Rob. It was two weeks after he invited her to dinner that they became intimate. ''I've always been heavy, and so I've always felt unattractive. But with Rob, I feel more attractive than I have ever with anyone, mainly because he's very turned on by what he calls 'the lush bod.'

''He likes great, heavy, hanging breasts. He says, 'God, you're supposed to play with this. This is wonderful stuff.' Meanwhile, I always thought, Damn, I want to cut it all off. But he loves my body. So now I don't worry about it.

''I worry more about wrinkles in my face. I think a lot

about that—I know a lot of women who are older than I am, in their fifties and sixties. I find them attractive because of their energy level. But their faces look old to me. That bothers me because you don't have any control over it. And I think Rob will look better as he gets older. I think a lot of youthful-looking men get a craggy look.''

Diane brings up the old bias that holds that women look older and less attractive as they age while the opposite is true for men. These are women whose bodies have the curves of individuality. Many of them, following our national trend toward physical exercise and good eating habits, are healthier than ever. But while the women may have learned to accept their bodies—wrinkles, flaws, et al.—they still worry initially that they will be compared to younger women. In addition to a general concern over the age difference, the first few times they sleep with their younger men, all the women worry about is what the men will think *after* they make love, when the lights are turned on and the women's well-worn torsos are on display. But that attitude is changing, again because younger men don't see it that way when it comes to responding sexually to a woman. In fact, their very different attitude toward a woman's body is a major reason why so many women are enjoying relationships with younger men.

It is the younger man's immediate response to her body that makes a significant difference to the older woman from the first intimate moment of the relationship. His unconditional acceptance of her body surprises and delights her. The discovery that the body she felt hesitant to expose—mainly because of a societal prejudice that says only the young and beautiful should be seen naked—is considered lush and sexy by the younger man heightens her self-esteem. "He taught me to look at my body with new eyes," said Diane, 45.

Said Stephanie, 43, of her sex life with Alan, 30, "At first, when it came to my body, I had great camouflage techniques. I got away with this camouflage pretty well until he said, 'Why don't we take a shower together?'

"I said, 'I've never taken a shower with anyone in my life.'

" 'What?' he asked me. 'Are you sick?'

"And then I felt terrible, like I'd really missed something.

"So I agreed, and he said, 'Good, it'll be fun.' And it was. It was great.

"I keep saying to myself, 'This can't work.' But seeing Alan, making love with him . . . I have this passionate addiction. Right now, I can't give him up."

Stephanie has been dating Alan for almost three months now. Even though she has reservations because of their age difference, their sexual compatibility is so remarkable that she continues to give the relationship a green light.

Another example of how easily body doubts are dispelled comes from Eric, who was 38 when he fell in love with Donna (now 65). That was four years ago. They have been married for three years. He is a square-jawed man with sandy hair and a medium build. Donna is a little shorter than her husband; her figure is trim and her hair lightly touched with gray. You might guess her to be in her late fifties or early sixties, rather than 65, but she doesn't hide her age. Instead, she exudes a warm charisma—her eyes sparkle when she talks, and her manner is soft but firm. When I told people about Donna and Eric and their 23-year age difference, many said, "Oh, that's too much," as if it's okay for a woman to marry a younger man, but not that much younger! To Eric and Donna, of course, it isn't too great an age difference. And it certainly isn't for women with older men. But that kind of response is why Donna needed assurance from Eric that her older body could be sexually appealing to him.

"It's really essence to essence that makes our relationship work, and that has nothing to do with age," said Donna. "What makes us a couple is what kinds of people we are."

Eric agrees. "I have a mental image of the ideal female body being about 25, blonde, and shapely. But I don't picture that ideal body as the person to have a good relationship with. It's just an image that I inherited somewhere or other in the course of my life. I measure the quality of our physical relationship and how wonderful it is to make love together, not whether or not Donna matches that image. And I would still have that image if I had met someone who was my age but brunette instead of blonde. She wouldn't fit the image either."

What the men find attractive in these women is their air of self-confidence, their outgoing and authoritative natures, their evident health, and the fact that they are attractive, sexy women promising adventure, new challenges, and a warm, easy responsiveness—qualities they find much more attractive than tight skin and tight buttocks.

Merritt, 42 (married to Tom, 33), described the response she once had from a man two years her senior. "We had been out once," she said, "and this guy told me that he found me very exciting and he wanted to sleep with me, but then he said, 'Don't get any ideas—it's just for the sex,' as if what existed above my neck didn't count. That's an insult, but I don't think it's an uncommon response from an older guy who thinks every woman is after the long-term commitment.

"Tom never once treated me that way. We responded sexually to each other, but we both recognized that that attraction happened on many different levels simultaneously. Because he wasn't afraid of that, I wasn't either—and that's something I think is different with a younger man."

The Older Woman
as the Sexual Aggressor

When people think of the sexual dynamics between an older woman and a younger man, the assumption is usually that she is the more experienced aggressor. Sometimes this is the case, but, even when it is, the relationships are characterized more by an equal-meets-equal attraction than by a student-teacher one.

Diane and Rob have been together for 8 years. At 45, she is 12 years older than he. "I think there's a real misunderstanding from outsiders of the relationship between a woman and a younger man—they think the woman is seducing the inexperienced man," said Diane. "I didn't think Rob was going to be that good in bed, but it had nothing to do with his age. It was more because he is almost androgynous in looks—not a macho-appearing guy. He's slender; he's very graceful in his movements. There's no swagger in him. This androgynous quality is manifested in his almost effete stand-offishness with women. I've watched him with women he's been interested in. He sort of stands back and assesses them. That's very different from the typical macho man style. It's also very sexy. He didn't do what I'm used to men doing when they come on to a woman, which is to be very obvious. He just made his statement and stepped back. With me, he told me how he felt about me and asked me out. When I said I had to think about it, he didn't push; he wasn't pulling any of the numbers I was used to. I found that intriguing. At first, I thought, Maybe he's gay. But I didn't think so after we had sex.

"It was about two weeks after he told me he thought he was falling in love with me that we slept together. And that was real good. I didn't expect it was going to be, but I really enjoyed that. And where I thought he was inexperienced, that was not the case at all."

Diane found that the lack of pressure from Rob, a very different response than from the older man she had been dating, proved provocative and exciting to her. Many women mentioned how not being pressured into sex suddenly makes them feel much more of an equal partner in the early expression of sexual interest. When the woman is allowed to be a more willing partner in the decision to have sex, she also tends to put more of herself into it. Since she gets to decide if she really wants it, she is more likely to make the decision that she wants it to be good, too.

Thus the old stereotype—that the woman is the more sexually experienced of the two—is frequently proven wrong by these couples, adding fun and mystery to the game for both partners. It also relieves either partner of feeling responsible for "showing the way."

The subsequent discovery that each brings different experiences and special interests to their sexual encounter serves to heighten the playfulness and pleasure between them. Attitude plays a major role here, as the women feel strongly that the younger men are better partners for them because the younger men are more open and accepting sexually, of bodies and of sexual practices, than older men. These are women who want more participation in the sexual relationship, and this—much to the surprise and pleasure of the women—is not viewed as intimidating or threatening by the younger men.

Donna, 65, and Eric, 42, reflected all these characteristics in the pattern of their early sexual intimacy. When he invited her to join him on his vacation trip even though their relationship had not yet blossomed into a sexual one, her reaction was spontaneous.

"When Eric said, 'Why don't you come with me?' my first response was, 'Oh, I can't,' " said Donna. "'But he said, 'Of course you can; we can talk about books for hours.' My reaction was that I had been with him for many hours over the years, and I knew him really well, but this changed our relationship. Maybe we had shared two dinners and one lecture, but suddenly everything was very, very different. It scared me to death.

"Here was a guy who is very responsive, very affectionate, and he doesn't have to do much to send out vibes. So when he called me the next day to say, 'Donna, I'm serious; I would just love to travel around the country with you,' I found myself saying, 'I can't promise to keep my hands off you.' He responded with the same enthusiasm. 'I can't promise you, either,' he said.'' Suddenly, they leaped from being teacher and student—as well as good friends—to being a man and a woman on their way to an unexpected adventure. And it was fun.

"I had absolutely no problem getting excited on that trip," said Donna. "I was wet all the time, constantly, and he had an erection for every 500 miles we covered. We had a good time—the sex was great—he was just wonderful.'' They had sex at least once a day on the trip. They were married a year later.

The older woman, unencumbered by fear of pregnancy and often sexually sophisticated due to years of experience and/ or having had several different partners, is quite likely to be a more responsive and interesting sex partner than a younger woman, as we've seen. Her frequent willingness to be the aggressor early in the affair is actually something the younger men find provocative and exciting.

Typically, the woman who feels comfortable taking the sexual initiative is a woman who is at ease with her sexuality and is *not* worried about her body. Part of what allows her to make the first move is her ability to recognize their intense mutual attraction; another is her ability to cope with rejection, especially since the union doesn't seem likely to be long-term due to the age span.

"I think we make the first move because we see an opportunity for truly enjoyable, no-pressure sex, since he is so much younger and not supposed to be someone to marry," said Michelle, 43, who is married to a man 16 years younger but had an earlier relationship also with a younger man.

"We just don't worry about all the details. The age difference made me feel very free about my behavior, and the result was a type of sexual experience different from the usual high-stakes gamble with an older man who was sure I was looking for a marriage partner so he wasn't loose himself. Frankly, I think it's sexier than hell to come on to a younger guy, if it's someone who is going to appreciate it.

"It's a real fantasy come true for two reasons. One, you don't have to sit around and wait for him to tune in. And why should you? An older woman knows she doesn't have time to sit around and play guessing games. Two, there's a feeling of power and control that I know men get out of initiating sex, and I do, too. It worked for me because my younger man wasn't threatened—he responded with as much interest in me. So suddenly you have two grown-ups who are very straightforward, feel good about themselves, and the sex is cataclysmic. Absolutely dynamite."

Michelle is typical of the type of woman who is enjoying her more sexually aggressive behavior. She is tiny, with jet-black hair and eyes, a very vivacious woman. She is also extremely articulate, a behavioral scientist who is considered a leader in her field internationally—a very self-confident woman and one that some older men of her acquaintance find rather intimidating.

Michelle extended the first invitation to a date after she and Henry, 27, met in an exercise class and Henry began walking her home. She sensed that her seniority in his department at the academic institution where they were both teaching made him too shy to ask her out. She and Henry became intimate on their third date when, after hours of discussing their mutual scientific endeavors, she finally interrupted the conversation to kiss him and say, "... why don't we just get a bottle [of wine] and go back to your apartment." Henry went along with the idea. They talked for another hour before Michelle interrupted to say, "I have one more question—are you ever going to kiss me?" They made love that night.

Michelle feels strongly that one reason she was open about her feelings and willing to sleep with Henry so soon was that she had learned to accept her body and her own behavior patterns as perfectly right for her. She felt comfortable in her sexuality, every aspect of it. Eventually, she and Henry married and had a child together.

"I felt good about myself—there was nothing wrong with my body when I met Henry," said Michelle. "I was 39, but it was no worse than when I was 25. I've always run and kept myself in shape. So I never worry about that. I'm going to let my body do what it wants to do. I stopped dieting the minute I got pregnant. And I lost most of the weight anyway. I figure if I'm five pounds over what I was when I got pregnant for the rest of my life and I'm not dieting, who gives a shit? Henry certainly doesn't."

For Terri, a spritely woman who was 30 when she met Denny, a 20-year-old-colleague who charmed her instantly, the appeal of being the one to make the first move stems more from the fact that she prefers to be in control of her relationship.

She remembers her first younger lover with great affection. From him she learned firsthand that age does not beget experience. (She still regrets that their love affair did not lead to marriage because their mutual sexual enjoyment—plus their work relationship and their friendship—was so terrific for her.) "Even though he was only 20, I kept saying to him, 'How did you learn to do these things?' " she recalls, smiling. "I'd been married five years, but I hadn't had those experiences in bed ever. When I was with him, he'd say, 'Let me tell you where to touch me and touch me this way' ... or ... 'that's too rough; this is how you have to do it—take your hand and put—.' I mean, he made me feel like a virgin at the age of 30.

"My former husband had been into just the usual stuff, and suddenly Denny was showing me a whole new way of making love. But it was wonderful, because we shared the lovemaking experience. Not just the sexual things; he taught me how to really love someone—to let the person be whoever he is and love him for it."

Terri often dates younger men as she discovers again and again that they think the way she does and act the way she likes to act, which is quite different from older men. And, knowing how much she enjoys these relationships, she feels free to make the first move. She says of one of her relationships: "We had been working together for six months when I ran into him outside the office and he gave me a big hug. You know how you just feel something? When he hugged me, I felt it. I didn't say anything, but a couple of days later, I called and invited him to lunch. After lunch, we went for a walk, and then, since he didn't have a car, I drove him back. What happened next I'll never forget as long as I live.

"We were sitting in the car, and it was dark, and I said, 'I had the greatest day with you. This is just what I needed.' And as he got ready to get out of my car, I said, 'Kiss me.' He said, 'How do you want me to kiss you?' And I said, 'Any way you want to.'

"So we kissed, and for three years I had an affair with him. That boy—that man—made love to me in my car, on the grass, in his bedroom."

Terri is honest with herself about her need to be the sexual aggressor. "I need to be in control," she said. "Maybe it's my own insecurities, my own craziness, but I need to be on top. When I'm with a younger man, it makes me feel that way—like the ball's in my court—and I like that."

Confident women, like confident men, see what they want and go for it. Some of these women enjoy the rewards of playing what has traditionally been a male role because they can face the risk of rejection; others are simply very open to, even eager for, new sexual experiences. Because there is such a strong sexual component to these love affairs, both the men and the women can be seen as sexual aggressors. As we've seen, who makes "the first move" is determined more by experience and personality than by gender.

What Happens When I'm over the Hill at 65 and He's a Virile 48?

What will happen to our sex life as I get older? As I experience menopause, but my husband is still in the prime of his life, will he leave me for a younger woman? Will I no longer be sexually appealing to him?

I agonized over those questions. Almost every woman I interviewed agonized over those questions, fearing that menopause, sure to occur sooner or later, would doom her relationship with a younger man. Some refused marriage because of that fear.

"When I'm 55, you will be only 42—that's my line to him," said Stephanie. "And that to me is more frightening than our current ages of 43 and 30. And then I think to myself, Does that mean I throw away this person because I don't want 10 good years?"

Stephanie's "10 good years" is a phrase that mirrors exactly what was on my own mind—what happens to Brant and me in 10 years when I reach the age of menopause? As "older women," must we concede that all we have left is "10 good years"? I could think of no woman over the age of 50, whom I have known personally, who appeared to me to be sexually active, much less even interested in sex. My mother was of a generation that did not discuss sex, that denied sexuality by treating it as something to be whispered about. My friends' mothers were the same way.

More than 10 years ago, I began to seek out older women among my acquaintances and colleagues who might serve as role models for the sexually active older woman. I couldn't find any. Then Masters and Johnson really depressed me when I discovered they hastily slot women over age 40 (that's me!)

into the appalling category of "The Aging Female," but don't put our male peers into their own old-age box until they are over age 50! And it didn't help that I couldn't find a single sign of a sexually active older female in any magazine ad or television commercial. (That, as we saw in the last chapter, has begun to change, but only very recently.)

I felt as though I must be exceedingly uninformed. And that surprised me because my work requires that I read dozens of newspapers and magazines regularly—but I wasn't seeing much on this subject. Was I somehow avoiding the issue?

Unfortunately, for too many of us, menopause does not mean change so much as *loss*. It has always had such a negative connotation for me, for example, that I simply avoided books and articles on it, thinking it would go away if I ignored it. I suspect many women do the same. Also, it isn't a subject we discuss among ourselves. If we are too close-mouthed on sex, we are even more so on menopause. (I'm told, by the way, that women in their twenties today are much more open to talking about sex. I hope so.)

When I met Lynn, 37, who has been dating Dan, 30, I hoped to get some answers to my questions about the sexual behavior of older women. Now here was a woman who would have the scoop—she works as a documentary filmmaker for a major media group and specializes in news-breaking, trendy subjects. I was hardly prepared for her to arrive with her own list of questions, and high on her list for me was "Do women have sex after 50?" I am not kidding. "I worry about dried-up organs," said Lynn, as she told me how much she loved Dan but was convinced there was no future in their relationship. "What do you do when you are no longer naturally and easily excited?" she asked.

Many of the younger "older" women I interviewed had several misconceptions about the future of their sex lives. These fears are not, of course, limited to women dating younger men:

- We lose our sexual appeal when we reach menopause. (No one can substantiate why, exactly, but most of us agree it mysteriously vaporizes the day we stop menstruating.)

- Fertility equals sexuality; i.e., if we can't bear children, we must be duds in bed. (We actually buy that line, even after years of using birth control in which we discovered quite the opposite: no worry over pregnancy means much more fun in bed!)
- Our vagina dries up, so sex is terribly painful. (This happens to very few women and is relatively easy to avoid.)
- We must take estrogen in order to keep some vestige of youth, i.e., smooth skin, etc., etc. (Someone has neglected to note that the gentlemen in our age group are also wrinkling and creasing at the same rate and are considered "handsome" for it; perhaps we need a new attitude instead of the pharmacy bills.)
- Older women are sexual neuters. (No one seems to put older men in the same category, though.)

"Well, everything is great right now," said woman after woman about her younger lover, "but I just don't know what will happen when I'm 50 and he's 40 . . . I'm 65 and he's 50 . . . I'm 60 and he's 44. . ."

As we've seen, there is a reason for their worry. We have a basic social bias against older women—we believe that they do not function as whole human beings in their later years. And that's a crime. Not only is that untrue, but it's hurtful. I suspect many women avoid relationships with younger men rather than face the pain of divorce later on because they do not have confidence in their ability to attract *and hold* a man as they age. It is past time for everyone to know the facts about older women's sexuality and the effects menopause does or does not have.

The Truth About Sex
After Menopause

If we believe menopause means the end of sex for women, we are making a terrible mistake. Not only will menopause not endanger our sexual activities, our sexual pleasures, our sexual interests (quite the opposite is likely to happen, and it's time all women knew it), but *as you get older, sex gets better, and the more you do it, the better it feels!* If you want to make love when you're 90, you sure as hell can—so long as you do it when you're 50, 60, 70, and 80.

The very first women I have met who have active sex lives in their later years or *plan to* were the women interviewed for *Loving a Younger Man.* However, all but one of us felt we were winging it because no one knew for sure what the scientific facts are. The only one who wasn't winging it was Michelle, 43 (married to Henry, 27), and she had a role model—her mother!

"I don't feel insecure about sex as I get older," she said, "because my mother may be 73, but she has had men in their fifties attracted to her ever since she's been widowed. She plays tennis every day and has an active sex life—so I don't worry about losing it."

Two months after talking to Michelle, my close friend Chris, 40, described to me films she had seen in a class on sexuality: "We were shown movies of three different couples making love. The first was two teenagers, the second a man and woman in their thirties, and the last an older couple. The last movie was the most sexually arousing to me because the older couple took their time and seemed to enjoy the love-making more. They were the sexiest of the three couples to watch."

I was amazed at how uniformly the women I interviewed reacted: while most were or had been afraid of postmeno-pausal sex, few actually experienced problems with it—and those problems encountered were minimal and easily solved.

The first woman over the age of 50 whom I interviewed was Elinor, 57. I hesitated before asking *the* question. I could sense my own reluctance to know the truth. I was terribly afraid that she might tell me that, indeed, her days with Brad, 39, were numbered. To my amazement and relief, she did not say any such thing.

Elinor's relationship with Brad is thriving. They have been together for nearly 10 years. Menopause was already behind Elinor when she first slept with Brad.

"Menopause has had specific effects," she said. "I'm not medically aware enough to know exactly what goes on, but there's a dryness of the vagina that I didn't have before. It really became a major issue for a short time because the dryness can make intercourse pretty damn painful. I talked to my doctor, and he told me to use an estrogen cream. I do not take the estrogen pills because of the link between estrogen and cancer, but I use the cream about once a week, and it takes care of the problem.

"I don't know if everyone has this dryness. That's the only problem I've had since menopause. Otherwise, I'm fine, and when it comes to my body, I like the way I look a lot more these days."

Her message was loud and clear: yes, there was a *slight* problem, but it was handled easily because a healthy solution is right at hand. No big deal. And yes, Elinor and Brad are a happy, quite sexually active couple.

Donna, 65, has been married to Eric, 42, for three years. "My only serious problem as I am aging is my thin skin that bruises easily," said Donna. "Otherwise, I simply checked with my gynecologist when I had a little dryness of the vagina.

"I take estrogen, and hormones are a help, but better than that is a vaginal cream that my gynecologist prescribed. I use it twice a week. It puts hormones right into the tissues. So if I am a little slow to get wet, I will use that. It's nothing I feel bad about. We use a lot of spit, too. Eric might put something on himself in a way that looks real sexy as though he's not only agreeing but is accepting that this is part of our making love. Or, sometimes, I put it on him. We make it one of the things we do for fun.

"When we make love, I keep thinking it's Eric who's the

wonderful lover, and he keeps saying it's me. I keep thinking that nobody kisses like Eric, and he keeps saying, 'Nobody kisses like you do.' Our relationship is so wonderful because of Eric, yet he thinks it's because of me—but he's such a joy to live with.''

Again, a singular truth that I have found in each of these relationships between women and younger men surfaces in her words as Donna describes how she and Eric enjoy mutual pleasures and a sharing of their feelings for one another—an equal partnership in the bedroom.

Today, 14 years since their first sexual encounter, Carolyn, 74, and Ed, 59, are an exceptionally attractive couple, very healthy and stalwart. She is recently retired from one top-level corporate position and has just begun a new career marketing a product of her own design. She is an excellent role model for women looking for examples of how to age gracefully, stay professionally active, and maintain a healthy, sexually rewarding marriage.

Ed is the manager of a small manufacturing firm. He courted Carolyn with unflagging enthusiasm even though she told him when they first met that, since she was 59 and he was only 44, she thought he was too young because "the age difference embarrasses me." They have been married 14 years.

"My first wife had a problem with lubrication even in her twenties, but Carolyn has never had that difficulty," said Ed. "Sometimes, if she is out of town for a while and we haven't had sex for a week or so, it might take her a little longer to build up her responsiveness, but she always gets interested. She tells me she really enjoys it. We try to have sex three or four times a week.

"She has these women friends who are surprised that she hasn't given it up. But we laugh because we figure half the reason they don't have sex is because their husbands gave it up a long time ago. I plan on our sex life going on for at least another 5 or 10 or 20 years!"

John, 57 (married to Lillian, 72), is outspoken about older men and their effect on women's self-images when he decries the attitudes of the men married to Lillian's friends.

"I think the only reason more women in my wife's peer group aren't having good sex," he said, "is because they can't get it from their lousy husbands." He has a point. Many women pointed out to me in our interviews that one reason they are attracted to younger men is their vitality and general good health.

"I'm 58," said Katherine, "and I have kept myself in good physical condition over the last 30 years, while many men my age have retired and gone to pot. I don't want to be with some old codger who wants to put his feet up in front of the TV. I'm ready to go."

The women interviewed for *Loving a Younger Man* are definitely "ready to go," and that energy is reflected in their sex lives. How they see themselves is clear from how they act.

New literature on the subject of our sexuality as we age reinforces what these women told me and explains why they are able to be sexually active as they age:

• *Age has been found to increase a woman's capacity for sexual enjoyment* due to the large and complex network of veins in the genital area that develop over time and lead to heightened feelings of sexual excitement, especially in women who have had children.

Even women who have not had children will enjoy this advantage if they stay sexually active by having sexual intercourse, masturbating, or achieving sexual arousal in some other manner several times a week.

Women have learned that regular exercise will keep their bodies fit and healthy—and attractive—well into old age. This principle also must be applied to the genital areas. Today's woman should look at masturbation or any form of sexual stimulation as a distinctly pleasurable "genital exercise," which will help her maintain vaginal health. She should not hesitate to use any aids that might facilitate this, such as films, magazines, books, fantasies, etc.

In other words, the news is that a woman has a choice: use it or lose it. It is the exact same choice faced by a man her age.

• *"Your vagina is not going to wither away with the pas-*

sage of time," says Susan Flamholtz Trien in her book *Change of Life: The Menopause Handbook* (New York: Fawcett Columbine, 1986).

Trien provides valuable insight into the physical changes that occur as you age. Perhaps the greatest service she provides is her dismissal of my fear—*our* fear as older women—of the frightening term *vaginal atrophy*.

"Indeed, many women are not even aware of any vaginal changes at all," said Trien. She describes how vaginal walls will become thinner and the vaginal secretions less acidic, and she explains a few problems that may result. None are serious. While the lubrication of the vagina in a younger woman occurs about 10 to 30 seconds after stimulation, a woman of 50 or 60 may notice that it takes 1 to 5 minutes and it may be less than she used to have.

"However," says Trien, "the decline in lubrication is not usually a sudden thing. A woman may begin to notice occasional dryness in her forties, but that it gets progressively worse in her fifties and sixties. Then again, some women never experience any noticeable changes in lubrication at all."

She cites a study by Masters and Johnson that inquired into the reason why several women in their sixties lubricated as quickly and rapidly as women ages 20 to 30, in spite of having vaginal walls that were very thin. "The secret to their youthful sexual functioning? All three had maintained an active sex life (intercourse at least one to two times a week) throughout their mature adult years. They were the only ones in the study to have maintained sex at that rate."

Thus, what Trien documents is also corroborated by other researchers when she says, "Regular sexual activity, at least once or twice a week, seems to keep the vagina moist and elastic, and more easily lubricated."

• *The mature woman often has fewer inhibitions and a greater knowledge of how to please her lover* than a less experienced younger woman.

We know this from earlier chapters of this book. However, the general public is just beginning to find this out. The point to be noted here is that the *menopausal* woman is in a particularly advantageous position because she is liberated from both the fear of pregnancy and the nuisance of birth control. However, women choosing new partners today will, in light of the AIDS epidemic, want to give careful consideration to the use of condoms.

• *The hormone levels of the mature woman undergo changes that increase both her libido, or sexual urge, and her sexual pleasure.* This occurs because ovaries and adrenal glands continue to produce her male hormones, known as *androgens,* or the "sexual turn-on" hormones, even as her female hormones, the estrogens, decline. This means the androgens are no longer opposed by estrogen and, consequently, exert a more powerful force, leading to a stronger sexual urge.

On the other hand, there is a great deal of confusing information out there on female hormones and their use for the woman in mid-life. I do not wish to get involved in the many controversial aspects of that—with an attitudinal change toward our bodies, such concern soon may be outdated. However, if the use of estrogen supplements interests you, please seek good medical advice.

Perhaps most encouraging are some statistics Trien cites in her book, statistics that are of particular interest to women involved with younger men. A study of 800 men and women aged 60 to 91 showed that these people were as sexually active as 40-year-olds.

Of the 478 women polled, *42.1 percent said sex was better after menopause,* 44.7 percent said there was no change, and only 13.2 percent said that it was worse.

Broadening Sexual Horizons

"Over the years our sex keeps getting better," said Diane, 45, who has been married to Rob, 33, for 5 years after living with him for 3. "I have less worry about getting pregnant. I think I'm becoming less concerned about how I look. I find myself getting freer about sex as I get older.

"Rob had a lot of experience with sex in college and afterward, while I had nothing like that at all. At first, he was more familiar with oral sex than I was, and it's been real interesting to get more into that. Also, Rob has this thing about pornography and a thing about tits. He buys tit magazines and tit movies, and I've kind of gotten into it. Sometimes we've filmed ourselves having sex and then get turned on by our own videotapes. I find it's interesting that the visual part of our making love turns me on, but hearing it really bothers me. I have to turn the soundtrack off.

"Sometimes we'll start our weekend with great sex. I'll come home from work on Friday night, and he'll be watching a tit movie and waiting for me—I have no problem with that."

You are likely to be struck by the women's willingness to try new things in the bedroom, whether it's using X-rated movies for arousal or enjoying oral sex.

These are couples who have been together for over five years, and it's exhilarating to see that the level of sexual excitement between them remains high because both partners keep spontaneity, fun, mutual satisfaction, and love uppermost on their list of reasons why loving one another is the best part of their lives together. Even more important, each sees the other as a sexy and exciting bed partner.

Merritt, 42, has been married to Tom, 33, for 5 years, after meeting 7 years ago. Her view of their sexual enjoyment is conditioned by her attitude toward her age and his.

"Now that we're married and life has settled down, we block out special times to really get into sex because it's one of the terrific things we love about each other," said Merritt. "We're like kids; we play around in bed. Sometimes we put up a mirror so we can watch ourselves make love. And he's the first man I've ever known that I could be open with about X-rated movies and books. I haven't felt embarrassed to share these with him. We really get turned on together reading those old Victorian sex novels, too.

"But on a deeper level, our sexual grounding is a very crucial element of our life. That's why, at first—and this was just before we got married—I was sort of hesitant because while we were having sex we would achieve this almost mystical union sometimes, and I thought my getting older ahead of him would diminish that in some way. I mean, it was so painful to think about that I ended up in tears. Finally I decided to go ahead and take the chance because . . . well, why not? I guess I could be killed in a car accident tomorrow just as easily.

"Our ages make a big difference between us in bed, and it's all great. He is someone who really knows how to perform oral sex, which I was very shy of. The other men I had slept with either expected blow-jobs as if this were part of my 'duty,' or they wanted to go down on me, but didn't really understand how delicate I am down there. I just found it all very awkward.

"But Tom had had more experience and a different understanding of oral sex. He had learned from women what *they* wanted. So he taught me this new approach that is truly pleasurable and exciting. He has a much slower, more fantasy kind of approach to it. And he never made me feel I *had* to do it.

"On the other hand, I'm the one who wasn't afraid to let go when we first started sleeping together. He told me that's different from younger women—that I'm comfortable with my body and I have orgasms easily. My nonchalance about that loosened him up because he had a tendency to hold back.

"Right now, our lovemaking is beyond what I ever thought a man and woman could experience. There are times when we are so close that I find myself able to totally cut loose of rational thought and float on this level of pure sensual pleasure with him. I'm not afraid to let go, he's not afraid, and we achieve a kind of sexual high, a level of physical and emotional ecstasy. I thought that happened only in novels. I didn't think you could really do that."

All of the women I interviewed shared what they felt was a unique, special sexual bond with their younger lovers. Physiologically, sex is getting better for the woman as she ages; a younger lover, still strong and with a higher libido than many men her age, matches her well. Sexually experienced, she is aware of her sexual needs, freer because she isn't worried about pregnancy, better able to please herself and a man because of her acquired skills, and more willing to experiment; all of these qualities appeal to a younger man. But the bond transcends physical desire when two loving people are able—through sex—to communicate deeply.

Michelle, 43 (married to Henry, 27), read an essay, originally published in *The Massachusetts Review* in 1974, when she was considering the possibility of marriage to Henry, part of which explains—as well as words can—the power of sex between a woman and a younger man. It was written by Dorothy Pitkin, two weeks before she died at the age of 75. She had been a wife, a mother, a worker, a writer, and an enormously strong woman—bucking the social attitudes of her time—and very perceptive about the meaning of a long love affair between her and a younger man. Her words were deeply inspirational to Michelle.

In the following paragraphs, you will find Dorothy's description of her feelings toward her younger lover to be filled with the same ecstatic wonder and the same agonizing pain that so many women experience when they first fall in love with a younger man. Like most of the women interviewed, she met her lover through her work. Their love affair, too, was grounded in the intellectual and emotional pull between them, as well as their strong sexual desire for each other.

Her love for him, deep, abiding, and sensual, lasted until her death. I don't know if she married that man. I don't know who he is and how he felt those last years. I don't think that is important. What matters is her struggle and her triumph as she deals with the stereotypes. She is open about her worry that he will see her as "the mother," and her magnificent writing shows how he turns that fear into a positive, sexual response.

I was twenty years older than he was. At first he was my student in the Photography Department at the college. He was then twenty years old and that would make me forty at that time. I was well known as a photographer of all the important happenings, he took my classes, and I became interested in his way of seeing things. He was direct and objective, not trying to make the oblique, the super dramatic angle. For instance, at the time of the mine cave-in, when men were trapped in the pocket of the mine, I would take a dramatic thing of it, like the faces of the relatives showing them contorted with fear, or something like a small child crying, or maybe the red jacket left behind the trapped in place. This he accepts as a way of showing the devastation, he accepts it as a way of showing the meaning of the experience, from a subtle way of doing it. He says, yes, this is interesting. Always the off-beat angle. He is with it, he says. He agrees with me, but never takes it over entirely. I am aware of his nonacceptance, unspoken, but there it is. One day I become outspoken, in my annoyance . . . "Look, you might be my son. I can ask you, why do you not come right out and tell me what you object to, it would be better if you came right out and say you do not like it, as you would if you were really my son." "Your son? Listen, I am not your son. You know how I feel about you. I am definitely not your son." And suddenly it happens. He tilts my head up and kisses my cheek. "This is the way a son would greet his mother. And this is the way I feel about you." Suddenly his lips are pressed with passion on my lips. "We may as well face it right now, you are not my mother. I am not your son." "Yes, Mother? Is this right, Mother?" Always the slight mockery, implied in everything he says or does. But now it comes out in the open. He is a lover. He never says lover, he shows how he feels by the passionate kiss, mouth on mouth. "Tell me, is this how you feel about me," he asks through the kiss, his mouth pressed passionately on my mouth. "Yes? Yes?" "Tell me yes." And I feel the passionate flood of feeling rush over me. He is not a son but a lover. "Yes," I whisper through the kiss, his mouth on mine. "Yes," I whisper helplessly. "And it has always been this way? Say yes." "Yes," I whisper with his teeth pressed on mine.

There was that walk which we took through the beech woods, and after that nothing was the same. Then it all came out—what we had both been hiding or rather we acknowledged the feeling we had always had. The beech woods had a small brook running along the middle. When we came to the dense part of the woods, he said, "Take a step towards the right of the brook. Never mind the rocks and stones, I have a hold of you." It seemed to me he had chosen the worst part of the brook. "Come on, you can do it, Mother." The "Mother" came out in a tone of sarcasm, though he had used "Mother" before. We had used it I kiddingly before, I once told him I thought of him as a son. "I have never had a son, now you can be one." That was when I was correcting one of the papers I had given him to do. A summary of what photography comprises today. "It is an art, and you must employ it as an art. Take the most significant parts of the picture and make what you can of them. That is the way it is done, son." And it was then that we jumped over the brook. And the beech woods walk became the symbol of our relationship. Son, lover, lover, son. . . . Now a lover.

Now in the Nursing Home, I see him so clearly. The way he looked when we jumped over the brook and the way he looked when he tilted my face to kiss my cheek and the passionate face when he kissed my mouth, and I thought things will never be the same. This is my lover. Now that I am in the Nursing Home, I see him so clearly, the male blond hair, his skin smooth as a woman's, but the male mouth, and his blue eyes. Some might say a killer's blue, sharp and clear, but a lover's blue too. Maybe the two went together, the killer's blue, and the lover's blue.

Now when I wake at the Nursing Home, I remember how I used to wake in the little apartment near the beech woods. I would wake and think something good is going to happen today. Then the happiness would steal over me. He is coming today. And I will set the table with the red and white tablecloth. And set the candles in the Italian candle holders. And the cheese will be provolone and oh yes, the wine will be Liebfraumilch, the wine he likes. Today there is going to be a celebration as today he is going to be forty, twenty years younger than me. And often before I would think twenty years younger. Now he is thirty and I am fifty, and this is the way it will always be, I am twenty years older than he.

We were sitting in the room in twilight. This was how we liked to sit, no lights yet. The evening light fell on his hair and it was a soft male blond.

After dinner we talked about this business of older? Younger? And how it affected our relationship. You might think it was something indecent, for a woman, to be twenty years older than the man she loved. Probably it belonged to the Victorian days, when a woman was supposed to need the support of the man she loved. She was supposed to be weaker than the male, in need of help in everything she did or did not do. The man must be older than the woman to give her that support.

She ends her essay with a few final phrases, and then she says, ". . . time is at the turning. Evening is turning into night. The arc of the sky is filled with great bands of sunset. Birds are flying high. . . ."

Sex may well be sweeter for a woman with a younger man because it tastes of the forbidden, because it is unexpected and unexpectedly wonderful, because, biologically, his needs are in tune with hers. But, as Pitkin suggests, deep sexual understanding with the one you love puts a woman at peace with herself and the world. That kind of understanding knows no boundaries of age or time. A Diane finds a Rob—who loves her body, her lush breasts—and he could be 24 or 54. Whether because of the age difference or in spite of it, sex between these men and women works. And that's all that matters.

6

The New Power Principle: How Women with Younger Men Establish Equal Partnerships

Male domination has had some very unfortunate effects. It has made the most intimate of human relations, that of marriage, one of master and slave, instead of one between equal partners.

—Bertrand Russell

Many professional couples say their careers have an energizing effect on their relationships . . . [they] say an arrangement that leaves them wanting more of each other is perhaps healthier than one that would seduce them into taking each other for granted.

—*New York* magazine

What happened between Brant and me is very typical of many older woman/younger man couples. In the beginning, our relationship was founded on and developed from our mutual interest in communications—specifically, newspapers. That was the kind of work we had individually chosen for ourselves and were involved in before we met. Then, like the other couples, our relationship was bolstered because we shared the same values, pressures, curiosity about the business, and career goals.

This became very apparent during the first two years we were together. Shortly after he moved to the same city where I was living, I became the chief spokesperson for a statewide political campaign that pitted two major American transportation groups, the railroads and the trucking industry, against each other. In a role much like that of a political candidate, I had to debate the issues on radio and television and lobby for legislation—politically sensitive tasks that put me under enormous pressure from the press.

Brant is a tough-minded and unrelentingly fair member of that press. Throughout the campaign, and especially when the issues were at their most sensitive, Brant gave me sound, expert advice that guided me through the hazards that mine a political arena where millions of dollars are at stake. His advice on how to be fair, balanced, and honest with the press was a major factor in our final victory.

At the same time, I was able to help him in his new position with a major midwestern newspaper. My many years in the community, my previous experience as a business writer, and my immediate involvement in the political campaign provided me with a base of contacts in business and politics that proved invaluable to Brant. Our ability to provide each other with advice, sources, and contacts continues today. The overlap between our two areas of media expertise has led to several joint projects. Since we are professionally in sync, our conversations are generally about things that matter to both of us.

Like many older woman/younger man couples, we have gotten to know each other best *because* of our roles in the workplace. We both work hard and like it and enjoy being able to talk our careers over with someone who cares. We have seen each other resolve tough work problems and learned that we handle job pressures in similar ways, which leads to a mutual understanding. If I had any unresolved questions regarding Brant's emotional maturity because of his age, they were answered after we guided each other through some tough work situations.

As you will see, our work and relationship patterns—and those of the couples interviewed—reflect a significant change in social patterns for certain men and women today. They signify a new power principle in which a man and a woman choose to be together because they discover they have the kinds of personalities that can *work* together as well as play together. They share equally in the rewards and demands of home and career. But it takes a new kind of woman and a new kind of man to want this and to be able to achieve it.

The women interviewed said again and again that a major difference in their relationships was that their new roles in the workplace did not threaten the younger men the way they did older ones. Several of them said they had been called "ballbreakers" by their male peers—either men working with them or those formerly involved with them in a personal relationship—while younger men simply do not respond to the women's ambitions and outgoing ways with such hostility.

As mentioned earlier, Lynn, 37, marveled at the immediate attraction she seemed to hold for her younger lover: "He's not angry at me," she said. It's an eloquent line—and one that makes it clear the younger man does not feel threatened, has the internal resources to feel comfortable with a talented, accomplished woman, and is willing to be half of a partnership in which equal power is wielded by both.

The women interviewed made it clear that, because they work and are happy to shoulder half or more of the burden of financing and running a home, they want men who have the energy to meet them halfway, the courage to share lives, the open-mindedness to be interested in new ideas and change, and the willingness to respect the goals, personal and professional, of both partners.

Because they meet at work, where the sharing of and the follow-through on responsibilities is crucial to gaining respect from fellow workers, it follows that the same expectation of equal sharing in responsibility and rewards should occur outside the office and within the relationship.

"One of the things that really annoyed me about my first marriage was that my wife was not contributing anywhere near a fair share to the upkeep of things. That really bummed me out,'' said Brad, 39 (living with Elinor, 57).

Brad's strong feelings are shared by Amanda, 41 (married to Steve, 32), who said, ''I have never been able to comprehend the role of the housewife—to be at home and fully financially supported is something I have a big problem with. And I cannot understand women who are at home complaining that their husband doesn't get up at night with the baby if he's the only one going out every day to earn a living. I've been out earning a living for 13 years, and it's not easy. To live with the strains of your job and also know you're the one everyone's depending on is very tough. And I never want Steve to feel he's the only one pulling the load—nor do I want to feel that way. So he knows that if he ever wants to quit this job in order to make a change, he can. I am happy to work full-time.''

The egalitarian quality of these relationships is a direct result of each partner's feeling that he or she carries an equal share of the financial responsibility for the joint household: equal money means equal power. Most of the women strive for this kind of equality in their relationships. As Michelle, 43 (married to Henry, 27), said, ''My first husband was very well-to-do, so I knew what I was giving up. This is a marriage with a much more equal balance of power. But Henry is a graduate student, and I do find that all this makes him tense, and when he is tense, he tends to withdraw. So I've committed the next two years to putting his priorities first. Any objective person can see that the sooner he finishes his graduate work, the better off we will all be. What that means is I'm trying to take up the slack, give him more time.

''So sometimes I'll be in the kitchen doing the dishes because I know he needs to veg out. But when I need it, *he's* in the kitchen. He's taken on a whole set of household responsibilities that my first husband wouldn't even discuss. There's no question that I feel I am really stretched to the limit. I'm exhausted when I get to bed at night. And it's not because I'm older—it's because I have too goddamn much to do.

''Sometimes I find myself thinking—when I'm feeling sorry

for myself—'Here I am, slave to another man and his fucking career.' But then I say to myself, 'This man deserves it. He's giving an awful lot back in return.' ''

It is no coincidence that we're seeing more equality in marriage as women have entered the work force and become independent, self-sufficient individuals. Their attitudes have become more like men's. Their needs also have converged with those of men.

That this is happening was illustrated by a recent study commissioned by *Cosmopolitan* magazine. ''The Report on the Changing Life Course of Women'' found that, as late as 1970, 18 percent of college women were in college to find a husband. In 1980, just 10 years later, the number of women in college to get their ''Mrs.'' degree had dropped to 1 percent! This means most women, like men, are attending college in order to prepare for the work world.

The same study showed that, in 1970, 21 percent of college women and 31 percent of college men considered career preparation the prime function of their college education, but by 1980, 40 percent of women and 43 percent of men said they went to college to pursue a career. This means that, while men's values have not changed much, today's women place much more emphasis on their careers than women did 10 years ago. Thus, men's and women's values are converging—becoming more equal.

The *Cosmopolitan* study noted another interesting change in women's attitudes: in 1952, almost 90 percent of college women said family life was more important than careers, while only 6 percent said career was more important. Thirty-one percent of college men placed career before family in that year, while 60 percent said family was more important. By 1974, a radical change had occurred: 23 percent of college women and 29 percent of college men placed career before family, while just 57 percent of women and 48 percent of men placed family before career. Again, the attitudes of women and men are converging.

While the *Cosmo* study reports on the attitudes of younger (nonworking) women, the college women surveyed reflect a change in the attitudes of women overall. It appears that the image of a "woman" is becoming one and the same with the image of a "working woman." The attitude of many of today's working women is exemplified by these words spoken by Elinor, 57 (living with Brad, 39): "I certainly wasn't looking for someone to take care of me [when I met Brad], which many women my age might be doing. That's never been a factor in my life—I've always supported myself. In my first marriage, we both worked and struggled together, and in my second marriage, I contributed more financially because he had a wife and children from his first marriage. So I have never been taken care of. In the later years of my career, I earned a very good salary, and I have my own retirement plan. I've never felt bad about taking care of myself, probably because of my background—not only have I worked all my life, but my mother always worked. So that has never been an issue."

Elinor is a woman whose attitudes are ahead of her time, relative to her age group. Yet she reflects exactly the attitude you will hear expressed by women in the work force today. I can't think of a single woman I know under the age of 40 who expects to be taken care of by a man for the rest of her life.

New Patterns in Intimacy

Even as her attitudes toward education and career become more and more like her male peer's, one personality characteristic of the older woman has not changed—and it is one that sets her apart from a man her own age. She refuses to discount or undervalue her role as a nurturer and caretaker. This is also a key personality trait that makes life with her very attractive to a younger man. Thus, she forges a new pattern for herself in work and love as she merges her traditional sex role as the nurturer, the person sensitive to the needs of others and responsible for maintaining familial and emotional relationships, with her new, more malelike qualities such as the capacity for autonomous thinking, clear decision making, and immediate action. It has been necessary and satisfying for her to incorporate the "masculine" and "strong" characteristics of personal autonomy and maturity in order to perform well, particularly in a managerial capacity, but all the women interviewed took care not to forfeit their feminine characteristics while doing so. Instead, each worked to combine the hallmarks of the decision-making role with the best of the traditional female role. This meant the women placed equal value on intimacy and love relationships, on their roles as nurturers and caretakers, and on their performances as successful career women. They want to have it all, and they work hard to balance the complex roles that are needed in order to succeed in the office and at home.

I think one reason this is so often true of women with younger men is that most of the women have had families or earlier relationships—they understand how important it is to them to be able to nurture. I know that living apart from my children for three months was a wrenching change for me. I simply could not abandon the role of nurturer. For the first time, I understood how deeply fulfilling being a mother was for me. What is true for me was true of many of the women interviewed: we want to be mothers. Motherhood was very fulfilling to the women who had children. Several of the women who had not had children regretted not having had the experience, while others said they had made their decision not to have children and were very content with that decision. Unlike younger women, who may not have resolved the question of whether or not motherhood is right for them, the older women who have had children *know* it was right for them. They are comfortable as nurturers.

This acceptance of the role of the nurturer is apparent in the woman's approach to the people around her. "She's so outgoing, so warm, so responsive," said many of the younger men about the older women they knew, and it is that quality of caring, of kind nurturing, that emanates from the woman who is at ease with her feminine traits. Such warmth was cited again and again as one big reason for the attraction of the younger man to the older woman, and, not surprisingly, it is a trait the woman values in a man as well. Elinor, 57 (living with Brad, 39), cited his genuine concern for his colleagues—his willingness to help them—as something she noticed and liked about him immediately. This was true of all the couples: an immediate and mutual recognition of a pattern of warmth and caring. It is particularly nice for the women that the younger men are more nurturing than older men since these women have learned how important it is to *be nurtured,* and they have learned to feel confident in expressing their need for nurturing as well.

Michelle, 43 (married to Henry, 27), is an excellent example of the woman who is both a leader in her field and a nurturer. She takes care to maintain an open, warm, constant communication with her husband. It was their mutual appreciation of their nurturing sides that also led them to decide to have a child of their own together. Michelle said she felt Henry would make a wonderful father, and Henry said that one reason he felt comfortable marrying Michelle was that he could see she "was a good mother" to her three children—a warm, caring woman.

"We keep our problems on the table," said Henry, appreciative of the value his wife places on harmony and communication in their personal lives. "You can't be married to Michelle and not do that. My natural instinct is not to be very open. But her makeup is exactly the opposite—she brings things out. That's one of the things I needed in my life. I will always work on that. And marriage to her certainly pushes me to do that. I think I knew that when I got into it. That's part of the reason I married her.

"I also think there's an attraction for certain men to women who are older, have children, play more of a motherly role than a 20-year-old who is just starting out in life. That is the truth for me. I have a positive image of my mother, and one of the things that certainly attracted me to Michelle was the knowledge that she was a good mother."

Like Henry, many of the younger men said they found older women to be sensitive to their needs for intimacy and skilled at reinforcing patterns of intimacy within the relationship. What is notable is that the younger men recognize the value of that intimacy. That reflects a new attitude among men, as older men traditionally consider a desire for emotional intimacy to be "weak" and "female."

Said Henry, "I think the men of Michelle's generation are very different from the men of my generation—and that difference is greater than if you compare differences between generations of women. The kinds of assumptions and values that I grew up with have changed so radically from the assumptions and values of men growing up in the '50s and early '60s. I think that's because they are more vested in the system, their careers, everything. So they have a harder time changing and developing as individuals than women do.

"Look at Michelle. She grew up as a part of that generation, but she has changed with the times. She's the career woman that is so unusual among her peers but who women of the '80s now take for granted. But as Michelle has changed and developed over the years, the men of her generation haven't. They've made certain assumptions, they've stuck with those assumptions, and it's much harder for them. When Michelle was looking for a relationship or marriage—a long-term situation—I think it was hard for her to find men her own age with whom she was compatible because of all the changes in her own life and because she knew the kind of life she wanted to lead. For me, it wasn't difficult to be with her. I have my own problems and my own issues, but they're certainly not those of the '50s generation. I don't have *that* much to get over. I'm much more flexible because I grew up when I did."

Elinor agrees with Henry's observation. She said, "Brad's generation didn't get all those awful values the men my age did. Because of that, I think he's an unusually unbigoted guy in lots of ways, but about women especially. He is intelligent and analytical—but he is also a *sensitive* person."

Why is this true for younger men? As we will explore in more depth in Chapter 9, the younger men who are attracted to older women not only display the traditional male sex-role characteristics (confidence, autonomy) but, as a result of being raised by mothers who were affected by the women's movement of the '60s and '70s, they also value intimacy, relationships, and the role of the nurturer and caretaker. Their mothers taught them two important tenets in life: that it is good to be independent and strong, but it is also good to understand and share your feelings. These mothers taught their daughters likewise, so younger men have come of age as the sons of women for whom life has changed significantly since the '70s and as the brothers of women who have been raised in a new age of feminism.

Some people think growing up in different decades would be a disadvantage for older woman/younger man couples, but these couples have been significantly influenced by the video revolution, which has meant that, even though younger men may not have lived through certain historic experiences with the women they love, they have been raised in the age of television and consequently exposed to news media coverage of events both current and historic. Because of ongoing revivals of interest in old television programs and rock and roll's "golden oldies," artifacts of years past are very much with us today. In that way, these couples do have a shared history (often from a better-researched perspective), not unlike couples in which both partners are the same age.

More critical to the shared values between these men and women is a second influencing factor: individual experiences such as marriage, divorce, parenthood, work experience, and personal traumas. The ability to share elements of these with another person in order to understand each other more fully has a significant impact on our relationships and on how we want to live our lives.

All the men and women interviewed have experienced the personal trauma of losing an earlier marital or love partner. And all of them felt that earlier difficult experiences in their personal relationships were the main reason they now value intimacy and time together over more material goals. It is probably the single most important reason they choose to overlook the age difference: they have learned through the difficult experience of ending previous relationships that, relative to all of life's rewards and joys, the value of a relationship with a person whom you can love and understand—and who can do the same for you—outweighs most other considerations.

"Sometimes it works so well," said Amanda, 41 (married to Steve, 32), of their mutual understanding of personal values. "I just lost a close member of my family, and Steve was so sympathetic and comforting and supportive. He surprised me with his insight, but this is so important to me—not whether I look good or worry about younger women, but that we're together on psychological issues. Some people can't handle things like death. But we think the same way, and we're closer today because of it."

The Premium on Time

Not surprisingly, most of the older woman/younger man couples interviewed choose to spend more time together rather than work overtime for more money. And, in turn, they choose to spend more of their money doing things together than on acquiring material goods such as houses and cars. Again and again, the women told me how they were delighted finally to find men who shared their own enthusiasm for quality, not quantity, in life.

"In the long run, I'm not very materialistic," said Michelle. "I want things that will make my life easier, and that's all—although I'm a woman, so I like pretty things more than Henry does. He's very nonmaterialistic, except he loves computers. I think we have very similar tastes."

Henry agrees. "I have a very strong sense of myself; I have a very strong sense of family, of what I want in a family, of what I want in my career. That means we can share a lot, but we are not competing. We struggle with the things all couples do. Each person brings certain strengths, certain weaknesses. With us, because of the difference in our ages, those issues are very up front. If we find we have different values in some area, we consider the age difference right away to see if we are looking at these things differently because of that. Then we agree to work it out.

"Whereas, I think, in relationships where the expectations are more traditional, all those things would only bring anxiety and a lot of confusion and a lot of people dealing with their egos.''

Materialism isn't as great an issue for a couple like Michelle and Henry where money is tight. Diane, 45, and Rob, 33, are in a different situation because her earning level is high and his business is thriving. Their annual income is close to $1 million, but their value system remains the same.

"We vacation a lot," said Diane, describing how important their time together is. "That's how we check in with each other to be sure we're having some fun in our lives. I think I'm a little different from many women my age because I don't want to own anything. I see owning as another responsibility. I don't want a car, I don't want a summer house, I don't want a mink coat. Rob feels as I do—so we agree on how to use our money, and that's to vacation together.'' They have found that three- and four-day trips are manageable within their work schedules, giving them the frequent breaks they need and can easily afford.

"Part of John's being different from other people is that he doesn't care about possessions; he doesn't care about prestige and status—all of which I like about him," said Lillian, 72, of her 57-year-old husband. "He has no competitiveness about him either, and he's not antifeminist. So our styles may be different, but our values are alike.''

Brad, 39, and Elinor, 57, also feel that shared values are important to the success of their relationship. "Basically, I think what makes a relationship endure or not endure has nothing to do with age," says Brad. "It's going to be about whether or not we want to do things together, whether or not we are paying attention to one another, and our different needs from one another.'' Says Elinor of Brad, "I love his sweetness. I like his manner, his professionalism, and how, in a low-key way, he is a very giving kind of person.''

Eric, 42, recalls how he fell in love with Donna, 65, during a time when he was trying to add a new focus to his life. "I wanted to be able to structure my life so that things happened more spontaneously—life could just unfold and happen," he said. "I'm able to live that way with Donna. I've found we have some days that are terrific and some that aren't, but we are able to stay together in the process of having things unfold. This is the best relationship I have found, ever, because it's part of how I want to live my life.''

No Ego-Bashing

A commitment to communication and mutual support is also important to these couples. Each man and woman I interviewed for this book expressed relief and pride that within their relationships they were able to establish an atmosphere in which an exchange of bad feelings could be handled as healthily and easily as the good feelings.

It's interesting how several of the women attribute their ease in this communication quite specifically to their age difference. ''My first husband was two years older than I,'' said Merritt, 42 (married to Tom, 33), ''and communication was a serious problem for us. He had an attitude that women basically have nothing of importance to say. And it wasn't just him. I felt this in his friends, and I frequently run into it among older men I work with. It has been such a frustration that I vowed—and this was before I met Tom—that I would never get myself into a relationship again where my opinions weren't as important as the other guy's.

''When I first met Tom, I was very up-front about my feelings, both positive and negative, and I've stayed that way. I am older, I've had certain experiences, and I know my opinion is important. He has never had a problem with this. I would say definitely that being older has made it easier for me to feel open about my ideas. It's like I can't be intimidated because I am older and I do know certain things from experience. At the same time, Tom is different from older men I know because he expects *all* women to have the right to voice their opinions, as long as they are fair and intelligent about it.''

Michelle, 43 (married to Henry, 27), expressed the same appreciation of her husband's willingness to keep communication open when she said, ''From the very beginning, I liked the fact that Henry *listened* to me. I have a tendency to talk a lot, and he listened with a lot of intelligence, so we spend a lot of our time talking.''

Elinor, 57 (living with Brad, 39), feels that her willingness to disagree with Brad is different from her pattern when she was younger. ''In my early relationships, I didn't feel that sure of my ground, so I wasn't open about my feelings. I didn't stand up for myself, and my relationships didn't work out. So this time, I felt strongly that I should say how I felt and not go through another period where I felt put down. I've made the mistakes, and I know what doesn't work, so I speak up. But it has taken me a long time to get to this point. I hope younger women today have more self-confidence and self-respect and argue more easily with their men, but I'm not sure if that's true.''

One reason women have traditionally been hesitant to speak up with their husbands or lovers is that a forceful woman is considered ''bossy.'' In the work world, she is considered to be unattractively aggressive (versus assertive). But because the women in these relationships have learned (through their work) that their word is valuable *and* valued, they extend that new self-confidence in expressing their opinions to their personal lives. And, time and again, women told me they found the younger men to be much more comfortable than older men with the woman who knows what she wants and is not afraid to say so.

Henry is very aware of the attitude older men often have toward women's opinions and addresses it in a way that reflects the responses of the other younger men interviewed.

''Sure, Michelle bosses all of us around sometimes,'' he said, ''but I feel that, if it's important, I can boss her around and fight back. That's what I think an egalitarian marriage is all about. You can't be equal or change relationships between men and women without having both people be strong, both people speaking out, both people saying what's on their minds. I think the whole thing about women bossing younger men around has to do with the fact that that's the way it was— men always bossed women around. Therefore, any woman who opens her mouth is necessarily going to be looked at as a bossy woman.

"It doesn't bug me to have a woman around who has had all these experiences. I think many other men of my age and certainly older men would feel incredibly insecure about having somebody else—like your wife—have all this knowledge that you don't have. But that just doesn't scare me. There are a hell of a lot of advantages to it. And I also know that what I bring to the relationship is different and important."

In a way, the openness and ease with which the older woman/younger man couples communicate—both in talking and listening—underscores a reinforcement of mutual self-esteem that is yet another deep expression of love. John, 57 (married to Lillian, 72), took pride in his role as the "listener" for his high-powered executive wife. "I think I contributed in part to her success," he said with a gentle smile. "Every Friday night for the first three years we were together, I would pick her up at the train and, during our drive to the farm, listen to her talk and unwind for an hour about all her corporate problems. I never charged her $75 an hour for it, either. But soon after we started doing this, she stopped seeing the shrink that she'd been going to at six in the morning!"

And so John, the younger man, became for Lillian the wonderful sounding board that many a traditional wife has been to her husband.

Not one man or woman in the couples interviewed was wholly dependent on his or her partner for support, emotional or financial. Quite the opposite was true, and intentionally so. In each case, because the woman worked, she was in a position to provide for herself if the relationship ended and, often, in a position to provide *for both of them* if needed. This made a big difference to the men because it relieved them of a feeling of carrying the full burden of responsibility for every aspect of the relationship.

"The fact that Amanda has a successful career and is financially independent made it easier because I wasn't suddenly thrown into being totally depended upon for the running of the house," said Steve, 32, of his 41-year-old wife. "So if things go wrong, which is a great fear of mine, she is there to pitch in.''

This ability to back one another up financially has benefits that extend beyond the handling of money. Whether you are a man or a woman, knowing that you have a partner who can help out if you choose to make a major career switch has to be one of the most emotionally supportive situations to be in. It means that you have the freedom to change your life—a priceless freedom to have.

On a daily basis, older woman/younger man couples find that the relationships work both ways: they share the pluses and minuses of being a two-career household. At times, the load can be almost too much, yet the rewards of making it work are all the more exciting and enjoyable when problems are conquered together.

''Both of us are under a lot of pressure constantly,'' said Michelle. ''I know there are times when he feels he will never complete his dissertation. Because of the kids and the house, he wonders if there will ever be enough hours in the day to do what he wants. And I'm in a position where I can't say no to more responsibility at the university. I like the prestige that I've earned, and they keep wanting to give me more— I can't be a member of a university community without taking on a heavier load. In the meantime, Henry and I are both anxious over money. We live on my salary, and it seems to be going down rather than up.

''So we have all these pressures, but we make our decisions mutually. In the long run, being together is wonderful. Henry is very alive and very bright, and I think we've been very stimulating to each other professionally.''

The same is true for a couple that doesn't face the financial and child pressures that Michelle and Henry must deal with. Diane, 45 (married to Rob, 33), said she and her husband design their vacations not only to be a pleasurable escape from their separate jobs but also as a time to be able to discuss the pressures they are under.

''We use our vacations as time to talk about how our life is going,'' she said. ''I think that is the most important thing we can do. One New Year's Eve we rented a place with no phone and no TV just so we could have time to talk. I asked Rob if he was having fun with his work, and he said, 'No, I'm really not. Everything is too theoretical; I want things to be more concrete.' So that's how we learned it was time to make some changes.

"When we got home, he changed his whole approach to his work, and that's when his own projects really took off. Now he has his own firm with lots of people working for him. But that doesn't mean we don't have the pressures. It really means that it's more important than ever that we always take time to get away and talk these things over."

The Joy of Work

Michelle and Henry have been married for three years. Both are scientists, and they met while completing research projects at the same university. They live with her two teenage daughters and their young son. Michelle is a tenured professor, teaching full-time while Henry completes his doctorate.

"Professionally, our life together is really wonderful," said Michelle. "Henry is very alive and very bright, and in many respects he has introduced me to new ideas and interests. I think we've been very mutually stimulating to each other professionally. It's been exciting for him to meet all my friends who are now the famous scientists in the field being studied by Henry and other grad students."

Henry points out that their initial attraction was so strong on a professional level that he almost failed to notice their age difference. "The only time I really thought of Michelle in terms of her age was when we first met, and that was just to note that we were in the same profession but she was further along than I was," said Henry. "I was at the university as a student while she was there as a scholar—that's why I found her interesting. I'd had other kinds of scholarly exchanges with faculty members, so that didn't scare me like it might other students.

"I think one of the biggest advantages of people in a marriage being different ages and having had different experiences is that you bring different perspectives to problems that come up, the issues that everybody deals with. It's helped me enormously when I'm pulling my hair out over my research to have Michelle here. She's gone through this. She has gone through nearly all the anxiety-producing experiences of starting a career.

"On the other hand, I think it's helped Michelle to have me around when we talk about doing things like moving to a new place or starting a new project or something that requires a little more enthusiasm and a break from the past. That I can provide, because I'm excited about new possibilities. I'm looking forward more. I'm not worried about breaking an old pattern as much. So I think it's helped both of us in a lot of ways."

Steve, 32 (married to Amanda, 41), appreciates the experience that she brings to their relationship, while she loves his enthusiasm and the bright future she feels certain will come his way. "A very important part of all this is that I'm learning so much from Amanda," said Steve. "I'm getting the benefit of all her experience in all these areas—money, sex, lifestyles. And she's got a wonderful wisdom, too. I think she was born with that. It's actually almost a privilege to be with her. I'm not walking in the dark. Somebody is throwing ideas at me that wouldn't be offered by someone in my own age group."

"I married Steve because of his youthfulness—his enthusiasm for life has not diminished," said Amanda. "People my own age tend to be so encumbered with burdens from work, from kids, from ex-wives. For us, the future is wide open. Anything is possible. And it's not because I want to ride on Steve's coattails, but he is thinking about a lot of different things he might do. It's not like he says, 'Well, here I am, and this is my life, and I'm not changing.' If you don't change, you don't learn, and that's not living.

"What I love about being with Steve is I'm in the kind of environment I love and I'm with someone who loves it, too."

I heard the sentiment numerous times from older woman/

younger man couples (and I feel this way about Brant) that the younger man's enthusiasm and energy fires the women up to make changes in their work. Brant often forces me to look at things in a new way.

"She has contacts and experience that have made some of my projects much more successful than they would have been otherwise," adds Steve, 32, of Amanda, 41. "We may be in different places career-wise because I'm still driving hard and she's ready to ease up, but we balance each other well."

There is no doubt about it—loving your work and working with the one you love pays off. With these couples, many of whom face undeniable pressures due to finances or still being in school or trying to "blend" families, the fact remains that both partners working in the same or similar fields serves to bring them closer together.

Sharing interests works particularly well when couples are totally in sync when it comes to work and money, which reflects ease with one another's work patterns and lifestyles. This is very true of Diane and Rob. "His business acumen is wonderful, and I really appreciate it," said Diane, who is still awed by her younger husband's financial success. "It's just one business deal after another. He thinks everything through very carefully. For example, now that we have all this money, I thought we should move. Rob drew it all out for me—how much more it would cost in so many ways—using financial concepts I knew nothing about. It was fascinating.

"I like what the money means to him. One of my colleagues had told me that his idea of rich was to pay a couple hundred dollars for a pair of shoes and not worry about it. But Rob says his idea of rich is 'to pay somebody to do everything I don't want to do.' He feels his time is the most valuable thing he has. He wants to use the money to make it possible for him to continue to do the kind of work he loves to do and for us to have time together. I agree with that, and we talk about it a fair amount."

Though she is on a lower rung of the earnings scale, Michelle, 43, also agrees that money can mean buying time, and she feels that she and Henry, 27, share that particular value. "For the first time in my life, money is what I need because I could pay for services that would make both of us less harried," she said. "I would hire a housekeeper—someone to cook the meals and clean the house—and that would make a profound difference in our lives. But otherwise I'm not very materialistic. I just want things that will make our life easier, and Henry agrees."

Lillian, 72 (married to John, 57), has struck an interesting compromise in style and work with her younger husband. "What I like about John is that, even though our styles are quite different, his style is one I admire very much. For one thing, he is very accommodating to our commuter marriage, which many men might find difficult. During the winters, I live in the city in a small apartment by myself because I started my own company after I retired . . . and I don't want to give that up. I need to be in the city weekly. But we're together every weekend and all summer when we work the farm together.

"And for a person who hated solitude when my first marriage broke up, now I love it. I crave it. So, since I'm lucky and I have a pension and I have John to help me, I can have this apartment and work on my writing, too. For a while we both lived in the city, but he doesn't like it. We both love the country. That's why I took early retirement—I was going to move to the country with him. Then I realized I still wanted the other, so we do it this way. I think, in his heart of hearts, John feels it's a good way to live, too. It's great. We both love nature and gardening, and that's how we spend a lot of our time."

Being Equal Partners

Sharing work interests doesn't mean you won't disagree, however. For example, age can make a difference when it comes to attitudes toward work and the rewards of a career. Steve and Amanda find themselves on opposite sides at times—because she has been in the work force a decade longer than he.

"Many of my friends are burned out or have dropped out or have been shafted by the companies they gave their lives to, so I'm a little jaded about the work world," said Amanda. "I know it's important to be conscientious and responsible, but to what degree? So when Steve plans to spend a weekend on work, I question the value of that. 'They won't be ready for it, so why kill yourself?' is my attitude—but, on the other hand, I don't want to dampen his enthusiasm.

"Steve is much more into thinking about 'career track' than I am. This may be because I see where my career is going, I like making the money, but I am over that hurdle of having to reach for the position. I'm here, and I don't find it all that great, so I'm ready to find satisfaction in some other areas of my life. He is still focused primarily on work. This is one way we balance each other, so I think our different points of view are healthy."

Steve agrees. "I'm working a lot right now, taking everything that comes along, working nights and weekends. Amanda sees some of that as bullshit because we're at different points in our work lives. I'm just coming into this in a way. Actually, I'm more a product of the '60s than she is. I was very antimaterialistic and all those things. Coming from that perspective, I have found that I *do* enjoy a career, do enjoy working, do enjoy feeling confident because I'm making money. To me, it's new and exciting, while she's tired of the whole racket. She thinks about the money differently and wants to use it so we can have more time for ourselves.

"But I'm learning from what she's telling me. In the long run, she's right, and what she's really saying is that I won't get rich or really do my best working for someone else. She wants me to go out on my own, but I'm not ready for that yet. But we both know that our time is coming; we'll have the money to be comfortable, and we'll be able to call our own shots. So I know I'm doing all this to get ready for that. And she spurs me on."

This conflict was voiced in slightly different terms by Henry, 27 (married to Michelle, 43), who said, "I'm experiencing so many different things in my work. Sometimes I can't share that with Michelle because she's been through it before. So she won't have the same enthusiasm or wonder about it that I do. I like going through the experience and letting it blow my socks off rather than having it explained to me by someone who has been there before. But that's a minor hassle compared to the amazing number of advantages we share work-wise.''

Brad, 39 (living with Elinor, 57), notices a difference—quite the opposite of Henry and Steve's feelings—in his attitude toward work versus Elinor's.

''I think the only thing that gives us much trouble is this generation gap that has nothing to do with emotional issues or physical issues,'' he said, ''but it's how I look at the world versus how she looks at the world. For me and my friends, work is something we do in order to get it done. We aren't deeply attached to any one organization. Or we will change our minds about what we're doing—just take what comes, what seems to work out. Elinor has always had this idea that she had to be in some paternal organization and have a title in order to be somebody.

''For example, this close friend of ours is a classic character who has gone from being a gardener to being a PR man to being a novelist—he has lots of different things he's interested in. Like, I can be this serious businessman, but when I get to the country all I want to do is chain-saw some wood or build on the house—and all that is part of me, too. Elinor has had to adjust to a certain way of looking at the world that's more my generation than I've adjusted to her way of looking at the world. She always thinks you have to worry about things or they'll all fall apart. I think you can let things go for a while, and they'll put themselves back together.''

Amanda differs with her husband on certain matters relating to money. ''One attitude we don't share,'' she said, ''is how we think about savings. Steve is more hyped about it than I am. I think travel and vacations are important, while he doesn't. One example would be our IRA. He wants to put more money into it, and I think there's enough there. My priorities are different from his.

"I don't want to be without money, but, as you get older and see people die, you know how precious every day is. You feel like *this* is the moment you have—this is it, right now. The more you deal with sickness and death in the people around you, the more you realize that you've got to enjoy yourself. You have to ease up a little.

"I think Steve is fortunate that I've done a lot and I'm satisfied with many things in my life right now. It's funny, but when you think about the age difference in terms of phases of life, you find that your goals can be very different. So many of mine have been attained; so many of his remain to be met. And yet, happiness is where my husband is. And if we're comfortable, that's enough. Who needs bigger, better? That's the trap of life. So we go back and forth—we balance each other with our different goals."

Separation of Sex and Money

We are all familiar with the image of the rich old guy with a flashy young babe on his arm—herein lies the origin of an identical stereotype for the older woman and younger man: he is her gigolo, her bought-and-paid-for lover. But most of the women interviewed for *Loving a Younger Man* couldn't afford a young male lover even if they wanted to pay for sex! Nor could they be pursued for their money—these are not rich women.

Ironically, when it comes to money and sex in the older woman/younger man couples, it is the *woman* who must step back and assess her economic future. After all, she has been conditioned by society to use her sexuality to "snare" an older man who would be able to provide for her financially. I remember well my thoughts about money in the months before Brant and I decided to marry. I had just seen two friends enter into second marriages with older men, well-to-do men, and move into large homes in prestigious neighborhoods. If I were going to marry Brant, his earning power and mine *combined* would hardly pay the ticket for such an upscale lifestyle—nor would it be likely to in the future, since we were both in occupations that do not lead to exceedingly high salaries such as those earned by lawyers and doctors. But while an expensive lifestyle was familiar to me and one that I might enjoy if I were to marry a man my own age or older, I knew already that it meant little to me. I had had it once and discovered that material comforts cannot take the place of love and respect from a person whom you also love and respect.

So I told myself that marriage to a younger man would mean that I would *have* to work and earn at least 50 percent of our household income in order to maintain the kind of lifestyle I wanted for myself, Brant, and my children. Also, I had the added financial burden of two children nearly ready for college, for which I would have to pay a portion. I resigned myself to the fact that I would probably have to rent a small house rather than own a home, have a less convenient kitchen than what I thought I always wanted, and budget much more tightly than I ever thought I would in my mid-life years.

But I had no doubt that life with Brant would be worth the trade-off: love rather than money. Having to work is no big deal—I love work. It's fun, it's always new and exciting, and the personal satisfaction I earn from it is boundless. And the very idea of equating a convenient kitchen with the priceless returns of a warm and loving marriage is absurd. But, like me, many of the women interviewed had to consider that trade-off from the traditional angle of the woman seeking financial security from an older man, before choosing to be with a younger man.

Most did so remarkably easily. The fact that they can support themselves means they can afford to be with men who might earn less than they do. For this reason, Lynn, 37, said that living with a younger man was the first time she felt comfortable just being herself, without worrying about stepping on a man's ego—she didn't "owe" him anything for supporting her, and she didn't have to apologize for making money.

As wage earners, most of the women interviewed made good, not great, salaries. However, they could maintain lifestyles that pleased them, so their levels of self-satisfaction in this area were high. Many had children and spent a major portion of their income on home and children. None of the women were independently wealthy. Those who earned the most were careful to point out that they had worked hard to get it.

Amanda, 41 (married to Steve, 32), had ended a relationship with an older, wealthy man who wanted to marry her just before she began dating Steve, whose career was just beginning.

"I knew that the only way I would marry again would be if I were financially independent first," said Amanda. "That's why I waited so long. I wanted to be sure I married for love, for the right reasons. I had had one very bad marriage, and I had had other opportunities to be married again, but I wanted to be sure I was marrying because *I* wanted it.

"My financial independence is very important to me. I felt when I was with the older, wealthier man that I was treated as if I were a belonging, a possession of his. Because of that, I value my life with Steve today much more. I do not miss the formal affairs and the cocktail parties and the charity balls. I don't miss it at all. It sounds crazy, but I felt like my identity was at stake. The reality is there is a lot of comfort in life with a wealthy man, but that's just not who I am."

Both Amanda and I married men whose personal styles—from possessions to clothing to living accommodations—were much simpler than our own had been. For me, life with Brant has meant a return to a casual kind of life, which I prefer. I may have spruced him up a little, but he has always been the tweedy type, which I prefer to pinstripes. The big change for him has been going from a lifestyle in which he could pack all his belongings in a car to one that now requires a moving truck.

Steve, 32, remembers his response to Amanda and her more formal way of living. "I felt so warm and comfortable walking into Amanda's house, it didn't make me stop," he said. "What mattered was what we had together. So when we decided to get married, I was in a small apartment without a lot of responsibilities or possessions. Amanda laughed at how I always made my dinners as simple as possible—one dish. But when I walked into her house and it was all put together, completely furnished and beautifully so, I felt like all the systems worked—for both of us.''

Amanda's attraction to Steve bears no comparison to the stereotypical concept of the older woman with a gigolo-type consort: "Choosing Steve was a major step for me. First, there was the hard work of getting into a new relationship, and, second, I had to drop that old identity of being rich and glamorous and part of a group of older people. Steve was no Peter Pan. He was very responsible, very mature, very sensitive, very hardworking, and extremely polite. Ethically and morally, I found him to be very unlike most 27-year-olds.''

While Amanda had little difficulty with Steve's significantly lower earning power and reacted positively to what it represented in terms of social identity, Maureen, 43 (married to Garrett, 31), whose first husband had been a surgeon, struggled with the choice. "The fact is, a younger man is less secure financially," she said. "I've already been through one man's career—getting a doctor on his feet. Could I go through all that again? The idea definitely inhibited me when it came to marriage, especially when I looked at my peers who have their second homes, are driving Mercedeses, belong to the club, take time off to travel, and are affording themselves all those wonderful things that presumably are due you in your forties. Could I go back to a little picket fence and a cottage and ironing my own shirts? I did not visualize having to do this again.

"So I took a big gulp and said, 'All right, a good reason to have a career of my own.' And I feel that I give back to my marriage and my home life because of my work, but it also makes me feel better to have resources of my own. I'm happy in my marriage, but when my husband asks me if I would work if I didn't have to, I say, 'Sure I would . . . but maybe not as hard.' ''

Meanwhile, the younger men are just as sensitive to "who provides for whom." Rob, 33, refused to marry Diane, 45, until he felt he could contribute a minimum of 50 percent to their living costs. "The one issue that I think [younger] guys do care about— and it's an issue that was important to Diane and me—is money,'' said Rob. ''When we got married, Diane was making twice as much as I was. Then things changed, and my business became very successful. So our 50/50 arrangement has changed.'' Later in this chapter, we will discuss how couples handle their finances, but for Rob it was critical that Diane *not* support him in any way.

John, 57 (married to Lillian, 72), also had to deal with that issue. Though he is comfortable with their arrangement today, at first he balked. Lillian, 15 years his senior, reached retirement age with a much larger nest egg than John and wanted to invest it in a home they could both enjoy. ''When we wanted to buy this house,'' she recalls, ''John could not have afforded it. But I couldn't have bought it without him because I could never live way out in the country by myself. It's scary. We're up on a mountain, two miles from the nearest neighbor. But we resolved the money issue easily. We talked it over, and I said, 'I don't want to live the way you can afford to. I want to live the way *I* can afford. Is that going to bother you?' And he said, 'No, why the hell should it? I'm grateful for it, if it's what you want, but I don't require it. I'm happy living on less, and you can save the money.' ''

John said, ''I'm amazed that I'm married to a woman who is essentially supporting me in this wonderful lifestyle. There's no way we could live this way without her financial resources. But I fell in love with her when we first met, and that was long before I had any idea of the extent of her corporate success.'' Indeed, John and Lillian met and were married 12 years ago—several years before she knew her ''early retirement'' agreement would provide quite substantial funds.

The Real Issues—
Power, Control, Money—
and How They Are Resolved

Relationships are like business partnerships. The person with the money has the power. In the past, the man made the money and controlled the marriage as the primary decision maker. One assumption, then, has been that in older woman/ younger man couples the woman must be the partner with the money and thus the partner in control. This isn't true.

But it is interesting that the question asked again and again by people interested in older woman/younger man couples is exactly this: Who has the power?

It isn't a naive question but one that evolves from the popular misconception that the older woman and the younger man are mutually attracted because of the woman's drive to be totally in control and the younger man's need to be dominated.

"You need someone you can boss around—that's why we think you married Brant," said one man, my age, who works with me.

Well, he's wrong. I need to be with a man who won't try to run every part of my life for me and doesn't want me running every part of his life. There are areas of each of our lives that we keep under our own individual control. Our work lives are a good example of that. But the life that we share is a life that Brant and I work hard to exert *mutual control* over—and this is what I found to be true of all the couples interviewed.

On TV's "Donahue," in a segment on older women/ younger men, the same question came up; Phil Donahue asked the couples which partner dominated the relationships. Each partner hesitated, then pointed at the other and said, "He does" or "She does." Then everyone reconsidered, and there was a simultaneous response from all three couples: "We both do." *Both* participate to an equal degree.

In talking to women in love with younger men, it becomes clear that the woman who falls in love with a younger man isn't trying to boss anybody around. Instead, more often than not, she stumbles into the relationship while seeking something as simple in concept as it is difficult to find: an equal partnership. She did not set out to find a younger man, just a man who will be her equal partner in every aspect of life: the intimate, the intellectual, the emotional, the professional, the cultural, the financial, and the practical.

However, things don't work out this way without a lot of

effort. Diane, a senior executive for one of the nation's top marketing firms, is 45 years old, 12 years older than Rob, her computer-whiz husband who has made his first million during the 8 years they have been together. It is interesting to examine how their relationship has had to adapt to the change in their incomes—how they manage their concern over power and control.

"I see the power angle as more important to Rob and me than the age difference," said Diane. "We've had a tremendous shift in our relationship because of the change in our incomes. What worries me specifically are the power plays I see between older men and younger women—the men taking control of the relationships because they make all the money. I don't want that to happen to us.

"When I first met Rob, he was working but making very, very little money. I was earning about $35,000 at the time. He was starting out on the ground floor of the computer industry while I was managing a full department of about 25 people. Right after we met, he took on some consulting but also took time off to develop his own software. I think that the first year we were together he finally made about $30,000—slightly less than I did. So the money part was something I was very comfortable with because we would just figure out what it cost us to live together and split it down the middle. I liked the 50/50 split."

During the same time, Diane and Rob were learning how to let each other know what they needed emotionally. It wasn't easy at first, but how they solved that problem had a significant impact on how they would resolve their situation when their financial positions changed drastically soon afterward. Like many couples, their feelings of emotional control or personal power are so closely tied to their perception of financial power that they had to feel comfortable opening up with one another on an emotional level in order to be able to deal with financial issues. In the beginning, however, Diane discovered that Rob was not a man who talked easily about what was bothering him. She, on the other hand, was very open.

"This was a problem for me early in our relationship,"

said Diane. "Rob has a tendency to remove himself emotionally from any situation he doesn't want to deal with. His eyes glaze over, and he backs away. I, on the other hand, insist that we have what I call our 'relationship review.' I want us to sit down, get back to basics, and ask each other if everything is still okay between us . . . ask ourselves if we know where we're going."

Diane was frustrated in her early attempts to get this communication going between the two of them. "So I tried to tell Rob, 'There's not enough exchange here. I'm giving it all, and I'm so intense but you're expecting everything will just happen and it will be fine.'

"And then he told me something that made me accept him the way he is. Rob said, 'I really want this to work, and I will talk more if you will try to feel more. I show you in a lot of ways how I care about you, but you don't get it.'

"But I still wasn't sure exactly what he meant," said Diane. "Then one day, a few months later, he met me at the train after work, and he said, 'I brought you a bag of M&Ms—I thought maybe you wouldn't have had a chance to eat.'

"And I started to cry. Because who would care enough to think of that? So I could see he *was* doing that all along, and I wasn't seeing it just because he didn't talk to me all the time. I've learned that I get a lot from Rob, I just don't always get it in ways I'm used to. I think it's because I'm a hard driver. At work, I'm very impatient and maybe arrogant about how I want things done. Those may not be good qualities on a personal level, but they are excellent qualities for my field. My boss tells me I'm very intense because I take everything so seriously.

"Now we are at a point where we talk together much more easily. Rob will say, 'Oh, oh, here you go with your life reviews again,' but he'll do it with me. And I've learned to temper myself. When we were first together, I had to address absolutely every single issue between us—I was convinced our relationship wasn't going to work. I had to resolve every disagreement between us before I went to sleep. I was a lot more demanding and structured then. Since we've been married, which is about five years now, I don't feel that way anymore. I think I've cried all of 10 times since our marriage. Of course, when I cry, man, I am *upset*. And when I'm angry, I am a furious woman, and there's no delaying things. Rob, on the other hand, will deal with anger differently. At first, he will sit on it and not say anything. He doesn't verbalize as much as I do. But he's changed, too. In fact, I got home late the other night, and he opened the door and said, 'I am pissed!' and I thought, Whoa, is this the man I married five years ago? So he had become a lot more open and straightforward. We just don't have any time to let things stew.''

As a result of Diane's early emphasis on "relationship reviews," the issues of control and power in their relationship continue to be addressed before they can become problems. Both Diane and Rob have grown comfortable with the dialogues. "Now it's easy for me to say, 'Come on, I've got to go to work tomorrow, and I don't want to be upset knowing something is wrong with you,' '' said Diane. "Or Rob will say, 'You've got to tell me what's bothering you. This is worth fixing. I really want this marriage to work. If you don't tell me, I won't know.' So we work as a couple because both of us have made a lot of adjustments.'' Money first surfaced as a major control factor in their relationship when they decided to marry.

"I remember how all of a sudden I wanted to get married after we had lived together for three years," said Diane. "We had never discussed it, but I just said one day when we were mulling over whether or not we would buy our house, 'Are you going to marry me or what? What are we going to be doing here?'

'' 'I've always wanted to do that,' Rob said casually.

'' 'Then why the hell don't you?' I said. 'Why don't you ask me?'

'' 'Because I don't make enough money,' said Rob. 'I want to feel that I can support you in a lot of ways, and I can't do that right now.'

'' 'So whether we get married depends on the prime rate?' I asked.

"And he said, 'Yeah, in a lot of ways it does. I really want to feel like my business life is together.'

"That was just as he was beginning to consult, and his computer ideas were about to find a backer, which happened pretty quickly, and then we just got married," said Diane.

"Money is an issue between us," said Rob. "At one point, Diane was making probably double what I was, and I really felt that I needed to be able to uphold my end of a 50/50 arrangement." Thus, Rob challenges the idea of the older woman supporting the younger man.

Now, however, things have changed, and Diane is the one who has had to make the major adjustment.

"A short time after we were married, we not only started to make the same amount of money," said Diane, "but suddenly his business just went through the ceiling. He has made an enormous amount of money in the last three years and will continue to do so.

"Until recently, I felt very uncomfortable with that. I didn't like it at all. It made me think how unusual it is to be married to a man that much younger who is really the breadwinner and now is taking care of me financially, even though I'm making a very good salary myself. I liked it better before because I was giving financially, too."

"So we talk a lot about our contribution. Rob equates what each of us puts in with more than money. Since I run the house, he asked me, 'How many hours a week does it take you to do this and this?' We worked it out. It takes 16 hours for meals and laundry, cleaning, and shopping. So he wanted to contribute more to house expenses to make up for that time.

"But now that he makes 20 times what I do, I began to feel a lot of conflict over it. Little things made me uncomfortable. I wondered what my motivation was to marry a younger man at a time when I was the main provider because I earned more. The roles are reversed now. I don't think this shift would be at all difficult for an older man with a younger woman. But this has been a dramatic shift, and I had a hard time adjusting to it."

What worried her? She wondered if she married Rob when she was earning more so that she could be sure of maintaining a certain amount of control in their relationship. Now that he was earning more, Diane feared a loss of that control. Even though her salary is excellent by any standard, the fact that it didn't equal Rob's million-dollar-plus income deeply concerned her.

"Where it bothered me was in our decision making," she said. "And I knew this was my own problem. Say Rob wanted to go to Paris, and I couldn't quite afford that on my salary. I felt like I had to ask, 'Gee, Rob, do you think it would be all right if we went to Paris?' because he's going to have to pay for it. Or if I needed a winter coat. It's like, all of a sudden, if something cost over a couple hundred bucks, I felt like I had to *ask* for it. I hate having to ask for things. So we went into this marriage as equal partners, and suddenly things changed.

"I found myself always looking to see what was happening between Rob and me. I couldn't see that there was a tremendous imbalance anywhere along the line, but I felt shifts that I denoted as losing my power. So for a while, the money had me quite crazed. I didn't have a problem with the success— it was just that our mutual share was not 50 percent anymore."

The solution to Diane's feeling of a loss of power and control in the relationship came in her old relationship review. This time the relationship review went further than emotions, however. The communication skills that Diane and Rob had developed made it easier to review their situation from the angle of a financial partnership as well as a marital one—exactly the focus Diane needed.

"I finally talked to Rob about all this. I told him that maybe what really worried me was that if we ever decided not to live together—I can't bring myself to say the word *divorce*— I have to understand how I am going to take care of myself financially. My salary seems fine, but I need to know where I am going with it. *If our relationship should end, I have to understand how I will take care of myself.*

"So we talked over all my feelings about the money and my conflict over what kind of power it did or didn't leave me with. Rob helped me figure it all out. We sat down with an accountant and worked out our joint ownership of this property and of a larger place. Then he showed me how I have certain percentages of other deals that he has put my money into. And that made me feel a million percent better.

"I know that I don't want to just turn my money over to him, but I also know I'm not capable of investing as wisely as he does. So now we have a system where he comes to me and says, 'I have this opportunity. I'm putting in this much and expect this back in 18 months. Would you like to be a part of this and you will own this percent?' So we do this jointly, and we sign agreements that show each person's percentage of ownership. This happened very recently, and I'm finding that because I am now part of those decisions my anxiety over the end of our 50/50 split has diminished."

Rob, in turn, feels very comfortable with the resolution of their finances and decision-making roles. "Our 50/50 arrangement has changed," he acknowledged. "That works when you're on a budget and have to be very wise about how you spend, but when you're making a lot more money, you can afford to contribute more. We're just jumping into another lifestyle right now, and Diane seems to be going right along. I don't see it making a major change for us in terms of power. Instead, it'll give us more freedom to enjoy ourselves. Financially, Diane does very well on her own, so I don't think our personal dynamics should alter. I like to think that we see things the same way."

Diane and Rob have found, as many of the couples interviewed have also, that feelings of power and control need to be constantly fine-tuned between them. This means keeping all lines of communication open. The couple that keeps in touch with what is working and not working in the relationship is the couple in which both members feel they have equal power. The women in these couples may have discovered that they have earned the right to contribute to the decision making in the household because they contribute to the financing of it, but an additional ongoing effort is required to keep the communication open.

Very similar to Diane and Rob's "relationship review" is the process by which Donna, 65, and Eric, 42, stay in touch with each other's feelings and maintain an even exchange, financial and emotional, on all levels in their household.

"We do this because I've been married before, I've been in therapy—as has Eric—and we both know there are lots of ways you can have power," said Donna. "You can have power that lets you make the decisions because you're louder and you make more waves. You can have power because you're the one with the money.

"So let's start with the money. I don't have a problem with money because we have decided to make this a 50/50 deal. Eric makes more than I do, and he does contribute more because he buys more extras. I'd have to say he isn't as much into the 50/50 split as *I* am, but it is important to me. I added up everything it costs us to live together—mortgage, water, electricity, gardener, repairs—and we split it right down the middle. So finances are not the source of a power struggle for us.

"Our problem is that I'm more outgoing, more outspoken. He's a very clear thinker, but he talks slower while I make more waves—I'm louder and faster. It's easy for him to feel that I'm going to override his decision, and I can sense when he feels that way. So then I hold back and feel bad because I'm too pushy. It's a tricky area for us because I want to be able to be myself; but, God knows, I don't want to be the 'mommy.' And I do butt in more than he does.

"The process helps us avoid what I call 'the powerful woman syndrome.' Women like me are powerful because we're used to being in charge, like I am in the classroom or in a lecture, but we need to have our men be powerful back to us. Otherwise, we're left being monsters. So what happens with our 'process' is that we both learn how to use power in different ways. I've learned how to be softer, how to trust more. And it pushes Eric to be louder. Louder is important, too.

"We use this process all the time," said Donna, "and it works well for us since Eric has a tendency to withdraw. And this isn't an age thing—I see it in the husbands of my friends my age. Men just have a tendency to hold back. So I accept the fact that Eric doesn't like confrontation and needs a safe space in order to talk things out. This process creates a safe space for him because it has rules—like we can't interrupt each other. We also set a time limit for our discussion, and we tell each other that our goal is to get to a place where we love each other—not tell which one of us is wrong.

"Sometimes we use a tape recorder when we do this because then we can go back to be sure we really listened to each other or to hear what we actually said. But there are four steps in our process. The first is to really let go about what's bothering us; the second is to say what we really want to have happen instead of the behavior that's bothering us; the third is to acknowledge what each of us did to get to this spot where we have a problem; and the fourth is to tell each other some things we appreciate about one another.

"And as many times as Eric and I say nice things about each other, it's really wonderful to look somebody in the eye and say something simple like 'I appreciate your doing the dishes every night' or tell them something you like physically or ethically about them. It really works!

"At first, Eric wasn't real sure if he liked the process, but after it worked very well for us a couple times, he changed his mind. Now he drags me by the hand and says, 'C'mon, I want to process with you. I don't know if I can do this because I'm too angry, but I'll do it anyway.' And it works for us."

I asked Eric if he agreed with Donna that the process helped their relationship or if he felt that she was domineering. "Not at all," said Eric. "It never comes up as an issue of dominance. I think that I have some ways that I like to be, and when those ways don't work out, we end up 'processing' them. I think I'm overly sensitive, so if I thought I were being dominated that might be the end of our relationship."

The 50/50 Split and Other Approaches to Evening Everything Out

Like Diane and Rob, most of the couples interviewed either shared finances 50/50 or adapted the split to accommodate one person's financial advantage in such a way that neither partner would lose something just as important: a 50/50 share of power and control in the relationship.

This is the financial arrangement that works for over half the couples interviewed, including Brant and me. I have strong feelings about this, as do many of the women I interviewed. After my first marriage, during which I did not earn any money comparable to my husband's income, I had to *ask* for everything. I vowed I would never allow myself to be so totally dependent on another person again. What a feeling of powerlessness!

Now, however, Brant and I earn approximately the same salaries. Even though we keep our finances separate, we decide on all purchases over $100 jointly. In fact, there's very little unilateral decision making in this house. Everything is 50/50. The only thing I do insist on is that Brant does not have to contribute to my children's expenses. Those financial responsibilities are strictly mine. Also, my clothing costs appall him, so I pay all those. But I'm in a customer contact business, and appearance is important. Overall, we try to run our house like a small business—take a full day a month for paying bills, going over the budget, deciding where we'll spend the money and how much each should contribute.

Elinor, 57 (living with Brad, 39), recently retired from her position as a senior management executive.

"Right after Brad moved in, we had a discussion about finances. It was clear that he would have to pay his own way. And I was aware, since we worked together, of what he was making. Since I made considerably more, I volunteered to pay a higher percentage of the rent. Now we are splitting it evenly because he earns more, and on my retirement benefits I earn less than I did. We're close to equal in our income."

"We are now," said Brad. "But, for a long time, she made

more than I did, and I relied on that to a certain extent. One of the things that had really annoyed me about my first marriage was that my wife was not contributing anywhere near a fair share to the upkeep of things.''

"We keep our finances separate and split everything 50/50," said Elinor. "We have our apartment, and we bought a country house jointly. We discuss our major expenses easily, but the house purchase had a lot of emotional overtones. Earlier in our relationship, we would wonder how committed we were—did we want to buy a house together? Since we are not married, making a commitment like this was a major decision.

"Finally, we did it, and it's come to represent a lot to us. We love the house. We do all the fixing up together, and we're happiest when we're there. We have the feeling that we built this together, and it's reassuring and good.

"So we have a strong partnership in all these things, and neither one of us dominates. I bring my work experience to Brad, and he, in turn, makes me feel like I'm living for the first time. Like the way we got our house. We rented a place for the summer, and I had never done that. I had never had a summer like most people seem to remember—with tennis and swimming and all those wonderful sunshiny days."

Michelle, 43, and Henry, 27, are struggling to live on her salary until his dissertation is completed. However, the handling of their finances is Henry's bailiwick. "He writes all the checks and manages everything on our computers," said Michelle. "I think he had no idea what it costs to run a family, so using the computer was extremely wise as it helps him forecast our needs. We do the financial planning together, and he does the projections. He gives me reports every month, and we find out how much over budget we are. It's been rough the last couple of months because of household expenses, but it'll be okay when he starts earning a regular salary."

On the other hand, Henry gives more than 50 percent when it comes to support in terms of helping with the household—from child care to cooking to housework. His contribution fluctuates, depending on the work pressures each one is under, but overall, he does not hesitate to pitch in.

This is also true in the household shared by medical students Ellen, 39, and David, 25. During the last semester, when Ellen's schedule was particularly grim, David took over all the cooking and the after-school care of Ellen's young son. Proud of the fact that his mother raised him to be self-sufficient in all ways, including housekeeping, David sees his assistance as a fair exchange.

My husband, Brant, like David and Henry, is the son of a working mother and consequently also shares their attitudes toward participation in household chores. We share the cost of cleaning help, but we also share the responsibility for daily activities ranging from cooking to doing the wash to picking up the dry cleaning or driving the car pool. Finances are shared, and so is the housework.

Once again, the younger men differ from older men as they do not hesitate to help with cooking, cleaning, and shopping, so that the home responsibilities are evenly shared by both partners. This was true of all the couples interviewed, and each couple had their own system: one husband might forgo doing laundry but compensate by handling all the household repairs. Always, the overall care and function of the home was not the woman's full responsibility, nor did she have to do battle to have it shared.

In an interesting variation on that sharing, Lillian, 72, sees the financial arrangement in her marriage to John, 57, as being a fair exchange even though she contributes substantially more money than he does. "Yes, I have more money than John," she said, "and it's because I had a bigger job than he ever did. It really was a big job—I was a vice-president and division head of this national company. But John has no competitiveness about him. He's totally free of that." Their exchange is one in which she is free to work and live away from home during the week, while he manages their country farm.

"We have a huge place with 125 acres in the mountains with woods and pastures and gardens. We cut our own wood, and we're vegetarians and raise all our own food. And we do lots and lots of work together—good physical work—and it's great. That's almost as important to me as the cultural and artistic and literary things. I think it's kind of a 50/50 split.''

What comes through loud and clear in these relationships is the emphasis on equality in all areas of the relationship as both finances and responsibilities are shared. The woman does not attempt to "boss" or control the younger man, as is often assumed. No one person ends up, as the wife did in the traditional marriage, being a subservient partner.

It is interesting to note in this respect that the financial situations for most of the couples are in flux. When they first meet, many of the men are in career tracks where incomes are still rising, although most earn less than the women. That changes over the next few years, since women still earn less than men do, even in higher-paid executive positions—so the younger men catch up. The couples interviewed provided a mix, income-wise, with some men earning less, some earning the same or some slightly more than their wives, while two earned a great deal more than the women. The amount of money didn't affect the balance of power in the relationship because so much time and effort went into communication patterns designed to prevent that. What keeps the relationships equal is the simple fact that *both* work. In addition, there seem to be three basic attitudes that successful older woman/younger man couples adopt.

First, from the earliest stages of the relationship, there is an avowed desire for equal input and a stated need for mutual respect for each person's opinions on all matters. Because each person had been in an earlier relationship where this didn't happen or was a point of serious contention, it is quickly and mutually acknowledged to be a critical issue between the two people.

Second, both move to "protect their interests" by establishing a 50/50 financial split of household expenses. This is true in most cases, regardless of how much each earns. This makes each person feel he or she has equal control over how things are run within the household.

Third, since both work, there is recognition of a drain on each person's time and energy from forces outside the relationship; thus, the complaint level is remarkably low—the couples understand the pressures that bear on each other. That makes it possible—and nonthreatening—for one person to take up the slack in household decisions if the other simply doesn't have the time or resources to be involved in some decisions due to short-term work pressures. That way no one's rights are usurped. It also works when one partner is willing to carry the full financial/employment burden because the other needs a break in order to make a job or career change. The bottom line: neither carries the full burden financially or emotionally.

If any motif runs through these pairings, it is one of equal sharing in everything from finances to household chores to planning for the future. A deep mutual respect and a strong desire to share in all decisions affecting their lives together characterized each couple interviewed. "This isn't a youth drive," said Deborah, 44, a prominent journalist, attempting to describe what drew her to a younger man, "it's a partnership drive."

7

After Hours:
Time Flies
When You're
Having Fun

The play was a hit, I was a hit, and, Mama, I married the good man. Mama, I married the best man in the world. We've just celebrated our thirty-seventh wedding anniversary. It takes courage. It takes believing in it. It takes rising above it. It takes work. It takes the dreaming soul of the human race that wants it to go right. Whatever you do, never stop dreaming. . . .

—the late Ruth Gordon, actress,
married to Garson Kanin,
16 years her junior,
from her autobiography, *An Open Book*

With her 1980 autobiography, Ruth Gordon did something no actress, no other woman in America's public eye, had ever done: she made being the "older woman" not only glamorous but synonymous with enthusiasm and excitement and fun. And it's clear from these words that her love for Garson Kanin, the younger man in her life, was for her as significant a source of delight as her work.

It's also clear that the age difference had no ill effect on the longevity of their marriage because, like the couples interviewed for *Loving a Younger Man*, Ruth Gordon and Garson Kanin knew how to enjoy life together on many different levels, both on stage and off. Trial and error, hard work, and luck are also necessary ingredients, but most of us will agree on what it is that makes relationships endure: the ability to communicate, a mutual physical attraction, respect for one another, the ability to share interests, good times, and intimacy. The last factors on this list—the sharing of interests, good times, and intimacy—are as important as all the others, and each builds on the other. Time and time again, as I interviewed older woman/younger man couples, they expressed the same exuberance and wonder that you hear in Ruth Gordon's words. They said that, even as they are drawn together because of shared work interests, they share the same pleasures in friendships, music, or other interests. They know how to have fun together!

Absence Does Make the Heart Grow Fonder

For dual-career couples like those interviewed, time is short. Ironically, the fact that both people work may be one of the biggest pluses for their relationships. Not only do their careers have an energizing effect on their relationships because as individuals with very separate identities they remain interesting to one another, but the squeeze that work puts on their time means that, unlike traditional couples who often take one another for granted because of easy availability, these couples find that a chronic shortage of time together leaves them always wanting more from one another.

In order to find time together after office hours, the couples try to streamline their approaches to friends and mutual interests. Some couples have settled into satisfactory routines, while others are still searching for a good balance between work and leisure pursuits.

Time and its use become important issues. Talking about how she initially felt about their age difference and her attitudes toward how she spends her time, Stephanie, 43 (dating

Alan, 30), said, "In these last few months, I've learned a lot about myself." Meeting Alan and discovering how much she enjoys him has changed not only how she thinks about younger men but also her attitude toward her own lifestyle and the way she wants to spend her free time. Like many of the couples interviewed, both Stephanie and Alan work under intense deadline pressures. "I used to have this rule never to date anyone younger than I am," she said, "but I've since learned that things I once held to be very true are not. All these rules that I've made about how I should conduct my life—I've been willing to throw those out. *And I know it has to do with the new sense of time.* Time is fleeting. On the one hand, I want to do too much maybe, but I also want to appreciate what I'm doing. That's where knowing Alan makes a difference.

"I have a lot of energy because I want to accomplish a lot: I wanted to have children *and* go to college, *and* I want to work *and* keep up with my children and their lives. I have found that, if you want to do all that, you have to develop the energy and maybe start being a little manic. Like, I find I need only five hours of sleep a night. I get up at five in the morning and get a lot done. Alan can't get over it. He looks at me and says, 'You have more energy than any 10 people I know.' That's good and bad. Sometimes I'm a little much for him. While I'm always up for what he wants to do, I might say, 'Okay, then let's do this and this and this.' And he'll say, 'I don't want to do all those things.' So I am learning to slow down and do things more his way. And I find that I'm having a lot more fun.

"My other life [before Alan] was always frantic with things I *had* to do, places I *had* to be, restaurants where I *must* eat because they're the latest . . . but with Alan it's all so different. He's more of a free spirit, and we're very comfortable together. I have found that I can really enjoy doing nothing when I'm with him. We'll order in pizza instead of going out. If we go to a movie, that's big time. We just really like to spend our time together alone."

Stephanie's newfound pleasure in enjoying more easy-going, quiet times with Alan is echoed by Lynn, 37, who is dating Dan, 30. "We have a lot of very nice open space together," said Lynn, "without my always thinking about what to do to fill up the next time slot. It's nice because it gives me a chance to really enjoy myself, a way of being together that I never knew before—with nothing going on. That's very different for me, but it's worth a million.

"For example, I've learned to relax and spend a whole day gardening with Dan or helping him build something. It's more a mental enjoyment than anything else and means that my mind is not in constant motion. I think it's because Dan is very present at that moment and he doesn't complicate things the way I have a tendency to do. When we go to the lumber store, we think lumber, not 'What does this mean, what about yesterday, what about tomorrow?' We just think lumber, period."

Several of the women felt that younger men have an easier time relaxing away from work because they grew up under the influence of the late '60s and early '70s, when the "hippie style" conditioned them to take a more laid-back attitude toward time. So while they may drive hard at work, they know when it's important to let up and relax—and the hard-driving women who live with them embrace that style with relief.

Certainly it's true in our household, where I was used to programming every minute among kids' needs and household duties and extra work from the office. Brant has taught me how important it is to take time away from *everything*, to take a day to do absolutely nothing—maybe read and listen to music. His attitude toward time—to use it as a gift to be enjoyed in a slow, contented way *together*—seems to be truer of younger men. I certainly heard the same feelings echoed by all the couples interviewed: they deliberately focus on finding ways to spend their time alone together, to maximize what little time is available to enjoy one another. A constant social whirl doesn't interest them, nor does the golf course or separate vacations. They make an effort to operate as two-person units, to share their activities and interests as a couple. And because the "work" of entertaining or doing something fun is shared, rather than the full responsibility of the woman (as has been the tradition), this mutual enjoyment is made even easier for her.

The Changing Role of Friendship

Brant and I have found few couples to socialize with who are not either people one of us has known for years or people we know through work. When it comes to knowing couples beyond those two circles, it has been difficult. I do not think that is because of our age difference but, rather, a result of the fact that we have so few opportunities to meet people because we spend so much time working. We're also finding that, as we get older, we are more set in our ways and more selective of the people we choose to spend our precious time with.

Several couples have told me that they wished they did know more couples to socialize with. However, they saw their lack of "couple friends" being a result more of heavy work schedules than of their age difference. This was a concern of Michelle, 43, and Henry, 27, as well as Ellen, 39, and David, 25. At first, I thought this might be more difficult for these couples because they also have children's schedules to cope with. However, Diane, 45, and Rob, 33, who have no children, felt the same way. Without doubt, the dearth of good friendships with other couples is a direct result of too many people of all ages having too little time outside of work.

Some couples are not bothered by this. "His friends seem very juvenile to me," said Maureen, 43 (married to Garrett, 31), "and he doesn't fit with them very well anyway. Fortunately, we are not social people. We don't feel compelled to get out every weekend or go to parties. We have entertained my friends, too, but Garrett feels uncomfortable with them, mostly because the men are so much more established in business that it puts him at a very different level conversation-wise.

"So even though I feel we have been accepted by both groups, we find it more comfortable to be just us. We're not reclusive, but we make it a point to pursue things that the two of us can do together.''

Sometimes a relationship with a younger man can mean learning to view friendships differently than you have in the past. Diane discovered this when she started living with Rob. He is very comfortable with other women as friends, which makes him quite different from the older men she has known. ''We decided to have this party and announce our relationship to our friends,'' recalled Diane. ''So I invited all my friends, and he invited *all the girls he ever dated.* It never occurred to me to invite the men I used to date. And he had dated a lot of women in a very short period of time. So when he told me all these women were coming, I said, 'Why did you do that?'

''He said, 'I'd kind of like to announce I'm living with you and have them meet you, and maybe, then, they'll meet somebody else.' As it turned out, one of his old girlfriends did meet a man at our party whom she is now dating. But I thought, Gee, he's got a whole different attitude about women and how you conduct relationships than I do. He's different from any man I've ever known.''

Friendships are very important to Brad, 39, and Elinor, 57. Like Diane, Elinor was initially taken aback by the number of women with whom Brad maintained easy friendships. At first she felt threatened by the specter of the ''younger woman,'' but as their relationship deepened, she learned not to worry, and their many friends include people of all sexes and ages.

''Our staying together has to do with a lot more than just working together or playing tennis together,'' said Brad. ''We both have a lot of interest in the creative life—creative people.

''I've introduced her to all my crazy friends who are painters and photographers and poets and people like that. She knows a lot of people, too, and we like to have some of the people we work with over.''

More than half of the couples interviewed stressed that their friends, like Elinor's and Brad's, come in all ages. I think this reflects not only the telescoping of age differences once we pass our 20th year but also how many more people we are exposed to in the work force. I know that when I wasn't working, my friends were people who had children the ages of my children or were the wives of the men working with my former husband. Because of my professional relationships, however, I now know people of a broad range of ages.

Side by Side

One of the early questions raised by people who wonder about the long-term compatibility of older woman/younger man couples is whether their lack of shared history will take its toll on their ability as a couple to appreciate different aspects of daily life.

As I mentioned earlier, the video revolution has spread knowledge of historic and cultural events to people of all ages and backgrounds. Says Michelle, 43 (married to Henry, 27), "I have to say something about Henry that is very odd. Despite the fact that he was born in 1959, he knows more about the '60s than I do. He knows so much about the politics and everything that happened that I can talk to him about things that happened to me then just as I would somebody my age."

More important than sharing experiences common to one generation, however, is the ability to enjoy—or learn to enjoy—similar interests.

Brad and Elinor are especially interesting in terms of shared interests because their age difference is significant (18 years) and the kind likely to raise questions of compatibility. Not only do they share friends of all ages, but their life together turns on a long list of shared interests as well.

"In September Elinor gets restless and says, 'We really ought to subscribe to the symphony,' " said Brad. "So over the years that's been a great experience for me because I tend to sit on my hands. We've ended up with subscriptions to the ballet and modern dance. We really know dance now. She has these records I always like to play—like *La Boheme*. Then we started going to the opera."

"We have a strong partnership in all our different interests,'' said Elinor. ''Neither one of us dominates. I might be more oriented toward the cultural side, but he's the reason we got our country house.''

A balance between interests shared and unshared covers the gamut of lifestyle decisions for Diane, 45, and Rob, 33. ''We live a very disposable lifestyle,'' said Diane.

''We are thinking of moving into a larger place, but we'll stay the way we are about possessions,'' she said, ''which neither of us is interested in. Otherwise, we don't always like to do the same things. I'm a complete opera freak, and Rob hates it. He, on the other hand, could spend a week in an art museum, and I can take about 45 minutes before I'm looking for the cafeteria. We also have different attention spans for different kinds of things. He loves to lie on the beach for hours, but when we went north recently, he took one look at the mountains and said, 'Nice, looks like fjords—let's go home.' ''

As mentioned in Chapter 4, sports are quite important to Brad and Elinor, who also play tennis and cross-country ski together. This reflects a common interest for many of the couples interviewed, as over 65 percent of the couples said they exercise together on a regular basis. This includes running, skiing, aerobics, and wind-surfing, in addition to tennis and cross-country skiing. I think this emphasis on engaging in sports together is notable, since many traditional couples tend to separate these activities—the men heading off toward the golf course, the women playing tennis in all female doubles groups. The participation of older woman/younger man couples in sports *together* not only highlights their desire to do things together but is also an example of their mutual interest in keeping physically fit.

During the interviews, I was able to clarify the impact of yet another fascinating connection for these couples: music. Popular music has the power to transport us immediately to a time and a place, to an unforgotten emotion in our lives. One line from an old Beatles tune and we can feel 14 years old again. If these kinds of shared memories can be valuable links for couples of the same age, how do they work for older woman/younger man couples?

"It's funny how we bridge that difference," said Brad, 39 (living with Elinor, 57). "We have very different frames of reference for something like golden oldies. What's nice is Elinor really relates to the period when she was a teen-ager, when World War II was on and all those songs were around. Those songs were near and dear to my father for some reason, but he only ever knew the first lines. Elinor has incredible recall and knows all the words, which is neat. The way we bridge the gap is by listening to Willie Nelson's *Stardust* or Linda Ronstadt's recent albums. But there are songs I relate to that she doesn't at all—the Doors, for instance. But she doesn't have a problem with the Rolling Stones. I recently discovered I'm an old fogy, anyway," laughed Brad. "I taught a class this semester, and I had to tell the kids who the Beatles were!"

"As we drive out to the house for the weekend, very often we sing in the car," said Elinor. "I love to sing, and I know the words to a million songs. I especially like classical music and the songs from World War II—funny ones like 'Praise the Lord and Pass the Ammunition.' So I sing, and Brad tries to sing along."

It's interesting how music can counter other disparities to be a unifying element for a couple with an age difference, as it does for Amanda, 41 (married to Steve, 32), who said, "Possession-wise, we have had to accommodate each other's lifestyle. Steve moved into my house with virtually nothing, while I was burdened with a lot of stuff. But it's kind of funny that the one thing we agree on is music. Music brought us together. When Steve invited me to a rock concert, our relationship moved from strictly business to the personal. That's when we found out that music was a big part of both of our lives. I used to meet once a week with a circle of friends to play music and sing together. Steve also listened to a lot of music with friends. We found we both like the same music— "oldies but goodies," Joni Mitchell, Neil Young, the Beatles, jazz, and classical. We will listen to the same things, though Steve knows much more about the rock scene than I do."

But it isn't just listening to music that works for these couples. Brant and I love to go to good rock concerts, to dance, and to really enjoy the music the way we did when we were teenagers. I remember my confusion as a young wife when my first husband announced that our dancing days were over. "That's just for kids looking for dates" was the gist of what he said. The hell with that! Dancing and a love of music, any kind of music, can help keep all of us young at heart. The only problem I've encountered returning to my youth with music this way has been with my children. It seems that we all want to hear the same groups, but they have an old-fashioned attitude about what parents should or should not do. So to avoid embarrassing them, I dance on the opposite side of the room.

The Best Is Yet to Be

The pleasures that all the couples experience are what make their futures together so promising. Maureen, 43 (married to Garrett, 31), expressed her confidence in the strength of their relationship when she said, "I look forward to the days when my kids are grown, which won't be too much longer. We get a great deal of satisfaction from doing things, just the two of us. We'll travel, and we're going to build a greenhouse. I'll paint again, and we want to take some art courses together. We want to expand our life as a twosome because we didn't have 20 years together like most couples my age."

It is satisfaction gained from shared work experiences, shared interests, and mutually enjoyed pastimes that I feel provides the strength needed to make these relationships endure. One couple exemplifies how these relationships can work over the long term. Both partners met after they had spent years working at jobs that provided each with a small retirement income. They pooled their resources—and their interests—and found great joy.

"I was 50 when I married Marie," said George, "and she was just short of 65. I had worked for 34 years and had a small pension. Marie had worked for 37 years, and she had

Social Security. We didn't have a great deal, but it was enough to keep us.

"We were married 28 years. Right after we married, she and I became gamblers—she loved bingo. And from bingo, we went further. On our honeymoon, we went up to Lake Tahoe, and that introduced us to Nevada. So every year after that, we went to Nevada to play the slot machines.

"I could say this: we had a honeymoon for 28 years. We were extremely happy together. And, in fact, on our trips to Reno, when we would come in, the people who ran the place would say, 'Here comes that honeymoon couple again.'

"On the day that she died, we had gone to play bingo. She was 92 then, but we played bingo just like we did every day. Then we came home, ate dinner, watched television for a couple hours, and went to bed. We had been asleep about two hours when all of a sudden she gave a deep sigh . . . and that was all. It startled me, and I spoke to her, but she didn't answer. I patted her cheek, and she didn't respond. I called 911, and they were at the house in two minutes, but there was nothing they could do. The doctor said it was cardiac arrest.

"I was told afterward by several people that they thought she was failing, but I never noticed it. I guess I was too close to her. We were so busy every day. Seven days a week we played bingo, getting up at 7:00 in the morning, leaving the house by 9:00, and getting back home by 4:30 in the afternoon and once a month going to Nevada for a week. Just a regular procedure."

In an endearing tribute to the "older woman" in his life, George expressed how he felt about Marie with this vignette: "One time Marie and I went to a Chinese dinner, and we got these little fortune cookies. Inside mine, it said, 'Among the fortunate, you are the chosen one.' And I thought that was so true that I saved the little slip of paper."

Eric is 42 years old and the husband of Donna, who is 65. "I have only one problem because of our age difference," said Eric. "Donna is likely to die before me. One of the images that I have of our relationship is that it's a continuing process. We are accumulating a history together that helps us form a tight bond, a closer relationship. I want her to share my retirement, to be my companion in old age. But I feel that, when I'm ready to retire, Donna might. . . . If she dies, I don't know what I'll do. How will I ever find someone like her?''

The kind of intimacy shared by George and Marie or Eric and Donna is not unusual for older woman/younger man couples. In fact, I thank God every day for Brant and all his blessed energy and sheer exuberance for living. Brant isn't hung up on the small stuff, not beaten down by the world. He's able to compromise, take time, and laugh with me over the small things. Laughter over the small things: the gift of intimacy. A treasure shared by all these couples. Whether they're dancing or singing, on skis or on the beach—they enjoy life better together. But over and over again, I'm asked, ''Can these relationships really last?''

Of course, no one can offer any guarantees. Older woman/younger man couples can suffer from the same problems as couples of any age; people are people. But in an article published in *Boston* magazine, California psychologists David Cary and Robert Lehrke were quoted on the results of a study they made of 56 couples in which the woman was older than the man.

They found that the quality of life together may be even better for these couples than for traditional ones for several reasons. ''Because the traditional role expectations are not there,'' Cary concluded, ''the couple can concentrate on mutual needs and interests and enjoy one another's company . . . from the woman's perspective, she is able to have a greater feeling of participation in the relationship. She can meet a man on her own terms. In a sense there's a role reversal, with the women in more control.'' Because the woman is able to participate more in several ways, including financially, Cary and Lehrke point out, she is also able to claim—as men always have—the privilege and responsibility of caretaking.

Simone de Beauvoir once called love a recognition of two liberties. Paraphrasing her in her book *The Woman Alone*, author Patricia O'Brien said, ''Put them together: I affirm, I am free; you affirm, you are free. Add generosity and tenderness, and you have the best of what goes into both friendship and love.''

The gift for friendship and a spontaneous generosity of spirit characterizes each couple interviewed for this book, along with a strong, childlike sense of curiosity, which was more developed the older the couple. Their shared warmth and deep interest in the world around them makes it a fact: these aren't couples growing old together—they are men and women who have learned the secrets of staying young together!

8

Children:
Dessert or Disaster?

Having a child was very important to me. Before we could even conceive of staying together, that issue came up. Michelle adamantly wanted to have another child; and I think that helped me tremendously. I think it would have been hard for me to think of myself as not being able to have my own child. Zach's birth has given me something that is new in our family, something that I share with Michelle and the girls. That's meant a lot to me.

> —Henry, 27, on the decision
> to have a child with Michelle, 43

Children—to have or not to have and how to live with them—can introduce real problems into the older woman/younger man relationship. Children (not the age difference) are likely to create the only real stumbling block in these relationships.

"The only reason I won't marry Paul is that I do not want to have another child, and I worry that a child is something he may want very much someday. That is the only thing that stops me from making a commitment," said Jane, 46 (living with Paul, 35). Her reluctance to have a child is understandable, as her son from her first marriage is in his mid-twenties, and Jane, who has a busy career requiring international travel, is definitely *not* interested in starting over as a mother.

Like many women interviewed who do not wish to have children but are involved with younger men who have not had children of their own, she is hesitant to commit to marriage because she feels that, even though he might say *today* that he doesn't want children, he could change his mind later—*and leave her for a woman who would have a child with him.* "I cannot bear the idea that someday he might resent me because I cannot have a child, but I know I don't want to go through the hard work of raising a child again," she said.

She is not alone. Nor is this the only way the very difficult question of whether or not to have children is raised in older woman/younger man couples. There are many variations on this issue of children:

- She does not want to have a child, but he is interested or undecided—the most common dilemma encountered among the couples interviewed. She is likely to be in her thirties or forties.
- She cannot have children, even if she wants them, but he is interested or undecided. She is likely to be in her fifties or sixties, old enough that adoption is also out of the question.
- She wants a child *soon* (her biological clock is running out), but he does not want a child ever or does not want one *yet*. She is likely to be in her thirties or forties. This is the second most common dilemma.
- She cannot have or does not want a child, nor does he. She is 30 or older. Children are not an issue for this man and woman.
- Both want to have a child and now worry about whether or not she can get pregnant safely because of her age. She is likely to be in her late thirties to late forties.

There is one other, critical issue to be dealt with by these couples—often a hidden one at first—and that is *his or her existing children.* Although over 70 percent of the women interviewed had children from an earlier marriage, few couples are fully prepared for the stresses that an eventual "blending" of the couple with children from earlier marriages will have on the relationship. (Note that while 10 percent of the men interviewed had children from earlier marriages, none had custody of their children. If men do bring children into the household, however, they should be prepared to face many of the same concerns outlined herein.)

Dealing with children can be a source of agreement and satisfaction for a couple, or it can lead to a situation fraught with tension and disagreement. The age difference can push the couple that wants to have a child *someday* into making that decision sooner rather than later. Or the issue may surface five or six years into a marriage, with devastating consequences if the man decides he wants a child but the woman does not, or cannot, consider having one.

Older woman/younger man couples, however, are not alone in having to deal with these questions. Couples of any age must make similar decisions. Therapists report that many couples who marry for the second time must deal with the same concern, because often one spouse has had a child while the other hasn't. It is also a factor for couples in which the *man* is much older.

The main difference for older woman/younger man couples, of course, is that the biological clock is ticking; she doesn't have much time left in which to decide whether or not to have a child. Time and experience can change what once seemed to be an unalterable decision. Health factors intervene. Whatever she decides, she is taking a chance.

Enough Already!

What happens when she does not want children but he is undecided? This is what happened to me. During the first years that I was with Brant, I definitely did not want to have more children. (In fact, it would be tough for me to have a child, because I had had a tubal ligation in my mid-thirties, which is very difficult to reverse.) I was uneasy; Brant is such

228

a warm, nurturing kind of person that I knew he would enjoy children of his own. He assured me, however, that having children was never a major issue for him. He said he didn't feel compelled, like some men, to have children to carry on his family name. All he wanted was for us to be together and to be happy. And so he told me one thing, but deep inside I suspected that if we had the opportunity to consider parenthood he wouldn't be against it.

I didn't realize how much pressure that awareness was putting on me until I went for a physical checkup just before our marriage. I asked my doctor if I could have the tubal ligation reversed and if I was healthy enough to have another child. She told me it was possible—but I'd better hurry. Then she left the room for a few minutes. I burst into tears.

That was five years ago. All the pressures that weighed on me as I sat alone in that stark, tiny examining room that day are hardly exclusive to couples in which the woman is older. But for older woman/younger man couples, the ticking of that biological clock is relentless.

I can't remember if I told Brant how desperate I felt when I tried to push myself toward motherhood at that time, but I know we did talk about having a child again. This time he responded differently, saying something I heard several younger men say in my interviews: *he knew he didn't want a child now, but he couldn't say how he would feel in five years.* In other words, he was honest about the fact that we would both have to risk his feeling very differently in future. We talked, then, about something equally important: the fact that, even if we felt we wanted to have a child together, no couple has any assurance that that can happen. And we knew that it was possible that either of us could change our mind. We decided to take a chance on each other. I was willing to commit to a relationship that seemed very right for me at the time and not try to second-guess what it would be 5 or 10 years down the road. Brant was willing to do the same, even though I was a particularly unlikely candidate for eventual motherhood. We married fully aware that this could be a problem in the future.

Now, five years later, we are a in a very different position—

we are trying to have a child! Our jobs are more flexible and will allow us to better support another child. Two of my children are in college, so the drain on my time is significantly less. And I have had my tubal ligation successfully reversed. However, after one year, I have been unable to get pregnant.

I couldn't be more sure that I want to have a baby with Brant. Everything I know about him tells me that parenting will be very different this time around: he will be an enthusiastic partner in everything that goes into caring for a child. I never feel that I'll be the sole caretaker of a child we have together. Without doubt, this will be more of a mutual endeavor. And I know Brant would love to have a child.

So what if this doesn't work? I'm mulling that over pretty seriously. Will we adopt? I don't know. I'm keeping my ear to the ground for news of mothers who conceive late—and when one of the women interviewed for this book told me that her mother was 50 when she was born, I was astounded and relieved. I continue to take my chances.

For Maureen, 43 (married to Garrett, 31), however, there is no "taking chances." She feels unequivocally that she does not want to have another child and took measures to ensure that she wouldn't. Like all the women interviewed, whether or not to have a child with her younger husband was an issue she dealt with immediately and head on. She was *not* willing to fit another child into her marriage, even though Garrett initially wanted a child.

"The one big problem Garrett and I have had is that not only do I not *want* to have another child, but I *cannot* have a child of our own because I had a hysterectomy 10 years ago," said Maureen. "He knew that when he married me. He had to decide for himself if he wanted to go ahead with this, knowing we would never have children. And he worked on that long and hard. He had to go off alone, struggle with it, talk about it, and come to a completely independent decision. I think it was especially hard because he comes from a family where his brothers and sisters are having children, and I think he felt some unspoken pressure on him to carry on the family name.

"But it was hard for me, too. I'm not into adopting because

I don't want all the hard work of motherhood again. My son and daughter from my first marriage are teenagers now, and I feel like I'm just getting out from under a lot of responsibility for them. My career has just taken off, and that's what I want to concentrate on for the next 10 or 20 years. So all I could say to Garrett was 'You've got to decide for yourself how much having a child means to you.'

"He went through a period several years before we married when he did feel he wanted a child. Then he decided that what he wanted really was a family, whether it was an already-made family or one he made with someone. Either way, he did not want to be without children. Since my children live with us, that seems to answer his needs."

When Nature Decides for You

For Elinor, 57, and Brad, 39, the decision of whether or not to have children hadn't been theirs to make, since Elinor was past the age of childbearing. Brad wonders if he wants a child when he sees his friends' families, but he is also deeply in love with Elinor and weighs his thoughts about children against their happiness together. In Chapter 7, we discussed how Brad and Elinor have established an extensive network of friends whose ages vary widely. Brad describes these friendships as "what we do instead of having children . . . sort of a family of friends."

"I was just about through my menopause when Brad and I started living together," said Elinor. "Since I was at the end of it, the whole children thing had been a bit of an issue with me. It was never in my scheme of things in my earlier marriages, but I have brought it up once or twice in recent years because I've seen Brad with his contemporaries, and quite a few have children. Most of their wives are in their thirties and having kids before it gets too late.

"I've often wondered if he was thinking, They're all having kids and I'm not, so I felt him out on the subject. But he said, 'Just because I have fun playing with them all the time doesn't mean I want the full responsibility.' Deep in his heart? I'm not sure. I don't see him pining away, but you never know.''

Brad is forthright about his feelings: ''I'm always wondering. All my friends have started having children, and there's a little curiosity on my part that isn't entirely resolved. I worry about it. What happens if I wake up one day, and I think I want to have children?'' He pauses. ''Having kids . . . I still view it as more of a curiosity than a driving force in my life. I saw this ad on TV last night that showed a little baby crawling around, and it said, 'By the time he grows up, it's going to cost $20,000 a year to put this kid through college.' Seeing that, I said, 'Oh, oh, never mind.' ''

Fundamentally, the issue remains unresolved for Brad, and at 57, Elinor will probably be too old to adopt should she and Brad later decide to start a family. But Elinor, like me, is willing to take the chance that their life together will satisfy them both.

When the Biological Clock Nears Midnight

Several younger men I interviewed said that their only hesitation about dating women who are several years older is the not-so-subtle pressure to get serious quickly, so they can marry and have children. It's a tough problem faced by many women who have delayed marriage and children because of their careers *no matter what age the man is,* and the man's being younger only exacerbates the situation.

Some women, it seems, push for marriage and children too early in the relationship simply because they feel ''on top'' of their careers and have the professional and financial stability that allows them to take on other responsibilities. Have these women fully examined their motives, or do they want marriage and a child so much that they are pushing for a relationship with a man they don't really love? The men seem to think that's the case.

They feel a pressure that can cause them to stop dating the

women. "I'm in my late twenties," said Frank, 28, "and I often date older women, but the ones who say they want to get married and have kids scare me off. I think they let their worry about the biological clock get in the way of their thinking about some other things that have to be right in the relationship first." Several younger men I've talked with say they feel the women are still calculating whether or not the men are good wage earners, etc., rather than loving them as human beings separate from their wallets.

If a woman wants a child badly and feels she has found the right younger man, but he resists, there is really nothing to do but give him time. Of course, the outcome can be disappointing if he continues to resist and the clock keeps ticking. That's what has happened to Diane, 45, and Rob, 33. Even though Diane is 45, which would seem to preclude her having a child, and even though she says that she agrees with her husband's decision not to have a child, she talks in a way that makes it clear she has mixed feelings about not having a child. Like several women I interviewed, her conflict is tied to two different issues—a feeling of loss at never having had a child and concern over the threat of a younger woman.

On the one hand, Diane expresses a genuine fondness for children, saying, "I think having a child must be real gratifying in a lot of ways. But when I weigh that against who I married and the way we run our lives, I'm comfortable with our choice. The decision not to have kids seems to be the right one—I happen to like kids, but Rob doesn't. Yet . . . I am not convinced that I never want a child."

"Once in a while Diane brings it up and wonders if we made the right decision," said Rob, who is aware of his wife's ambivalent feelings, "but at this point it's pretty late to have kids. So we really don't see eye to eye on this issue. I don't want kids at all, but I know if I wanted to have a child, I could definitely convince her. And there have been periods when I felt I was ready to have kids. Who knows? It could happen."

Rob's ever-so-slight air of uncertainty explains Diane's trepidation over the decision, which surfaces when she confronts her feelings about the possible threat a younger woman could someday pose to their marriage.

"One of my fantasies in my insecure times," she said, "is that Rob will divorce me, marry a younger woman, have a baby, and be really happy. Who knows? That could happen." She senses that she is vulnerable in her position as the older woman because the one role she can't fulfill as she ages will be the role of a mother. Many women may worry about this, and some, like Ellen, 39 (married to David, 25), use it as one of their reasons to get pregnant even though the timing may seem poor in light of other pressures.

Ellen was not convinced that David wouldn't want a child someday and, consequently, was much more in favor of her pregnancy than he was. The baby is due just as they begin their residencies, hers in surgery, his in family medicine.

At first they disagreed on the issue. "My reason for wanting this baby may not have been very rational," said Ellen. "But I had my first child on my own, so I don't feel that I have had the experience of having one with someone I love. That's important to me. And I really like kids. I probably would have wanted to have more when I was younger if things had worked out differently for me. I really think that in the future David and I would want a child—you know, when our financial situation is much better and we have more time than right now—but I'm almost 40. I can't say, 'Let's do it later.' I don't want to wind up four or five years from now saying, 'Now we're ready, but my time is past.' "

She is fully aware of the problems the baby's birth presents. "This will be more difficult, but I'm planning to take a month off and then go right back to my residency. Then I'll have another four years before I'll be practicing and really making some money," she said. "I know David doesn't feel as strongly as I do about this, but I don't want him to *not* have a child. I guess it worries me that he might want to be with someone else later to do that with. He will deny that, but how can he know that now?"

I think it is important to note that, unlike the younger men who merely resented pressure to consider having a child when they did not feel ready, David acknowledged his misgivings, listened to Ellen's reasoning, and ultimately feels cautious but supportive of their decision to have a child. And when he talks about the impending birth, his enthusiasm is obvious. "The age difference is significant in only one way that is hard on us," he said, "and that is here and now with the reproductive issue. We're forced into having a child now if we are going to do it at all. I wasn't very excited about it at first. I had never really thought about having kids, before I got married or after. That was not one of my priorities. Maybe that was the result of my parent's message: 'Take care of yourself, your career; don't overextend yourself.' That's valid, but it's also selfish.

"If Ellen had not wanted a child, that would have been fine with me. But now that we've gone ahead, I'm happy about it. We went for amniocentesis and got to see the fetus with the ultrasound. They used a new machine that has very good resolution, so it was pretty exciting to see it moving around, and we could almost make out a face. Children are cute. They're fun to be with, so even though they're expensive and time-consuming, I do know they really do give a lot back. However, I'd be crazy if I didn't realize this will be pretty stressful."

Pas de Deux

If some women, like Elinor and Diane and Ellen, wrestle with ambivalence, others are spared that indecision because their mates feel strongly that they don't want children.

Donna is 65 and has five grown children from her previous marriage. Her husband, Eric, is 42. "I am most definitely interested in *not* having children," said Eric. "I don't know exactly why I feel so strongly about this. I have watched other people have children. I can see that they get some joy out of having those children. But I can't relate to that joy. I am more aware of how children interfere with life. I just don't want to spend the amount of time that I would feel obligated to in the raising of a child. I guess it's more of a time commitment than I have ever wanted to make.''

For Donna and Eric it's the perfect solution, not only because of her age but also because her strong mothering instinct is well satisfied by her own children and grandchildren.

However, the age of the woman is not the only reason that couples agree to bypass motherhood. Thirty-seven-year-old Lynn is a successful documentary filmmaker who has never wanted children. She is relieved that the man with whom she has fallen in love, Dan, age 30, feels the same way.

''We hadn't talked about kids per se,'' said Lynn. ''Then it came up when we were on a shoot and there were several little tykes screaming in the same room we were in, and Dan said, 'I'm just glad I don't have a .45 with me.' That's when I explored the issue, because I'd been afraid to bring it up, thinking that he would feel the opposite. But he made it clear he doesn't like kids. He doesn't like the noise they make, and I agree. I don't know why we feel that way, but we do.''

The Older Mother

Twenty percent of the older woman/younger man couples I interviewed chose to have children in spite of the fact that the wife is older. This decision is not as awkward today as it might have in the past; motherhood for the ''older'' woman is becoming a fact of life—not something extraordinary that might be a source of embarrassment—for the many women who have postponed childbearing to pursue careers. Not only has their average age at marriage increased, but there has been a 36 percent increase since 1980 in the number of women over age 35 having babies, according to the National Center for Health Statistics.

This is just one of several factors that make having a child a more popular option for older woman/younger man couples than it was in the past. Another factor that makes the decision to have children later easier is the availability of amniocentesis, which has made it possible to determine the likelihood of serious medical problems such as Down's syndrome and other genetic defects. In addition, current research is revealing more positive physical data about older mothers. In 1986, *USA Today* reported that a recent three-year study of 1,023 women over 35 and 5,343 women aged 20 to 25 by Dr. Roger K. Freeman (and his associates at the Women's Hospital of Long Beach, California) showed "very few" statistical differences in pregnancy and labor complications between the older and younger groups.

And the article pointed out that in her book, *The Timing of Motherhood*, author Carolyn Ambler Walter found that the older mother, who had worked an average of nine years before having her first baby, often described herself as more achievement-oriented, autonomous, self-reliant, and individualistic, which underscores the reason some experts think the older mother is better prepared for parenting. A recent *New York Times* profile of older parents cited Dr. Jerome Kagan, an expert on child behavior and a psychology professor at Harvard University, who said, "Older mothers tend to be calmer, more rational and are more relaxed with their children." As a result, there is likely to be "less conflict and anxiety in the child," he said.

Joanne, 53, said that her career/marriage pattern had worked extremely well for her personal happiness and for the well-being of her family. First, she established a successful career she enjoyed. Second, she married a man 10 years younger and took a brief "retirement" of 7 years, during which time she gave birth to two children. Third, she returned to a full-time career. At age 52, she is now in the midst of a full-fledged, demanding career, yet she still has plenty of time and energy for her family life. She has discovered the secret to "having it all."

Joanne and Hans have been married for over 20 years, during which they raised two daughters. Their courtship and decision to have children happened at a time when marriage to a younger man and Joanne's subsequent pregnancies, at ages 35 and 39, were quite unusual. The results are inspiring for all couples where the woman is older, has a career, and is considering having a child.

"We met when we were dancing together," said Joanne, a talented dancer whose career has taken her around the world. "After we were married, Hans wanted to have children right away. And for the first time, I found I did, too. I had had a very successful career in dance and felt satisfied with that part of my life. So I didn't hesitate. Our first daughter, who is 18 now, was born two years after we met. At first, since I was older, I worried about the health of the child during the time of my pregnancy. But she was fine. My physical condition was excellent as well, perhaps because I dance and dancers age more slowly. I did have morning sickness all the time until I was five months pregnant, but so did my mother and sister, so that had nothing to do with age. The same was true with my second pregnancy four years later—I was sick at first, but my baby was fine. I never gained a lot of weight, either.

"I think it's been wonderful that I had my children later. I have no regrets. I had a wonderful dancing career; I did everything I wanted to do; I traveled all over the world. Then, when I wanted to have children, I knew I *wanted* to have children, and it was very important to me."

Not only did Joanne feel that the decision to have children was made at the right time in terms of her career, but she supports the experts when she says that she felt emotionally better prepared than if she had been younger.

"If I had done it earlier, I would have been a terrible mother. I wouldn't have had the patience to handle children," she said. "My husband was thrilled. Together we really wanted to have children. He continued to dance another 10 years while I took time off to have the children. During that 7 years off, I did some part-time teaching, but I also did all the other things that I never had time for when I was working. I had all the time at home with the children, and it was lovely. I did all the things I never had time to do when I was young. I enjoyed it, and then suddenly one day I got caught up into working full-time again, and you know, I love that, too.

"Today I have a full-fledged career with commitments around the world again, but I still have lots of time with the kids. My children love it. My daughters told me just the other day, 'You know, we're so glad you're working because we don't want you to be like some mothers of friends of ours—all they do is go to the hairdresser and have nothing to talk about.' "

Like many of the younger men interviewed—and unlike many men in older generations—Joanne's husband, Hans, has shared the household responsibilities with her over the years. In fact, he does most of the cooking. Because of the nature of their professions, both of them have had periods during their careers when travel commitments were heavier for one than the other, but still they have balanced the demands on their time in order to share the load of home and children.

Michelle, 43, and Henry, 27, were also thrilled to find that they would be able to have a child together, something they had agreed from the beginning that both wanted. For Michelle, who has two teenage daughters from her first marriage, this meant she had an opportunity that men her age or older traditionally enjoyed—the chance to start a "second family."

"I am so happy having Zach," said Michelle. "There's a very nice feeling to it. Something happened recently that summarized how I feel about this. I was on campus on my way to the elevator, and I passed an office where an older graduate student, a man in his late thirties, was holding an adorably responsive little boy. I used to be able to walk by babies and not bat an eyelash—now I can't. Every time I see a baby, I have to say something. I didn't even do that in my twenties when I had the girls. It's really funny what happens to you. I think I have a better sense of how life deals out blows, and I appreciate more. So I said to the man who was holding this child, 'He's wonderful; he's adorable.'

"The guy must have known that I have a baby too, because he said to me, 'Isn't it great? Don't you think they should pass a law that no one should be allowed to have a child before the age of 35?'

"I agree with him absolutely," said Michelle. "What we both meant was how good it feels to bring all our life experiences to childbearing."

However, Henry and Michelle are willing to admit that

having another child at a time when finances are tight, the work load is heavy for both of them, and they have had to adjust to life with two adolescents in the household has not been easy.

"We wanted a baby, but Zach came a year sooner than we had planned," said Michelle. "We were going to wait a year. But thank God that baby was born, because I think the timing might have felt all wrong if we had waited. As it is, his birth made for a lot of extra tension. But I also think that the older the baby gets, the easier life is. We might have decided the following year that things were too hard because of all our problems with the girls, who are in the tough stages of being teenagers, and then we might not have had a child. And I think Henry would have missed out. Henry should have 10 kids."

Henry agrees that the baby has added stress to their daily lives, but he also sees the pluses, including seeing his youth as a positive factor. "I think the age difference has helped. It has certainly been a plus with Michelle's desire to have a child at 40—I don't think she could have done that with a husband her own age. I think it would have been much harder for her because I'm willing to do more than a lot of guys her age.

"Another benefit is that I'm experiencing different things by being a first-time parent. I think all my enthusiasm helps us deal with the problems that come up. I think I bring to Michelle my wonder, my love for the newness of it. It helps her. While she's getting her own things out of having a child at 40, I'm getting my own things out of having my first kid. Together we can be excited about the total package: it's more than just our individual experiences. And the only time age comes up is when we think about having another kid. Once in a while, when Michelle's back goes out, she'll say, 'If I was 30 or 25, this wouldn't happen. . . .' "

But Michelle doesn't pay much attention to the physical aggravation. Her enthusiasm for her chance at a second family with a man she loves and who helps out with the child care and the housework remains high. "I'm not sure that I might not have another child," she said. "I was so sure Zach would be my last, but the pregnancy and the birth were wonderful for me. To be pregnant by a man that I really love and who was excited about the pregnancy has been so nice."

Can He Live with My Children?

Merging a new partner into an existing household is the most difficult adjustment, bar none, to be made by the woman who has children from an earlier marriage. The fact that a husband or lover is older or younger does not change things: the new, blended family is a tough adjustment for people of all ages. In couples where the man is younger, there is an immediate tendency to feel the resulting problems are due to his younger age. However, according to recent research I have done on the blended family, the problems are not related to the age difference. It is extremely important that older woman/younger man couples recognize this and approach their problems in a way that does not place blame on the age difference or on the younger partner.

The problems encountered by each of these blended families are complex, but the basic issues are accepting that each person in the household needs to define his or her "territory" as regards space and time and the need to establish guidelines for decision making and discipline even though one partner is not the natural parent. This can be a hassle that can threaten the health of the relationship unless the areas of strife are acknowledged and dealt with.

"No one really understands our problems," said Henry, 27. "We live in this crazy system that includes her kids, her ex, their relatives, my relatives, our ridiculous work and family schedules, tight finances. . . ."

The most obvious problem that confronts a new family is the sheer complexity of finding a place in the household for the new member. Young husbands try to lay claim to their own territory in the household, while kids are often shifting back and forth from one family home to another. Even the traffic patterns in the house can be sources of strife because of noise or lack of respect for closed doors.

Steve, 32, is married to Amanda, 41, who has two teenage daughters from her first marriage. "I've had to adjust not only to a marriage," said Steve, "but also to two grown kids who seem to be constantly present, have needs, and are a responsibility for me.

"But the biggest change was the lack of privacy. I need a lot of quiet time and time to read, and that's changed almost totally. It's very hard to do that now."

Steve said that it was easy to feel overwhelmed at first because the pace of life was so different with four people instead of just one. When Merritt, 42 (married to Tom, 33), saw the same thing about to happen in her household, she made an immediate attempt to try to help Tom adjust and feel a part of the family by encouraging him to live with her and her teenage daughter and son before they made a final decision to marry.

"The most important thing I did to help the situation," she said, "was to ask him to move in with me and my kids for a full year before we married. I know that most women don't want to do this because they think it sets a bad example, but I just felt too shaky in terms of the age difference, and I had to give myself some assurance I was doing the right thing. After all, Tom and I were making some significant financial as well as personal commitments to each other.

"So that was how I was able to prepare all of us for this. He found out the kids drove him nuts because they raced through our bedroom, they played his records, and they wiped out the refrigerator. The kids discovered he could be cranky and unwilling to bend about a lot of stuff that I might give in on. I was distressed to find they could all band together and ruin a completely nice afternoon.

"But after a while, we learned to look at each other as human beings who aren't perfect. We know where our problems are, and yet we still love each other. My kids really respect him. I think he knows that, and it makes him feel good. We have our good times and our bad times—but no nasty surprises.

"I can tell you one thing for sure: this man may be nine years younger than I am, but emotionally he's light-years ahead of my first husband, the father of my kids. My kids are the lucky ones—they now know that divorce isn't the end of the world and it takes hard work to make a marriage."

The issue of territory in the household came up frequently as I talked with women and younger men. "It's a problem for us," said Maureen, 43 (married to Garrett, 31), "because at first my kids [a son and daughter in their mid-teens] did what they always had done and kept walking in and out of our bedroom and our bathroom. Garrett felt very encroached upon by this, especially when my son borrowed his razor. To me, everything belongs to everyone, but he felt invaded. Garrett was used to living alone, and some of our sharing really bothered him. He needs his own territory. I've asked the kids to respect that, and they do."

Hand in hand with the issue of personal space goes the issue of stepparenting. Henry, 27, and wife Michelle, 43, live with her two teenage daughters, 13 and 16, in addition to the young son she and Henry have had together. Henry sees stepparenting, particularly defining his parenting roles, as his major adjustment to life with Michelle.

"Today I think the biggest issue for me in our marriage has been stepparenting," said Henry. "It is clearly a much more difficult thing than I thought it was going to be. There's no real way to anticipate it, particularly with teenagers. Sometimes I wonder what happened to those sweet young girls I knew when they were 12. All of a sudden they've become these difficult teenagers."

"When we first thought about getting together, I tried to warn Henry about this," said Michelle. "I would say, 'Do you realize there's less difference in age between Amy, who was just 16, and you than between you and me?' And he would smile.

"The girls liked him a lot when they met him, partly because he was very wise. He didn't try too hard; he just hung back and let them slowly get to know him and figure him out. So Henry didn't think living with them would make one bit of difference. And I think he was very naive. I was not so naive, but I sure wanted to listen to friends who said it wouldn't matter. And I did have people I trusted, people who are educated in family therapy and family issues, who said that. They did not tell me I wouldn't have problems; they just didn't think the problems would be any worse than normal life with adolescents, if the basic relationship between Henry and me was right. And you can never tell until you go through a long time anyway.''

But the ''normal life'' with teenagers is one in which a parent has had the experience of raising the child from birth, and this isn't true for a new husband. The younger husband, unlike some older men, is less likely to have had children of his own, so he often has less experience with children.

''I have even more of a problem than a parent would in dealing with his own teenagers because my relationship was not as solid with them before they entered that period,'' said Henry. ''That's been a problem for me. And it's been a problem, I think, because I've had to move into Michelle's world. I came here—it was her house, her kids, her relationship with her ex-husband. All of those things were part of her life, which I then adopted. Yet Michelle had to adapt to very little of my lifestyle, and I think that has made me feel uncomfortable and not as rooted as I would otherwise. So when an issue with the kids comes up, I often feel that I'm at a disadvantage in dealing with it because I don't have the same kind of shared history with the kids that she does. This is not familiar territory to me.

''The kids are not bad; they aren't terrible teenagers,'' said Henry. ''They're probably much better than most. But I think it's also been hard for me since their world is my world, and they take up so much time. And it's been difficult for me to etch out my own role in the family, particularly when they're changing and developing. But the positive side of all this is that we do have Zach, and I think that in spite of the great chunks of time he has taken from all of us, he's also brought our family together in a way—in very special ways—with each individual person.

''One problem I have with the girls is that Michelle and I were raised in different households. There are different values involved, different expectations. A good example is the volume in the house. Michelle and the girls—their volume is much higher than mine, than my family's was when I was growing up. People are yelling at each other up and down the stairs, and I just can't deal with that sometimes. It's hard for me. I can say, 'Please keep it quiet,' but it's difficult because I know for better or for worse it's a habit Michelle has with the girls. The stairs are there—you don't want to go all the way up or down the stairs to talk to somebody, so you just holler. And it's hard to change that habit.

"On the other hand, having Zach, we can say to each other, 'Do we want the baby screaming at the top of his lungs?' And if we don't, we're going to have to change the way we do things. Sometimes we can work those things out, but it's hard for me."

One way Michelle and Henry have developed to help work everything out has been to set a specific time to be together.

"The kids are here all the time," said Michelle, "so that makes it doubly important to set aside time for just us. Like Sunday night is our night. By hook or by crook we go out, and the girls are responsible for baby-sitting. If they have a test or something, they have to work it out between them. That helps all of us feel like the girls also have to take responsibility for something around here. It's sort of a payback for all the time Henry gives to them.

"In Henry's mind, I think there's still a question—he hasn't acquired that middle-aged sense that I have that you never get anything you want anyway, so therefore why bitch about it? If I get to take a bubble bath once a week, that's about the level of my personal wants that get fulfilled. I think that's much harder for him to accept. He's young, he's got his whole life before him, and he feels there's got to be something better than getting to watch a movie with your wife once a week. 'Is this what I got married for?' So I think in that sense it's hard."

Maureen and Garrett have the same problem. "I know that Garrett has had to give up a tremendous amount to be with me," said Maureen. "Ironically, since we've been married, he has had to give up having me to himself even in a dating situation. Because the kids are always here, he feels like he sees me less now that we live together.''

Brant and I have the same problem. We always have at least one child in the house. The only solution is to realize how important it is to have time together and go after it. Like Michelle, I find it hard to balance everyone's needs for space, time, and attention, but letting everyone know that it is a problem and that you are working on it does seem to help.

"I do feel—I know—there has been goodwill all around," said Michelle. "I think we're working with two healthy kids who are basically loving and giving. Neither of them has any extraordinary problems—just the normal ones that teenagers bring into your home, which is that they're all-enveloping, they fill the room, they're loud, they're demanding. But I think there's mutual respect among all of us."

That mutual respect Michelle refers to is the result of that great effort she and Henry exert in the area of decisions and discipline. Michelle feels strongly that Henry must be an equal partner in the decision making regarding the girls, even though this is difficult at times. I found that the families who seemed to have best resolved the blended family situation are those in which the mother takes care to include her younger husband in all the household decisions and discipline matters.

"I've included Henry in the parenting from the very beginning," said Michelle. "In some ways I wish he would do more. I think there are a few things that he could do. He's still feeling his way in terms of assertiveness, authority, 'when to,' 'when not to.' Sometimes he gets angry when he shouldn't, and sometimes he doesn't get angry when he should. I think we'll all work more smoothly as we get these things straightened out."

Henry has been willing to try hard to fulfill the role of stepfather. He points out that some of their conflict in this area stems from guilt feelings that Michelle has as a result of her earlier divorce and the pain it caused the children.

"I think that Michelle has a residue of guilt left about the effect the divorce had on her kids, whereas I have a much harder time identifying with what happened in her household six or seven years ago. Therefore, I have less patience with the girls. She's more open to understanding them and giving them a certain amount of room. I think Michelle realizes it's hard to break her old habits with the girls. Meanwhile, I'm demanding that habits be broken. That's been tough for us.''

"The hassle with the girls is similar to what any man joining a family would experience, except that Henry has so much less emotional experience with parenting,'' said Michelle. "After all, he's only married for the first time—he's a father for the first time. So in terms of handling emotional situations, he's new at all this stuff.

"Intimacy for him is a fairly new experience on an adult level. It's not as if he's tried and failed 25 times the way my friends and I have. Not only that, but the intimate relationships he had before me were on his age level, which means that he didn't have to deal with the kinds of things that you have in blended families, like 'whom should I give time to,' 'why do I never see my wife,' 'why do I care more about my son than I do for these two girls whose father is a schmuck,' or differences in parenting style.

"He didn't love her when she was a baby, so when Amy is obnoxious now, he doesn't have that whole history to temper his feelings. It may be that he's so young that he wants to be perfect, and he doesn't have a perspective on failure yet. I'll say it again: parenting in the blended family is tough.

"We have been in counseling, on and off for a year, to help both of us deal with everything. This blended parenting stuff hit me like a ton of bricks, too. I didn't realize how complicated it was. I'm amazed that I didn't. But I don't know anybody who talks about it.

"Meanwhile, we're really trying to have some sort of egalitarian marriage, which it isn't in some ways because of my girls, but it's a hell of a lot better than my first marriage. Henry's fairer than my first husband ever was. And he wants to be involved more, but he is completing a dissertation. I remember what I went through. I couldn't have survived if I'd had to handle what Henry has had to handle—not just emotionally and physically, in terms of responsibility, but the driving around of kids, the 'this' and the 'that' of family life.''

Because Henry will be seeking a position when he completes his dissertation, Michelle has made it clear that she is quite ready to move where and when he wants. Both of them see this as a partial solution to family problems since they will have territory that is new to everyone and not just to Henry.

"Believe me, I know the stepparenting is very burdensome for Henry, and he wants to get out of here," said Michelle. "He wants to be in a new place where we can start together on an equal footing. As a stepparent, I don't think he feels that he's doing as good a job as he could, and he isn't. He did a much better job the first year, but he did that with an enormous amount of self-sacrifice of his own needs. Now he's really got to buckle down to his own work first. Now we have a son, and he's a very good father for that son. And that's about all he can handle in terms of time."

Maureen and Garrett experience a very similar kind of strife between them and her children. However, Maureen has not been as open as Michelle has to *sharing* the parenting role with Garrett, perhaps because Maureen and Garrett have not had a child together as Michelle and Henry have. This affects the relationship by making her seem less understanding of his needs.

"In our household right now the issue is power, and it isn't financial power, but it has a lot to do with past history," said Maureen. "It's like Garrett feels he is in a position to have shared input regarding my children, shared decision making, but at the same time he feels he is excluded because the children and I were a unit and he's the outsider. It's usually the case that the children come to me first—they don't seek him out for permissions and other parent-type decisions. So I'm caught in the middle.

"I know Garrett tries to leave the parenting to me. And he does try to be supportive of whatever dogma I set as far as house rules. He comes across as kind of passive-supportive, but I know it frustrates him because he would prefer to take a much more active role. And this is a constant issue between us.

"My kids like Garrett. They have a great deal of respect

for him, and they know they can count on him. He is a very consistent person. On the other hand, he tends to be too structured in some ways—not as flexible as I am.

"When I have to deal with a crisis involving the kids, he just hasn't shared the family history, so I end up battling with him on the issue at hand and on how to deal with the kids— just when I really want him on my side. Yet what it comes down to is that he's not going to be on my side unless he acquiesces to my parenting."

Clearly, Maureen sees herself as the primary parent, unlike Michelle, who wants Henry to be an active, governing member of the family. But Maureen is not cold-hearted. "I always try to catch myself and learn to be more aware of taking care of him—more sensitive to where he is on this because it makes him feel so displaced," she said. "Garrett is jealous of the time and attention I give the kids. I'm always aware of that. So our big problem has nothing to do with our age difference—it's the children, and it's constant. Our situation is that we don't have 'ours'; we have 'hers.' I'm always on the defensive, and yet I feel—and I've been to my therapist because of this—that I have a loyalty to Garrett that I need to be more aware of. All of us are really trying hard."

She recognizes that she has only just begun to deal with all the issues involved in blending their family. To her credit, she is seeking professional help, which she hopes will enable her to share the parenting of her children with Garrett.

It is also important for parents to understand the children's position on the issue of the blended family. We looked at the issue in depth in Chapter 3, but it's worth a brief mention here. David, 25 (married to Ellen, 39), discussed with me what he perceived to be his stepson's point of view. Ellen's son had not had a dad before David.

"Before we got married, he was real excited about it because he wanted to have a daddy. He had never had one before. He wanted to show me off. When we started living together, I think it was a real shock to him. Being an only child, he'd always been the focus of attention, and he really didn't have to do any sharing. On the other hand, we pretty much just do family things that are mostly geared toward what would interest him, not necessarily us, but I know that I'm also kind of a burden to him. Meeting some of my needs means some of his have to be excluded. Like the fact there's an extra person in the house who may want to go to bed early or later—so that will control his behavior more. Or eating used to be a constant battle. He was a picky eater, and when I began to do all the cooking because of Ellen's schedule, I refused to do what she did—I would not make two different meals—so he had to adjust.

"But most of the time things work out. You need to separate the family problems from the rest because, if we didn't have this child and another on the way, I think the issue of age difference would be minimal. Without kids, we'd start fresh and new together and steer our own course with no regard to age."

Helen Swan, a noted family therapist, explains why these family problems can be so difficult. "Often, blended families come together so quickly that the tension level in the household can be very high. Everything is trial and error as each family member seems to carry around a mental image of the perfect 'nuclear family' that he or she aspires to. Blended families are not nuclear families. They have few workable models to use for examples or to gain perspective on their own problems."

Yet many couples, including Michelle and Henry, even though they acknowledge their difficulties, feel very positive about their future. "After we had Zach together," said Michelle, "we were able to counter the negative aspects of life with the girls. Henry's enthusiasm and thrill with the newness of being a parent combines wonderfully with my own experience. I can calm him down when he thinks the baby is sick and the worst is at hand, and he reminds me of how wonderful and amazing it is to have a cute new baby. The baby means something special to my kids, too, so maybe this little kid brings us all together in a better way."

In our household, Brant and I share the decision making on all issues, particularly those that involve my children. Many times he's been on their side, forcing me to taking a more flexible and less "parental" approach, such as giving

250

them more freedom in their late teens. Other times, he feels, like Henry, as though too much of their noise and activity spills into the quiet time he wants for reading. Or, conversely, he will want to play the stereo full-blast just when a kid wants to nap.

So we work it out. We argue, we laugh, we get angry—but we talk about it every step of the way. And because blending a family is so very difficult, I cannot imagine a better partner than Brant to help meet the challenge because, like all the younger men interviewed, he's more open to basic communication—not only about what aggravates him but also about what pleases him, such as when he is touched by a small gesture of appreciation from one of the kids. And, *always,* he has been willing to help out—with the driving, with the meals and household stuff, and in those rare moments of panic when I have been terrified that something has happened to one of my kids.

I really can't offer a reassuring answer or alternative to a woman who is involved with a younger man but for whom all the problems surrounding the issue of children have not been resolved. Whether she desperately wants a child but he does not or the situation is reversed, there's no easy answer—only a risk. You must consider the strength of the love you share, the reason you value one another, and decide if *that* merits staying together.

9

His Mother/Our Future

*Many couples agree . . . that the men in these relationships
are more egalitarian than older males—in part because they
were raised by a generation of women who grew up in the
age of feminism. "Intimacy and sharing," says Freudenberger, "are not threatening to younger men."*

> —*Picture Week* interview with psychologist
> Dr. Herbert Freudenberger

*Women tend to love their lovers and best friends about the
same, but actually like their best friends more than their lovers. Further, liking someone, they discovered, was a better
predictor of long-term success of a relationship than loving
someone.*

> —from a recent study by Dr. Robert J. Sternberg
> and Susan Svajeck of Yale University,
> as reported in the *Hartford Courant*

Another woman figures prominently in relationships between
older women and younger men: his mother. But not the way
that people expect when they assume the attraction reflects
an Oedipal complex, the classic search for a mother figure.

Initially, most of the women interviewed were on guard in their new relationships, afraid that outsiders would view their relationship as one in which they played the role of the mother. But not one couple interviewed showed any evidence of the man's seeking a strong mother figure in the older woman. Brad, 39 (living with Elinor, 57), spoke to that point when he dismissed the idea by saying that we look for some characteristics of both of our parents in everyone we meet and become attached to. He felt on solid ground making that statement because he has been in therapy and hasn't found in working with his therapist that his relationship with Elinor derives from an extreme need for mothering.

"There may be some mother thing going on," he said, "because every relationship a man forms has something to do with his mother—even if a woman is younger. I have a male therapist, and I think of him as making up for all the things I felt I got shortchanged on from my father, so maybe Elinor is compensating for my mother in some way. But they have nothing in common."

In my experience, I was unaware of any overtones of the "mother-son" stereotype. In fact, I had begun to suspect that Brant's relationship with his mother had, in fact, made it possible for him to look at women as his intellectual peers and as potential good friends.

I became aware of this early in my relationship with Brant, although I initially pulled back, thinking that he might be looking for a mother figure. Even though he made it quite clear that was not the case, I had my doubts; there's such a strong societal attitude toward relationships like ours.

But as I got to know Brant better, and I became aware of his remarkable relationship with his mother, I saw I had nothing to worry about.

Brant has a wonderful relationship with his mother. They talk at least once a week, like good friends, covering the unusual and the trivial, the myriad details of life that everyone likes to share with friends. His father is very much a part of his life as well. They are three people—parents and son—who are very good friends and among whom information is shared on an equal basis. There is no father/son exchange, for example, that excludes his mother, and no mother/son confidences that exclude his father.

A major topic of conversation among them is work. All three deal with exhausting work schedules. Each one is involved in a fascinating, fast-paced career. They have helped each other through times of intense pressure. Helping is *expected* of the men in the family. What sets his family unit apart, along with most of the families of the younger men interviewed, is that Brant's mother completed her education and has worked full-time since his birth. Even during the few years that she was an army wife and not in school or working, she was very active in the community and had responsibilities that required her presence outside the home. She and Brant's father have balanced their demanding schedules and shared their home responsibilities for years. As early as elementary school, Brant was a part of this mutual support team, caring for himself for several hours after school each day and in charge of the dusting, vacuuming, and garbage disposal.

I was curious about my mother-in-law's motivation to work and how she was able to balance her role as a working wife and mother. "When I was 11, I wanted to be an attorney," she said. "I was incensed by inequities in the world around me, and I was impressed by another woman, a lawyer, who was my mentor in high school. Later I was directed more toward social work, and that has been my field since. Even though my parents were very supportive, I still found it difficult to convince others that I wanted to be more than the traditional housewife. My husband, however, has always been very, very supportive of my work."

I think their relationship, with its obvious evidence of an equal partnership in marriage and career goals, shows that the older woman/younger man isn't the only marriage where equality is possible, but few older men are as enlightened and supportive as Brant's father. Yet it is the few men and women like my in-laws, with their more traditional age difference (he is one year older than she), who have broken with traditional attitudes and helped make it possible for all of us to have other options in life. Even though I focus on the mother's relationship with the son in this chapter, the father's role is critical. His support is crucial if she is to change and grow out of outdated patterns and roles.

In talking with Brant's mother about this book, I told her that I felt her close friendship with Brant was one reason he and I seemed to communicate so easily and so well. I couldn't get over how easily we could talk about so many things—and understand each other—because I had always found it hard to talk to men.

"Brant was a very mature little boy," his mother said. "His father was in the service and gone for months at a time. Our families were far away from the base where we lived, so even though he was just five years old, Brant was my confidante. I talked to him as if he were my peer."

I think it was from that that he learned respect for the individual. He also learned that it was okay to feel emotions and to talk about them, to be sensitive to the emotional needs of others. In addition, the first woman who was important to Brant was also someone for whom education and career were an integral, accepted part of daily life. Brant is very proud of both of his parents, but being aware of how much she has accomplished during a time when women were just beginning to become self-sufficient gives him a deep respect for his mother, which carries over to all women. It's the same respect that, traditionally, family members have reserved for the male head of a household. My in-laws share that role, and they share recognition of their successes from their son. Ultimately, that explains why Brant has never questioned *my* need to work and to achieve. Nor does he see anything unique in his attitude, because it's an outlook that other men his age grew up with. Brant and his peers are the sons of pioneers— sons of the women who entered adulthood during the early years of feminism and adapted many principles of the women's movement to the way they raised their sons and daughters. They grew up around women—mothers and sisters and friends—who were discovering they had new options in life beyond being wives and mothers. And their new options have meant new options for the men around them, too. These options include sharing the financial load as well as the housework in dual career families, communicating easily about feelings and worries, and establishing friendships with people of both sexes that are grounded in mutual respect and understanding.

"My generation doesn't put people into boxes," said Brant when I asked him if he agreed with me on this. "A box is thinking that someone in his or her forties must act and be a certain way. I don't believe that. How can I believe it when my own mother, who is 52, was just promoted to a top-level management position? Does that sound like a typical woman in her fifties? I have learned from my mother to approach women as vital, interesting, challenging people. The people I choose to be around are ones who are smart and work hard. That's what I value in all my friends, male or female."

So I give Brant's mother a lot of the credit for the wonderful changes in my life that have happened because of my relationship with her son. Even if we had never married, his acceptance of me reinforced my self-esteem so much that, had we stopped dating, I still would have walked away feeling good about myself. Brant is very, very different from my first husband, who maintained that my role was always to be subservient to him, that my personal goals were not to be respected as highly as his. He felt that he should always be the sole caretaker of the household and, consequently, that made him the most important person in the family. I wanted to be important, too. I wanted our children to feel important. I wanted all of us to share in those feelings of being special and contributing to everyone's success.

Brant shares those kinds of feelings with me. I am convinced that it is due to his mother's early influence that he understands something many older men do not—that to truly care for others is to acknowledge the importance of each person's sense of independence and to understand how feelings of positive self-worth grow out of the knowledge that you can be self-sufficient, that you can contribute to the world around you. Brant learned from his mother, and he shares that with me. I think his attitude is one found more often in younger men, but I am confident that men my age and older are beginning to understand that the independent working woman can be a strong, loving, supportive partner, not a threat.

The New Mother-Son Relationship

At first I thought Brant's relationship with his mother was unique, but as I interviewed other younger men involved in successful relationships with older women for this book, I found the same pattern recurring—a warm friendship with their mothers and respect for their accomplishments. In fact, I soon realized that a good mother-son relationship almost always preceded an older woman/younger man relationship. The mothers of the younger men in these relationships not only make it possible for their sons to establish friendships with women more easily—friendships lacking in age discrimination—but at the same time may have provided a strong basis for enduring, long-term love relationships.

"Rob adores his mother," said Diane, age 45, of her 33-year-old husband. "She works. She's not traditional in any sense. She doesn't cook. But she keeps up with family life on the personal side and would like us to do more family things. She's very friendly and often stops by without her husband, and we have a great time. She might stop by in the middle of a party we're having, and she fits right in, giggling and laughing and having a good time.

"Her background was very rough. She was put in foster homes growing up, she had to immigrate to this country, and she learned to take care of herself, to be independent. Perhaps that's why I've never felt her to be critical of me and my independence."

"I had a very comfortable relationship with my mother," recalls Eric, 42 (married to Donna, 65), whose mother died recently. "I think my experience with her was that she supported me; she was very accepting. I always found her easy to talk to.

"She was pretty traditional—she worked occasionally, but

given the strong bond between my parents, she was also fairly independent and traveled a lot with women friends.''

Stephanie, age 43, dating 30-year-old Alan, says of his mother, ''I still haven't met her, but I've talked with her on the phone. I think she could be a good friend. It's bizarre— after I met Alan, I couldn't wait to tell a few good friends that I'd met this really terrific guy. I got on the phone right away, *but I didn't tell my parents.* Now he went home, and he didn't tell his friends—but he told his mother. He barely made it home before he told her. I thought that was really neat.

''They have a terrific friendship, which is always a plus, I think. And she works. He said I reminded him of his mother, and I don't take that in a negative way because he said it after he found out that I had gone back to school in my late thirties, really stuck to it, and I'm out there now working hard and really accomplishing something. In three years I've made a good reputation for myself. He said it's my spirit that reminds him of his mother.''

The friendship between the man and his mother is easily extended to include the new woman in his life. Almost all of the women interviewed who had had an opportunity to meet the mothers of the men they loved found it as easy to like the mothers as it was to like the sons.

''One of the things I like so much about Dan is his mother,'' said Lynn, 37 (dating Dan, 30). ''I like his mom a lot. She must be well into her sixties, but she could be a contemporary of mine. She is a very sharp woman. We go at one another because we have varying opinions on different issues, but she's a person who could easily be a friend of mine outside my relationship with her son.''

"Younger" Has More to Do with Upbringing Than Age

Of the older woman/younger man couples interviewed for this book, 80 percent of the men are the sons of women whose critical stages of adult development—their twenties and thirties—occurred during the 1960s and '70s, a time of tremendous social change in this country that was affected by the women's movement. Because of this, these women were the first to benefit from social acceptance of new roles for women beyond the traditions of marriage and motherhood. Most of the men interviewed are the sons of women who work or have worked. Some of them are sons of women who married younger men.

Henry, 27 (married to Michelle, 43), has a mother who is four years older than his father. Even though that doesn't seem to be a large age difference, relative to social attitudes at the time when they married, it was significant for his parents. Henry's mother was a true pioneer, one of a small percentage of women then marrying younger men. She was also unusual in the way she timed her marriage and the pursuit of her career.

"Although my parents are traditional in many ways," said Henry, "my mother is 4 years older than my father. She married at 30, fairly late for a woman of her generation. She has always had her own career, and she has always made more money than my father. Even when I was born, she took only two weeks off work. So there are a lot of things that helped them deal with my relationship with Michelle and, I'm sure, helped open my mind to marrying someone who is older, earns more than I do—that sort of thing. When I introduced my parents to Michelle, my mother knew what I was doing was unconventional, but she didn't think it was an important issue."

Says Michelle, "It's clear to me that Henry's mother—and his parents' relationship—made ours possible. His mother has always been the primary breadwinner in their family. She is better educated than his father, and she has been the stronger force in decisions on the family's lifestyle. She is a very strong-minded woman, yet Henry's father is not emasculated. He is also strong. A quiet, interesting man. Even though the mother is strong, she is old-fashioned in the sense that she's very careful about men's sensibilities. She's not a shrew. She's very family-centered. They have been a very interesting model for Henry."

Even the mothers of the younger men who married older or same-age men or chose not to work benefited from societal changes. They began to feel more valued as individuals. In turn, because they have learned to value more highly the traditional feminine characteristics such as emotional, familial attachments and the open expression of emotion, they have been less hesitant to encourage the development of these qualities in their sons. An indication that the expression of emotion, once discouraged in young boys and considered strictly a feminine trait, is now more acceptable for men is the fact that, in modern family therapy today, responsibility for family "feelings" has shifted from being a concern primarily of the mother to being a mutual concern for both parents, just as the financial support is a mutual concern in the majority of families today.

It is for these reasons, perhaps, that a man in his twenties or thirties is a marked contrast to men my age and older, whom I have known to be much more detached from their mothers, not comfortable with frequent, intimate conversations with them, not likely to share their concerns with them, not apt to count them among their good pals, and—in my experience—not particularly respectful, either. In fact, a lot of the men I knew in my late teens and early twenties tended to poke fun at their mothers and even treat them as if they were silly, foolish, bothersome women. Others treated them as goddesses, distant images to be revered.

Says Henry, 27, of his 43-year-old wife's peers, "I think the men of Michelle's generation are very different from the men of my generation. That difference is greater than if you compare differences between generations of women. The kind of assumptions and values that I grew up with have changed so radically from the assumptions and values of men growing up in the '50s and early '60s. I think that's because they are more vested in the system, their careers, everything that was socially prescribed during those years. So they have a harder time changing and developing as individuals than women do."

But age is really not the primary issue here; there are 20-year-old men who can't really relate to women and 70-year-old men who are wonderful, sharing partners. What characterizes any healthy relationship—but particularly between older women and younger men—is friendship. It is a friendship that is often dual in nature: first, the man experiences a friendly, supportive relationship with his mother early in life that is maintained into adulthood and reinforced with regular contact. Secondly, friendship emerges again and again as a hallmark of the relationship the man shares with the women he loves. And that openness to friendship with women often extends beyond the love relationship. Brant has many women friends, as do Brad, Henry, Rob, and Eric.

The pool of men who are young—young at heart and the type of men with whom women can develop lasting partnerships—is growing as more and more women demand equality for their children. And equal partnerships beget kids who, when they grow up, look for equal partnerships. Things are indeed changing.

A latecomer to the women's movement, I nevertheless tried to break with the stereotype as I mothered my children, making sure that my daughter had the same opportunity to develop her abilities and responsibilities that my sons did and concentrating on instilling a basic acceptance of equality between the sexes. And at the same time, I tried to convey the importance of feminine values, too. As much as I wanted my daughter to be prepared to be independent—financially and socially—and my sons to recognize that this is wise and acceptable for a woman to do, I wanted all three to understand and value fully the traditional female traits by which we learn to be considerate, to know that it is healthy to acknowledge our emotions, and to feel comfortable with the concepts of love and intimacy.

I made the same toys available to both, and I enrolled both in the same sports—including track, baseball, and soccer. Sometimes I had to fight to get my daughter on the team, as when I first enrolled her for track and the coach looked at me and said, "No girl is going to run on my track." Years later, when he was her basketball coach and I reminded him of that statement, he was shocked to recall he had said it. Times have changed indeed.

I also made damn sure my daughter had the same academic

opportunities as my sons: I have never forgotten asking my dad for a dentist kit for Christmas only to watch him give it to my younger brother instead. That did not happen in our house. Today my older son and my daughter are outstanding scholars, my daughter is oriented toward linguistics and business, and both of my sons are interested in the performing arts. All three are very good pals, and they play basketball together.

What is even more telling, however, is that *all three have large circles of friends that are both male and female*—far different from the days when I was in school, when you knew a man as a boyfriend or almost not at all. We have learned to raise our daughters as the equals of our sons—and good friendships are made between equals.

We all learn as we grow older that friendship knows not the boundaries of age. We meet men and women, young and old, in our daily lives and from them select those who will be a part of the fabric of our lives for many reasons. I firmly believe that a strong friendship provides the cornerstone of a good marriage, of a delightful, expressive sexual relationship, and of a pairing of two people who will enjoy growing older together.

10

Loving A Younger Man:
Is It Right for You?

Love does not consist in gazing at each other but in looking outward together in the same direction.

—Antoine de Saint-Exupéry

Is loving a younger man right for you? Think it over. It isn't a question that's easy to answer. I know, because it took me years to feel I had made the right decision. On the other hand, my reason for writing *Loving a Younger Man* was to make that question much easier for everyone to answer without taking years to do so!

As you consider the question, I'd like to share something with you. I've spent at least 20 years watching other people make their decisions in order to figure out who was doing it right—who was succeeding in marriage and life—and why. Here's what I found: the people who didn't pay attention to social conventions, who didn't follow the rules but found their own way, who lived by some innate personal honesty, were the people who were happiest.

When I did make my decision to marry a younger man, I tried to arrive at it by listening to my own heart and following my own intuition. And guess what? I did the right thing. I'm

263

happy. I enjoy my old friends and the new ones I've met through Brant—and the same goes for him. Becoming an "older woman/younger man couple" has turned out to be such a natural pairing for both of us that I wonder why on earth it took me so long to say yes.

So read the following and don't do what I did—if it's right for you, don't procrastinate.

Love and Sex

Let's answer one of the big questions right away. Is sex _really_ better with a younger man? It sure is. For those of you who skipped right to this chapter, it's not for the reasons you think. It's better simply because he's the guy most likely to love you, and love making love to you, not for _what_ you are, but for _who_ you are. The younger man today is a new kind of man, as you have discovered in the pages of this book. He's a man with whom sex and love and life can be terrific because he's more likely to bring out the best in _you_. Together you have a better chance at a love affair that may be sexy, sweet, sensible, and satisfying. It is also more likely to be based on equal sharing on all levels.

Will The Real "Older Woman" Please Stand Up?

As I interviewed men and women for _Loving a Younger Man_, I discovered certain recurring personality traits and behavior patterns. To recap:

The woman who chooses to risk a long-term relationship with a younger man tends to be the kind of person who stands out among other women—and men. Self-sufficient and financially independent, she is a woman who has worked her way up in her field. Whether she is in her early thirties or her mid-seventies, she has achieved some measure of career success. All of the women interviewed were achievement-oriented and had pursued careers as business executives, doctors, and lawyers, or they were independent professionals such as tenured college professors, performers, producers, artists, or writers. Not one had achieved wealth or status because of a family inheritance or a prior marriage. The woman who fell in love with a younger man was a self-made woman.

When it comes to physical attributes, whether she is short or tall, slender or chubby, this is a woman whose strikingly attractive appearance is less a product of cosmetic efforts than a high-energy attitude that radiates self-confidence. Direct and well-spoken, she presents herself the same as any man holding a responsible, well-paid position. Her sense of self-esteem is derived from pride in her willingness to take risks, to set and meet difficult goals. As the type of individual who has been able to adapt to change that she felt was necessary in her personal and professional life, as well as change that might have been forced on her through various personal traumas, such as divorce, illness, or death, she has learned to be unafraid of, even to value, change.

Indeed, it's the knowledge of how tough, short, and unpredictable life is that leads her to eschew conventional behavior such as considering only men her own age or older as potential partners. She has a strong awareness of what matters most in life. She is able to pinpoint the advantages of relationships with younger men, such as their easy ways of communication and intimacy. She feels that to have found a "kindred spirit" is worth more than money in the bank or the security a more conventional marriage would provide.

Because she has experienced serious losses in her life, she has a sense of urgency, of how important it is to enjoy the relationship *now*. The woman knows exactly what she values in her marriage or relationship with a younger man and why. She does not hold back from telling her partner how much she cares, and she does so while acknowledging just how tenuous that satisfaction and pleasure might be. She is willing to risk any problems the age difference may present in order to be with him.

A Profile of a Man Who Is Forever Young

At the very beginning of their relationship, as flattered as the woman is by the man's interest, he is equally flattered that she is willing to go out with him. This is because he sees her as an accomplished, talented professional—often a woman in a position of leadership in his field—while he may see himself as someone just starting out.

At first glance, the "younger" man looks no different from other men. He may be 16 or 60, tall or short, bearded or clean-shaven. He just happens to love a woman who is a year or 10 or 20 years older than he. Perhaps because he is the son of a working mother or the brother of an independent, self-sufficient woman, he is more likely to see a woman as his equal—and that is a new way of thinking. For example, George was 80 years old, but he thought of his wife, 92-year-old Marie, with the same respect and love and affection that Henry, 27, lavishes on 43-year-old Michelle. Twenty-seven or 80, the numbers make no difference, so long as the man is young at heart, so long as he loves and accepts a woman not for *what* she is but for *who* she is.

Most of the men are 10 to 20 years into their careers; some are completing graduate school. Those married to women over the age of 50 are established in their careers but may see their wives or lovers as having achieved higher positions and incomes in their own careers. However, the younger man is not a person without accomplishments. He may be younger, but, like the woman he is with, he tends to be very independent and in a position that allows for a great deal of autonomy—often a self-employed, entrepreneurial type such as a computer specialist, writer, lawyer, business owner, artist, or physician.

Whatever his field, the woman finds the man to be her peer intellectually, to complement her kind of analytical thinking so that they establish an easy dialogue from the first—most often meeting one another through their work. In fact, it is the work environment that helps a woman set aside one of her main concerns—whether or not he is mature enough.

One trait that the men have in common is something one woman described as her husband's "eccentricity" and another described by saying, "He's not at all like other men I've been attracted to." These men are different from the men the women grew up with: "He can be a friend more easily" . . . "I can't put my finger on it, but he's not that good ol' boy kind of guy we all went to college with and thought we were supposed to marry" . . . "He's more comfortable with women as his peers" . . . "He's got a strong little kid in him."

Another personality trait that all the men demonstrate is the ability to communicate uncommonly well with women. They listen and talk and feel comfortable discussing subjects ranging from the professional to the personal, the everyday to the intimate. Again and again the women state that the younger men, unlike many older men they have known, are willing to talk over problems and discuss issues on both an intellectual and an emotional level. All the women point out the greater degree of intimacy they experience with their younger lover as a result of the ongoing communication between them—significantly more communication than they had in previous relationships.

And every woman interviewed said that one of the things she likes most about life with a younger man is the opportunity he represents—the fact that he isn't totally settled into a career and a set way of doing things, that facing the future with him makes everything a little less certain, a lot more exciting.

Quiz: Is Loving a Younger Man Right for You?

I developed this questionnaire to help you assess your own potential in an older woman/younger man relationship. It may be perfect for you, or it may be totally wrong. The questions are similar to those I asked in my interviews.

Independence

	YES	NO
Are you over age 25?	☐	☐
Do you adapt easily to change in your job?	☐	☐
Do you adapt easily to change in your daily life?	☐	☐
Do you view new challenges with eagerness and anticipation?	☐	☐
Have you been married before or lived with a man at least once already?	☐	☐
Are you free from undue anxiety over what your family thinks of you and your lifestyle?	☐	☐

	YES	NO
Can you accept failure and be willing to start over?	☐	☐
Do you take risks in your professional and your personal life?	☐	☐
Do you think of yourself as a reasonably happy, well-adjusted person?	☐	☐
Do you worry about the future?	☐	☐
Do you want your life to change significantly between now and 10 years from now?	☐	☐
Do you feel you have control over your environment?	☐	☐
Can you say that money is not all that important to you?	☐	☐
Have you been forced to make some painful decisions in your life, such as choosing to divorce?	☐	☐
Have you experienced a life-threatening situation or severe trauma?	☐	☐
Have you lost a close family member to death?	☐	☐
Do you consider yourself an independent thinker?	☐	☐

Friendship

	YES	NO
Do you enjoy conversation?	☐	☐
Does your list of friends include many different kinds of people?	☐	☐

Is Loving a Younger Man Right for You?

	YES	NO
Do you like to meet new people?	☐	☐
Do you have friends of all ages?	☐	☐
Do your friends include people of both sexes?	☐	☐

Family

	YES	NO
Do you have a younger brother?	☐	☐
Do you have a good relationship with your father? Your mother?	☐	☐
If you have children, do you communicate easily with them?	☐	☐
Do you feel that your children can communicate easily with you?	☐	☐
Do you think a man should be able to cry?	☐	☐

Body Image

	YES	NO
Can you cope with a wrinkle?	☐	☐
Do you feel good about your body?	☐	☐
Do you use a minimal amount of makeup?	☐	☐
Do you think you will look good as you age without plastic surgery?	☐	☐

Quiz

	YES	NO
Are you able to live with your weight?	☐	☐
Are you physically fit?	☐	☐
Can you look at yourself naked?	☐	☐

Sex

	YES	NO
Do you enjoy making love?	☐	☐
Do you maintain an active sex life through intercourse or masturbation or both?	☐	☐
Do you believe in sex after age 70?	☐	☐
Are you sexually experienced?	☐	☐
Do you believe in trying new things in the bedroom, including oral sex or the use of pornography?	☐	☐
Have you had more than one sexual partner?	☐	☐
Do you feel comfortable saying ''no''?	☐	☐

Younger Men

	YES	NO
Have you ever felt attracted to a younger man?	☐	☐
Have you been asked out by a younger man?	☐	☐

Is Loving a Younger Man Right for You?

	YES	NO
Has a younger man ever paid special attention to you?	☐	☐
Does your work environment bring you into contact with younger men?	☐	☐

Interests

	YES	NO
Do you like rock and roll?	☐	☐
Do you like different kinds of music?	☐	☐
Do you like outdoor activities?	☐	☐
Do you enjoy movies?	☐	☐
Are you athletic?	☐	☐
Do you like to try new sports, new interests, new ideas?	☐	☐
Do you read a lot?	☐	☐

Career and Education

	YES	NO
Do you have a college degree?	☐	☐
Do you work?	☐	☐
Are you in a traditionally male occupation, such as medicine, business, or law?	☐	☐
Do you plan to work until retirement?	☐	☐

Quiz

	YES	NO
Do you plan to work after retirement?	☐	☐
Do you consider yourself successful?	☐	☐
Did you take this quiz because you believe everything is possible?	☐	☐

All the questions have been phrased so that "yes" answers mean you might be happy with a younger man. The women I interviewed who answered "yes" to questions like these were the women in thriving relationships with younger men. That means you should give careful consideration to your "no" answers, perhaps reviewing the chapters that deal with the issues involved. Be sure you really mean "no" and that you aren't a victim of outdated stereotypes, of old attitudes, that can affect your thinking if you aren't aware of their source.

Quiz: Is He the Younger Man for You?

The questionnaire that follows has been developed to help you decide if the younger man who interests you might be a good partner in a long-term relationship. Is he young in age only or young at heart? Every "yes" answer is a positive sign for the future of your relationship. Every "no" answer means you had better think it over carefully.

	YES	NO
Was he attracted to you first?	☐	☐
Does he think you're brainy as well as beautiful?	☐	☐
Does he listen to your opinions?	☐	☐
Do you talk things over easily?	☐	☐
Do you talk a lot?	☐	☐
Has he asked you how old you are?	☐	☐
Has he refused to be embarrassed by the age difference between you?	☐	☐
Does he offer to share expenses?	☐	☐

Quiz

	YES	NO
Does he have other women friends—platonic relationships?	☐	☐
Does he have friends of all ages and both sexes?	☐	☐
Does he get along with his mother?	☐	☐
Does he get along with his sisters?	☐	☐
Did you meet at work?	☐	☐
Does he work well with others?	☐	☐
Has he ever said he admires your work?	☐	☐
Do you share any similar interests?	☐	☐
Does he know how to clean house, do the laundry, or cook?	☐	☐
Does he do any of the above regularly?	☐	☐
Can he match his socks? Can he match yours?	☐	☐
Has he ever taken care of a child?	☐	☐
Has he ever taken care of you when you were sick?	☐	☐
Is he someone you would be willing to share finances with—50/50?	☐	☐
If you have children, do you think he could adapt to them?	☐	☐
Do you think your children would respect him?	☐	☐
Does he have a gentle side to his personality?	☐	☐

276

Is He the Younger Man for You?

	YES	NO
Do you find him sexually attractive?	☐	☐
Have you answered most of the above with a "yes"?	☐	☐
Has he asked you out?	☐	☐
Do you want to ask him out?	☐	☐

What are you waiting for?

Profile Statistics

The following couples are those described and quoted most frequently in *Loving a Younger Man*. Please note that all names have been changed in order to protect their privacy.

Amanda, 41, and Steve, 32, (met at ages 35 and 26). Amanda and Steve have been together for six years and were married four years ago. They live with her two teenage daughters. Both work. *Nine-year age difference*

Carolyn, 74, and Ed, 59 (met at ages 59 and 44). Married for 14 years, Carolyn and Ed met shortly before her sixtieth birthday. They have no children. Both work. *Fifteen-year age difference*

Diane, 45, and Rob, 33 (met at ages 36 and 24). Married five years ago, Diane and Rob have been together for eight years. They have no children. Both work. *Twelve-year age difference*

Donna, 65, and Eric, 42 (met at ages 58 and 35). Married three years ago, Donna and Eric have been together for four years and have known each other for seven. She has five grown children. Both work. *Twenty-three-year age difference*

Elinor, 57, and Brad, 39 (met at ages 47 and 29). They have lived together for nine years. Both work, no children. *Eighteen-year age difference*

Ellen, 39, and David, 25 (met at ages 35 and 21). Married for three years, they have known each other for four years. They live with her son, aged seven, and are expecting their first child soon. Both work. *Fourteen-year age difference*

Joanne, 53, and Hans, 43 (met at ages 33 and 23). Married for 20 years, they have two teenage daughters. Both work. *Ten-year age difference*

Lillian, 72, and John, 57 (met at ages 60 and 45). Married for 12 years, she has one grown child and he has two from their previous marriages. Both work. *Fifteen-year age difference*

Lynn, 37, and Dan, 30 (met at ages 36 and 29). Currently dating and seriously considering marriage. No children. Both work. *Seven-year age difference*

Marie, 92, and George, 77 (met at ages 65 and 50). Married for 27 years, she has seven children and he has two from their previous marriages. Though they were retired in their later years, both had worked full time. *Fifteen-year age difference*

Maureen, 43, and Garrett, 31 (met at ages 31 and 19). Married for 6 years, they have known each other for 12 years. They live with her two teenage children. Both work. *Twelve-year age difference*

Merritt, 42, and Tom, 33 (met at ages 35 and 26). Together for seven years, they have been married for five. They live with her two teenage children. Both work. *Nine-year age difference*

Michelle, 43, and Henry, 27 (met at ages 39 and 23). Married for three years, they have known each other for four. They live with her two teenage daughters and have one son of their own. They are considering having a second child. Both work. *Sixteen-year age difference*

Stephanie, 43, and Alan, 30 (met recently). Still in the early stages of their relationship, they continue to see each other at least once a month—not a bad schedule since they live on opposite coasts. *Thirteen-year age difference*

Bibliography

Books

Bianchi, Suzanne M., and Spain, Daphne. *American Women in Transition*. New York: Russell Sage Foundation, 1986.

Blotnick, Dr. Srully. *Otherwise Engaged: The Personal Lives of Successful Career Women*. New York: Facts on File Publications, 1985.

Gilligan, Carol. *In a Different Voice: Psychological Theory and Women's Development*. Cambridge, Mass., and London: Harvard University Press, 1982.

Gordon, Ruth. *An Open Book*. New York: Doubleday, 1980.

Lawrence, Frieda. *Not I, but the Wind*. New York: Viking Press, 1934.

O'Brien, Patricia. *The Woman Alone*. New York: Quadrangle/The New York Times Book Company, 1973.

Peter, Laurence J. *Peter's Quotations*. New York: William Morrow & Company, 1977.

Pickford, Kaylon. *Always Beautiful*. New York: G. P. Putnam's Sons, 1985.

Bibliography

Reitz, Rosetta. *Menopause, a Positive Approach.* New York: Penguin Books, 1979.

Sarrel, Lorna J. and Philip M. *Sexual Turning Points: The Seven Stages of Adult Sexuality.* New York: Macmillan Publishing Company, 1984.

Scarf, Maggie. *Unfinished Business: Pressure Points in the Lives of Women.* New York: Ballantine Books, 1981.

Trien, Susan Flamholtz. *Change of Life: The Menopause Handbook.* New York: Fawcett Columbine, 1986.

Articles

"About That New Grandmother," *American Demographics* (March, 1987).

Berger, Amy. "Spring-Autumn Romances," *Woman's World* (November 18, 1986).

"Breaking a Taboo," *Picture Week* (August 25, 1986).

Dorsey, Gray. "The Love Doctor," *Northeast/The Hartford Courant* (February 8, 1987).

Faludi, Susan. "Wedding Bell Blues: How the Media Fooled Around with a College Study on Marriage," *The Hartford Courant*/Knight-Ridder Newspapers (October 1, 1986).

Gavzer, Bernard. "Why More Older Women Are Marrying Younger Men," *Parade Magazine* (May 24, 1987).

Gross, Jane. "Single Women: Coping with a Void," *The New York Times* (April 28, 1987).

Hessburg, John. "Here's to You, Mrs. Robinson," *Pacific Northwest* (November, 1986).

Hodge, Marie. "Why Women Lie About Their Age," *50 Plus* (February, 1987).

Jacobson, David. "The Age Barrier," *The Hartford Courant* (December 14, 1986).

Johnson, Janis. "The Boom in Later Babies," *USA Today* (May 27, 1986).

Jong, Erica. "Is There Sexy After Forty?" *Vogue* (May, 1987).

"The Marriage Crunch," *Newsweek* (June 2, 1986).

Pollitt, Katha. "Being Wedded Is Not Always Bliss," *The Nation* (September 20, 1986).

Prince, Dinah. "Marriage in the '80s," *New York* (June 1, 1987).

Rosener, Judy B. "Coping with Sexual Static," *The New York Times Magazine* (December 7, 1987).

Rushefsky, Carolyn. "More Older Women Seek Out Young Men," *Chicago Sun-Times* (October 15, 1986).

Tweeton, Leslie, and Lyons, Suzanne. "In Praise of Younger Men," *Boston Magazine* (July 1986).

"Women's Concerns Shift Toward Self," *Inside Print* (March, 1987).

Yarrow, Andrew L. "Older Parents' Child: Growing Up Special," *The New York Times* (January 26, 1987).

Other Sources

"The Cosmopolitan Report on the Changing Life Course of American Women, Summaries of the First and Second Reports," prepared by Steven D. McLaughlin, John O. G.

Billy, Terry R. Johnson, Barbara D. Melber, Linda D. Winges, and Denise M. Zimmerle of the Battelle Human Affairs Research Centers, copyrighted 1986 by the Hearst Corporation.

"Older Women/Younger Men," "Donahue" (May 5, 1986).